— S̲ultans and M̲osques —

— Perween Hasan —

SULTANS AND MOSQUES

The Early Muslim Architecture of Bangladesh

I.B. TAURIS
LONDON • NEW YORK • OXFORD • NEW DELHI • SYDNEY

I.B. TAURIS
Bloomsbury Publishing Plc
50 Bedford Square, London, WC1B 3DP, UK
1385 Broadway, New York, NY 10018, USA
29 Earlsfort Terrace, Dublin 2, Ireland

BLOOMSBURY, I.B. TAURIS and the I.B Tauris logo
are trademarks of Bloomsbury Publishing Plc

First published in Great Britain 2007
This paperback edition published 2024

Copyright © Perween Hasan, 2007

Perween Hasan has asserted her right under the Copyright,
Designs and Patents Act, 1988, to be identified as Author of this work.

All rights reserved. No part of this publication may be reproduced or
transmitted in any form or by any means, electronic or mechanical,
including photocopying, recording, or any information storage or retrieval
system, without prior permission in writing from the publishers.

Bloomsbury Publishing Plc does not have any control over, or responsibility for,
any third-party websites referred to or in this book. All internet addresses given
in this book were correct at the time of going to press. The author and publisher
regret any inconvenience caused if addresses have changed or sites have
ceased to exist, but can accept no responsibility for any such changes.

A catalogue record for this book is available from the British Library.

A catalog record for this book is available from the Library of Congress.

ISBN: HB: 978-1-8451-1381-0
PB: 978-0-7556-5360-7
ePDF: 978-0-7556-1385-4
eBook: 978-0-7556-1384-7

Typeset in Garamond by Stilman Davis

To find out more about our authors and books visit
www.bloomsbury.com and sign up for our newsletters.

To my parents:
Afifa Huq and Syed Azizul Huq

Contents

List of Illustrations	ix
Picture Credits	xiv
FOREWORD	1
PREFACE	3

Chapter 1
THE GEOGRAPHY, HISTORY AND CULTURE OF BENGAL	7

Chapter 2
ORIGINS OF BENGALI MOSQUE ARCHITECTURE	23
PRE-ISLAMIC TEMPLE ARCHITECTURE	27
THE SULTANATE MOSQUES	32

Chapter 3
CATALOGUE OF SULTANATE MOSQUES IN BANGLADESH	71
AREAS WHERE MOSQUES ARE CONCENTRATED	72
EARLY SULTANATE PERIOD	75
MIDDLE SULTANATE PERIOD	77
KHAN JAHAN STYLE	114
LATE SULTANATE PERIOD	147

Appendix 1
INDEPENDENT MUSLIM RULERS (SULTANS) OF BENGAL	207

Appendix 2
DATED SULTANATE MOSQUES OF BANGLADESH	209

Appendix 3
SULTANATE MOSQUES BY DISTRICT	211

Principal Abbreviations	214
Glossary	217
Select Bibliography	221
Index of Mosques	229
General Index	231

List of Illustrations

1	Map of Bangladesh with main rivers and Sultanate mosque sites	6
2	Bagerhat, a *do-chala* thatched hut	23
3	*Shikhara-shirsha bhadra* temple in *Ashta Sahasrika Prajnaparamita*	24
4	Hmawza (Burma), Bebe Paya Temple, eighth century	24
5	A *chau-chala* thatched hut	25
6	Sonargaon, bamboo frame for a *do-chala* hut	26
7	"Alexander Receiving Dara's Daughter Roshanak" from *Iskandar Nama* of Sultan Nusrat Shah, 1531-32	26
8	Votive *shikhara* temple from Dinajpur, ca. tenth century	27
9	Ashrafpur bronze *stupa* with *bhadra* temple in front, ca. seventh century	28
10	Dhyani Buddha Amitabha seated inside a *shikhara-shirsha bhadra* temple, Dhaka, ca. eleventh century	28
11	Hmawza, Lemyethna Temple, eighth century	29
12	Hmawza, Lemyethna Temple, plan	30
13	Hmawza, Bebe Paya Temple, eighth century, plan	30
14	Puthia, *chala* Govinda Temple, eighteenth century	33
15	Shankarpasha, thatched hut-mosque	34
16	Pandua, West Bengal (India), Eklakhi Tomb, early fifteenth century, plan	35
17	Pandua, Eklakhi Tomb	36
18	Sonargaon, Goaldi Mosque, 1519, plan	38
19	Sonargaon, Goaldi Mosque, southwest view	38
20	Dinajpur, Gopalganj Mosque, 1460, plan	39
21	Dinajpur, Gopalganj Mosque, vaulted verandah	39
22	Gaur, Darasbari Mosque, 1479-80, plan	40
23	Gaur, Darasbari Mosque, southeast view	41
24	Patuakhali, Masjidbari Mosque, 1465-74, plan	41
25	Bagerhat, Nine-domed Mosque, mid-fifteenth century, plan	42
26	Bagerhat, Nine-domed Mosque, southwest view	42
27	Tribeni, West Bengal (India), Zafar Khan Ghazi's Mosque, 1298, plan	44
28	Tribeni, Zafar Khan Ghazi's Mosque	45
29	Munshiganj, Baba Adam's Mosque, 1483, plan	45
30	Munshiganj, Baba Adam's Mosque, reccesses in the exterior south wall	46

31	Pandua, West Bengal, Adina Mosque, 1375, plan	47
32	Pandua, Adina Mosque, central aisle with collapsed vault	47
33	Shaitgumbad Mosque, Bagerhat, mid-fifteenth century, plan	48
34	Bagerhat, Shaitgumbad Mosque	49
35	Sonargaon, Fath Shah's Mosque, 1484, plan	50
36	Sonargaon, Fath Shah's Mosque	52
37	Kishoreganj, Qutb Shah's Mosque, late sixteenth century, plan	53
38	Kishoreganj, Qutb Shah's Mosque, southeast view	53
39	Sonargaon, Muazzampur Shahi Jami Mosque, 1432-33, mihrab motif on exterior west wall	54
40	Habiganj, Shankarpasha Mosque, 1493-1519, mihrab motifs on exterior west wall	55
41	Narasimha Vishnu from Rajshahi, seventh-eighth century	55
42	Vishnu from Dhaka, twelfth century	56
43	Pandua, Adina Mosque, terracotta decoration on tympanum above mihrab	57
44	Rajshahi, Bagha Mosque, 1523-24, corbelled brick pendentive in interior	60
45	Tughra inscription of Sultan Shams al-Din Yusuf Shah dated 879/1474-75	61
46	Naogaon, Kusumba Mosque, 1558, mihrab	68
47	Mahasthan, Mankalir Bhita Mosque, reconstructed plan	74
48	Mahasthan, Mankalir Bhita Mosque, ruined interior piers	76
49	Sonargaon, Muazzampur Shahi Jami Mosque, 1432-33, plan	77
50	Sonargaon, Muazzampur Shahi Jami Mosque, interior	78
51	Dhaka, Binat Bibi's Mosque, 1456-57, exterior north wall	80
52	Dhaka, Binat Bibi's Mosque	80
53	Dhaka, Binat Bibi's Mosque, reconstructed plan	81
54	Shahzadpur, Makhdum Shah's Mosque, mid- to late fifteenth century, minbar	84
55	Shahzadpur, Makhdum Shah's Mosque, plan and top view of minbar	85
56	Shahzadpur, Makhdum Shah's Mosque, northeast view	86
57	Shahzadpur, Makhdum Shah's Mosque, interior	86
58	Barguna, Bibi Chini's Mosque, mid- to late fifteenth century, ruined interior	88
59	Barguna, Bibi Chini's Mosque, plan	88
60	Chittagong, Faqir's Mosque, 1474-81, plan	90
61	Chittagong, Faqir's Mosque	91
62	Chittagong, Faqir's Mosque, *chau-chala* entrance vault	91
63	Gaur, Darasbari Mosque, 1479-80, central aisle	93
64	Gaur, Darasbari Mosque, interior northwest	94
65	Narayanganj, Bandar Shahi Mosque, 1481, plan	96
66	Narayanganj, Bandar Shahi Mosque, north view	97

LIST OF ILLUSTRATIONS

67	Narayanganj, Bandar Shahi Mosque, interior northwest	97
68	Munshiganj, Baba Adam's Mosque, 1483, mihrab pillar	99
69	Munshiganj, Baba Adam's Mosque, exterior mihrab projection	100
70	Sonargaon, Fath Shah's Mosque, 1484, interior, arched vault on south side	102
71	Sonargaon, Yusufganj Mosque, late fifteenth century, plan	104
72	Sonargaon, Yusufganj Mosque	104
73	Gaur, Dhunichak Mosque, late fifteenth century, northwest view of ruined interior	105
74	Gaur, Dhunichak Mosque, plan	106
75	Gaur, Khania Dighi Mosque, late fifteenth to early sixteenth century, interior mihrab wall	107
76	Gaur, Khania Dighi Mosque, plan	108
77	Chittagong, Badr Awlia Dargah Jami Mosque, late fifteenth century, prayer chamber	110
78	Chittagong, Badr Awlia Dargah Jami Mosque, plan	110
79	Faridpur, Shatoir Mosque, late fifteenth century, interior	112
80	Faridpur, Shatoir Mosque, plan	113
81	Bagerhat, Shaitgumbad Mosque, mid-fifteenth century, interior	115
82	Bagerhat, Shaitgumbad Mosque, *chau-chala* vaulted roof in central aisle	116
83	Bagerhat, Shaitgumbad Mosque, pediment over central entrance on the east	117
84	Bagerhat, mosque adjoining Khan Jahan's tomb, mid-fifteenth century, south view	118
85	Bagerhat, mosque adjoining Khan Jahan's tomb, plan	119
86	Bagerhat, mosque adjoining Khan Jahan's tomb, renovated interior	119
87	Bagerhat, Ranbijoypur Mosque, mid-fifteenth century, plan	121
88	Bagerhat, Ranbijoypur Mosque	121
89	Bagerhat, Ranbijoypur Mosque, mihrab wall	122
90	Bagerhat, Ranbijoypur Mosque, before conservation	122
91	Bagerhat, Bibi Begni's Mosque, mid-fifteenth century, plan	124
92	Bagerhat, Bibi Begni's Mosque	124
93	Bagerhat, Shingra Mosque, mid-fifteenth century, plan	126
94	Bagerhat, Shingra Mosque, before conservation	126
95	Bagerhat, Nine-domed Mosque, mid-fifteenth century, mihrab	129
96	Khulna, Masjidkur Mosque, mid-fifteenth century, plan	131
97	Khulna, Masjidkur Mosque	131
98	Khulna, Masjidkur Mosque, north mihrab	132
99	Barisal, Kasba Mosque, mid-fifteenth century, plan	134
100	Barisal, Kasba Mosque, southwest view	134
101	Barobazar, Satgachhia Mosque, mid-fifteenth century, plan	136
102	Barobazar, Satgachhia Mosque	136

103	Barobazar, Galakata Mosque, mid-fifteenth century, plan	138
104	Barobazar, Galakata Mosque, southeast view	138
105	Barobazar, Galakata Mosque, central mihrab before conservation	139
106	Jhenaidah, Sailkupa Mosque, mid-fifteenth century, southeast view	140
107	Jhenaidah, Sailkupa Mosque, plan	141
108	Patuakhali, Masjidbari Mosque, 1465-74, southeast view	142
109	Patuakhali, Masjidbari Mosque, interior of verandah *chau-chala* vault	143
110	Patuakhali, Masjidbari Mosque, interior southwest	143
111	Bagerhat, Chunakhola Mosque, late fifteenth century, plan	145
112	Bagerhat, Chunakhola Mosque	145
113	Bagerhat, Chunakhola Mosque, interior mihrab wall	146
114	Bagerhat, Chunakhola Mosque, terracotta pattern within rectangular frame of eastern entrance	146
115	Gaur, Chhota Sona Mosque, 1493-1519, plan	147
116	Gaur, Chhota Sona Mosque, northeast view	148
117	Gaur, Chhota Sona Mosque, platform in interior northwest	149
118	Gaur, Chhota Sona Mosque, exterior west wall	149
119	Habiganj, Shankarpasha Mosque, 1493-1519, plan	152
120	Habiganj, Shankarpasha Mosque, southeast view	153
121	Khulna, Aroshnagar Mosque, 1501-2, reconstructed plan	154
122	Khulna, Aroshnagar Mosque	154
123	Narayanganj, Baba Saleh's Mosque, 1505, reconstructed plan	156
124	Sonargaon, Goaldi Mosque, 1519, central and south mihrab	158
125	Bagerhat, Ten-domed Mosque, early sixteenth century, plan	160
126	Bagerhat, Ten-domed Mosque, interior northwest corner	160
127	Rajshahi, Bagha Mosque, southeast view	161
128	Rajshahi, Bagha Mosque, plan	163
129	Rajshahi, Bagha Mosque, mihrab	164
130	Rajshahi, Bagha Mosque, terracotta panel with mango tree motif	164
131	Faridpur, Majlis Awlia's Mosque, early sixteenth century, plan	166
132	Faridpur, Majlis Awlia's Mosque, corbelled entrance vault	167
133	Faridpur, Majlis Awlia's Mosque, exterior mihrab projection	168
134	Faridpur, Majlis Awlia's Mosque, south mihrab	169
135	Barobazar, Gorar Mosque, early sixteenth century, plan	171
136	Barobazar, Gorar Mosque, part of exterior south wall	171
137	Barobazar, Manohor Dighi Mosque, early sixteenth century, plan	173
138	Barobazar, Manohar Dighi Mosque, ruins	173
139	Barobazar, Pirpukur Mosque, early sixteenth century, plan	174
140	Barobazar, Pirpukur Mosque, ruins	175
141	Sirajganj, Nabagram Mosque, 1526, plan	176
142	Sirajganj, Nabagram Mosque, verandah facade	177

List of Illustrations

143	Barobazar, Jorbangla Mosque, early sixteenth century, plan	178
144	Barobazar, Jorbangla Mosque, northeast view of reconstructed mosque	179
145	Barobazar, Noongola Mosque, early sixteenth century, reconstructed east facade	180
146	Barobazar, Noongola Mosque, plan	180
147	Barobazar, Pathagar Mosque, early sixteenth century, plan	181
148	Barobazar, Pathagar Mosque, interior mihrab wall	182
149	Barobazar, Shukur Mallik Mosque, early sixteenth century, interior mihrab wall	183
150	Barobazar, Shukur Mallik Mosque, plan	183
151	Satkhira, Parbajpur Mosque, early sixteenth century, plan	184
152	Satkhira, Parbajpur Mosque, exterior west wall	185
153	Bagerhat, Rezai Khan's Mosque, early sixteenth century, ruined interior	186
154	Bagerhat, Rezai Khan's Mosque, plan	187
155	Chittagong, Hammad's Mosque, 1532-38, plan	189
156	Chittagong, Hammad's Mosque, southwest view	189
157	Sylhet, Osmanpur Gayebi Mosque, early to mid-sixteenth century, plan	191
158	Sylhet, Osmanpur Gayebi Mosque, interior east	191
159	Dinajpur, Sura Mosque, mid-sixteenth century, plan	193
160	Dinajpur, Sura Mosque, mid-sixteenth century, northeast view	193
161	Dinajpur, Sura Mosque, central mihrab	194
162	Naogaon, Kusumba Mosque, 1558-59, plan	195
163	Naogaon, Kusumba Mosque	196
164	Naogaon, Kusumba Mosque, platform in interior northwest	197
165	Barisal, Shialghuni Mosque, mid-sixteenth century, mihrab facade	198
166	Barisal, Shialghuni Mosque, plan	199
167	Kishoreganj, Qutb Shah's Mosque, late sixteenth century, *makara* head in ornamental vine motif at entrance	200
168	Bagerhat, Zinda Pir's Mosque, late sixteenth century, northeast view	202
169	Bagerhat, Zinda Pir's Mosque, plan	203
170	Jessore, Shubhorara Mosque, late sixteenth century, plan	204
171	Jessore, Shubhorara Mosque, interior mihrab wall	205
172	Jessore, Shubhorara Mosque, exterior west wall with mihrab projection	205

Picture Credits

1: Drawn by Kazi Ahmedul Islam
3: Cambridge University Library Ms. Add.1643, fol. 59. Reproduced by permission of the Syndics of Cambridge University Library
5: Courtesy George Michell
7: British Library Ms. 13836.f.32. Reproduced by permission of the British Library
8: Bangladesh National Museum Acc. No. 1118. Courtesy:Bangladesh National Museum
9: Drawn from S. K. Sarawati, *Architecture of Bengal* (Calcutta, 1976), Bk. 1, Plate 1, by Naushad Ehsanul Huq
10: Bangladesh National Museum, acc. no. 43. Courtesy: Bangladesh National Museum
16: After Catherine B. Asher
27: After Catherine B. Asher
31: After Naseem A. Banerji
41: Bangladesh National Museum, acc. no. 76.505. Courtesy Bangladesh National Museum
42: Bangladesh National Museum, acc. no. 66.37. Courtesy Bangladesh National Museum
45: Varendra Research Museum, acc. no. 2661. Courtesy Varendra Research Museum, Rajshahi
90: Courtesy Department of Archaeology and Museums, Government of Bangladesh
94: Courtesy Department of Archaeology and Museums, Government of Bangladesh

Foreword

Our knowledge of Islamic art and architecture is in a constant state of flux. It changes, of course, as new information, archaeologically retrieved data, discoveries of hitherto unknown or poorly known buildings, better reading of texts, more sophisticated analyses of existing monuments, sometimes simply accurate drawings and complete photographic surveys are made available to students and amateurs alike. Sometimes even this new information is not easily accessible, because it appears in rare periodicals or in languages that are only read by a few. But, on the whole, one can be secure in the notion that the new information is somewhere, even if hidden in the offices of archaeological institutes or departments of antiquities, that it can be seen, and that some day the marvels of modern technology will bring all these monuments to everyone, at home or in their place of work. The old libertarian dream of a total knowledge in the hands of all men and women and without significant cost can easily be imagined. But we are not quite there yet. In the meantime, any book, like this one, that gives access to buildings which were little known, at times not known at all, is an essential addition to scholarly literature and should be welcomed by all.

But the study of any art and architecture does not depend only on information. It is also affected by changing attitudes towards the arts, by new expectations from knowledge, and new paradigms of interpretations. Attitudes, expectations, and paradigms can be universal, as they often are in our allegedly global intellectual world, but they can also be restricted, constricted, or even enriched by the particular needs of separate cultures. Thus, the study and understanding of Islamic art requires that attention be given to features or questions that may not be as significant in other cultures. A few examples will illustrate my point.

One instance of a fairly universal query with peculiar Islamic details is regionalism. Fifty years ago or more, very broad geographical categories—the Muslim West, Iran, the Indian subcontinent were sufficient to categorize and classify a monument of Islamic art. Today we cultivate dozens of separate traditions, at times reasonable geographical or historical entities and at other times simply reflections of contemporary political divisions. The advantage of seeking to define such smaller units are obvious. Precision of study is required in every detail of a building, as each monument's differences are analysed. Thus accuracy and precision are necessary components of the best regional studies. Also, local pride can be strengthened, not necessarily as an exercise in vanity or chauvinism, but rather as the recognition of the idiosyncrasy and uniqueness of every space created by man on earth. The disadvantage is that the forest is no longer visible, only the trees. Broad cultural commonalities of faith, government and social practice have been transformed into masses of details uniquely valid for one building alone. And no easy mechanism exists to justify such generalization as may emerge. Thus, if we seek what social scientists used to call "the big picture", we end up by neglecting the reality of thousands, millions, of lives, expectations, dreams, frustrations and achievements that make up the history of human nature. To take an example from the book, I was struck by the observation that the majority of the early mosques of Bangladesh were built between 1450 and 1550. For a historian of art, this is sufficient to establish a roster of techniques, decoration and functions for a specific time, and to define a "period style". But for the historian of culture it is important to imagine how the continuous maintenance of buildings from one period affected the further development of an art of architecture. Did the fact turn people away from architecture as a profession? Did it create a sense of pride and common values within communities? Did it affect over the centuries the practice of the many activities which take place in a mosque?

Or, to take another example, how should one explain the relative absence of minarets in Bangladesh? Does the presence of minarets in Delhi, Cairo, or Istanbul assume a different kind of Islam from the one practised in Dhaka? If it does not, is the minaret an unnecessary appendix for mosques, significant only for reasons of vanity, prestige, or some function that does not deal with the practice of the faith?

A book that presents for the first time the architecture of an area clearly circumscribed in time and in space leads to such questions. It strengthens our awareness of what makes one area different from another one. It also identifies the architectural features that, by their presence or by their absence, their originality or their commonness, are the important vectors in the architecture of all those who claim to be Muslims. Created as a labour of love, this book is both an invitation to know Bangladesh better and to meditate further on the brilliant history of Islamic architecture everywhere.

Oleg Grabar
Aga Khan Professor of Islamic Art Emeritus, Harvard University
Professor Emeritus, School of Historical Studies,
Institute for Advanced Study, Princeton

Preface

This study deals with the mosques of Bangladesh built between the independent Sultanate of Bengal (from 1338 to 1538) and the end of Afghan rule in 1576, when Akbar conquered Bengal and it became a *suba* or province of the Mughal Empire. These Sultanate mosques form a homogeneous group of Muslim monuments in the area, in sharp contrast to those of the Mughal period that followed: while the Sultanate architecture of Bengal differs markedly from that of Delhi, the buildings of the Mughal period show the powerful influence of the Delhi style.

The purpose of this study is to collect all the documentation available in an effort to fill at least some of the gaps in our knowledge of these mosques. While the catalogue of mosques is as complete as possible, the inadequacy and occasional absence of documentation required that emphasis be placed on fieldwork and on the physical aspects of the mosques. This meant visiting every monument to make measured drawings, and establishing a standardized formal vocabulary to rationalize the wide divergence in the use of terms in earlier works. In many of these buildings the original structure is either in ruins or has been completely obliterated through remodelling, and the floor plan is the only original feature that has survived. In such cases every effort was made to investigate what the floor plans might reveal of the original structures.

Fifty-five mosques were surveyed. The plans for seventeen of them are being published for the first time, and a few formerly published plans have been corrected and redrawn to metric scale. North is indicated at the top of each plan, and the qibla is due west. The mosque was singled out for study for several reasons. First, by definition the *masjid* (mosque; place of prostration) is architecturally representative of Islamic culture by its association with collective prayer. Second, of the various types of buildings that must have been a part of the architectural landscape from the fourteenth to sixteenth centuries, mosques have survived in the largest number. Third, buildings with a common function are well-suited to historical investigation, as their architectural features can be readily identified as imported Islamic-style or indigenous pre-Islamic-style.

Sultanate architecture forms a continuum with both pre-Islamic Buddhist and post-Sultanate Hindu temples. Although the shapes of the mosques vary, from the square of the small and medium-sized buildings to the rectangle of the large ones, the basic element is always essentially a square-domed unit. In a few of the large rectangular mosques, an axial aisle running down the centre changes the usual organization of the interior space, and a verandah might be added to the front of the building. However, these are minor variations in a plan that shows the same distinctive regional style throughout.

My fieldwork covered the geographical limits of the state of Bangladesh (East Bengal before 1947, and East Pakistan 1947-71). The mosques of the modern Indian province of West Bengal are not included here, although the frontiers of Bengal, variable during the period in question, usually included them. This is partly because the large number of monuments in Bangladesh seemed adequate for a single study, and partly because of the practical difficulties involved in carrying out fieldwork in India; however, the Indian mosques are discussed wherever relevant.

In Bengal, a mosque takes the name of a patron, a local saint, or a location; in this text, the mosque name is usually followed by the name of the village, town or general area, whichever is more commonly used. In the catalogue entries the names of the village, police station, and district are also given. In Bangladesh, villages and urban areas are grouped into administrative units under the control of a police station, which serves as their centre. Several police stations make up a district. To locate a place, it is important to know both the administering police station and the district to which it belongs.

The orthography for transliterated Arabic and Persian names generally follows the conventions of the *Encyclopaedia of Islam* (2nd ed., Leiden: E. J. Brill, 1960 onwards), except for the substitution of j for *dj*, z for *dh*, and q for *k* and the omission of diacritical marks. For place names in Bangladesh, the standardized spellings of the *Statistical Yearbook of Bangladesh 2000* (Dhaka: Bangladesh Bureau of Statistics, Planning Division, Ministry of Planning, Government of the People's Republic of Bangladesh, 2002) are used, with the Bengali pronunciation guides in parentheses in the catalogue. As the English version often evolved from transliterations from Urdu or Persian they are sometimes phonetically different from Bengali, e.g., several place-names end with the word *bazar* (market), although the z sound does not even exist in Bengali. The name Bengal is used to denote both Bangladesh and West Bengal. Dates are given in Common Era years unless they are quotations from original texts.

Several scholars have studied the monuments of the Sultanate period, but an adequately documented comprehensive study of the mosques of East Bengal has never been done. M. M. Chakravarti in 1910 and S. K. Saraswati in 1941 studied some of the buildings from plans, but their efforts were sketchy, the drawings inadequate, and the monuments they dealt with were limited mainly to West Bengal. A. H. Dani's *Muslim Architecture in Bengal* (1961) includes a selection of Sultanate buildings from both East and West Bengal, and is the only comprehensive work available. In larger volumes on Indian architecture and history, the architecture of Bengal merits a few pages or a small section. J. Fergusson (1876), E. B. Havell (1913), J. Marshall (1922) and P. Brown (first published 1942) selected monuments mainly from Gaur and Pandua to illustrate a provincial style. Syed Mahmudul Hasan's *Mosque Architecture of Pre-Mughal Bengal* (1971), is mainly a compilation of previously published works by scholars and surveyors; and his classification of monuments based on shape is confusing.

Catherine B. Asher's "Inventory of Key Monuments" in *The Islamic Heritage of Bengal* (1984) is very useful for its brief descriptions of monuments both in Bangladesh and West Bengal, arranged in alphabetical order according to site, and accompanied by excellent photographs and plans. Abu Sayeed Mostaque Ahmed published (1997) his dissertation on the Chhota Sona Mosque in Gaur with excellent drawings. Although it is a detailed study of only a single monument, he includes a number of other mosques in a catalogue. However, like Mahmudul Hasan he classifies according to shape, and thus restricts the usefulness of his catalogue. Earlier monographs on individual sites by Creighton (1817), Ravenshaw (1878), and M. Abid Ali Khan (1931) are more comprehensive, but also dated. A dissertation on the monuments of Khalifatabad by M. A. Bari (1980) deserves credit for adding some new material.

Historians like Abdul Karim, Mohar Ali, S. Mukhopadhyay and Richard Eaton disagree on the chronlogy of a few of the sultans. I have generally followed Eaton as his work, *The Rise of Islam and the Bengal Frontier* (1993) is the latest and seems well researched.

The basis of this study was my dissertation written in 1984 for Harvard University. Thanks are due to several colleagues and friends for their help in putting together that original work, particularly my supervisor Professor Oleg Grabar who initiated me into the study of Islamic architecture and has been a source of inspiration ever since; Professors John Rosenfield and Pramod Chandra, who taught me how to look at objects and guided my studies in Indian art; to Catherine and Frederick Asher who took me on my first field trip, to Shireen and Ishtiaque Ahmed who provided me with a home away from Dhaka; and to the late Margaret Sevcenko for doing the final editing of the manuscript.

Most of my graduate education at Harvard was supported by the JDR 3rd Fund of New York. The Aga Khan Program for Islamic Architecture at Harvard and MIT and the Asian Cultural Council of New York provided financial assistance for completing my dissertation. In Bangladesh, Professor A. B. Musharraf Husain of the Department of Islamic History and Culture of Rajshahi University first suggested the topic of research and was one of my dissertation readers, and Firdous Azim read the first draft of this manuscript. To all these people and institutions, I am deeply indebted.

The Department of Archaeology and Museums in Bangladesh made available to me their entire collection of plans and photographs, and provided pre-conservation pictures for all the mosques under their care. My sons Zeeshan and Zahin had to be left several times with their grandparents while I travelled and was in residence in Cambridge, and I am beholden for the love and care they were given. Finally, my deepest thanks go to Zahed, without whose inspiration, encouragement and constant support, this work would never have been completed.

The section titled THE SULTANATE MOSQUES may be read as the Conclusion.

Perween Hasan
Dhaka, Bangladesh

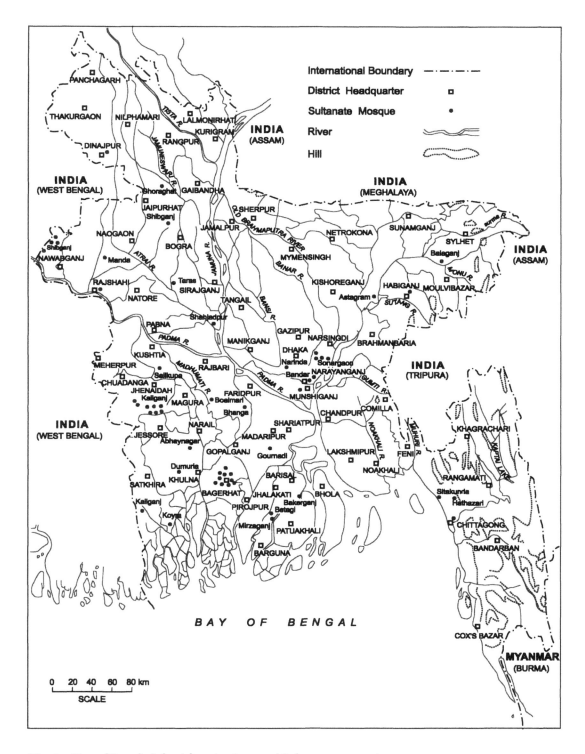

Fig. 1. Map of Bangladesh with main rivers and Sultanate mosque sites

1

The Geography, History and Culture of Bengal

The geographical position of Bangladesh has largely determined its history. Comprising an area of 144,000 square kilometres, it is on the northeastern side of the Indian subcontinent. It is bounded on the north, east and west by India and on the south by Myanmar (Burma) and the Bay of Bengal.[1] The flatness of its terrain is so absolute that areas 150 kilometres away from the sea are still less than nine metres above sea level—the slope of the land is less than eight centimetres per kilometre. Three raised areas, nowhere higher than thirty metres above sea level, are the only exceptions; these are known as the Madhupur Tract (in the Dhaka and Mymensingh districts), Barind (in the north), and Lalmai (southwest of Comilla town). There are hills only along the eastern and south-eastern border; the great mangrove forests of Sundarban are in the south.

Small and large rivers crisscross the vast flat alluvial plain, and marshes (*bils*) dot the land. On a map showing the physical features of the land, the numerous rivers present a formidable and bewildering sight. To the Bengali, the rivers are not barriers but links connecting the outlying territories with the centre; from time immemorial they have been considered the highways of the land. The Ganges flows into Bangladesh as the Padma (Pawdda in Bengali) from the west, the Brahmaputra (also known as the Jamuna) from the north, and the Meghna from the north-east (fig. 1). These three with their numerous tributaries drain this delta. The confluence where they empty into the Bay of Bengal is more than 11 kilometres wide; it is also less than 200 years old, the result of the frequently changing river courses in the area.

This propensity for the rivers to change course is a remarkable feature that has affected human settlement in Bengal throughout its history. When the English geographer James Rennell surveyed Bengal for the East India Company in 1764-72, the first modern geographical study of Bengal, he showed the main stream of the Ganges flowing

---

1   For the geography of Bangladesh, see Haroun Er Rashid, *Geography of Bangladesh* (Dhaka, 1991) and Nafis Ahmed, *An Economic Geography of East Pakistan* (London, 1968).

down the river Arial Khan to the bay, a course which is to the west of the present river.[2] Earlier still, the main channel of the Ganges flowed through the Bhagirathi-Hughly rivers in West Bengal, a course that was even further to the west. At that time, the Padma probably represented the most northerly spill channel. Then the Ganges began its eastward movement and, in the process, gradually shifted the active stage of delta formation eastward, leaving the rivers in the western districts to dry up. Thus while the Bhagirathi or the main channel of the Ganges shrank, the tributaries running east and south into the present delta area expanded. Geographers assume that by the beginning of the sixteenth century, the main stream of the Ganges had definitely taken on a southeasterly direction. This shifting of river courses continues over a vast area to this day.

The average annual rainfall is heavy (about 254 centimetres) and completely inundates much of the area during the monsoon months (June-September). Where the current is not swift, the silt-laden rivers deposit their load on the banks, forming dykes that allow the water level to rise above the surrounding area. When the bank finally gives way, the water floods onto the lower land beyond. In the process, the large rivers are continually eroding one bank and depositing silt on the other, over time changing course. Markets and junctions shift from place to place almost every year, following the shifting rivers.

Although thick vegetation once covered much of the land, forests now account for only 24,820 square kilometres, or 16 per cent of the total land area, and even these remaining forested areas are continually being reduced. The largest is located in the Chittagong district and the Chittagong Hill Tracts, where *jhum*, or slash-and-burn cultivation, over several centuries has reduced the forests. Next is the Sundarban Forest which covers the southern part of the Khulna district and the southwestern corner of Barisal and is completely inundated during the rainy season. At the advent of British rule, these forests were twice their present size, but were denuded when landlords (*zamindars*) on the northern boundary were allowed to clear as much of the jungle bordering their lands as they required.[3] The Madhupur Forest in the Dhaka, Mymensingh, and Tangail districts is located in the middle of a vast market and consuming area that has caused its reduction in size. Finally, the Sylhet forests located in the north and south of the district are also being denuded by urbanization.

Bengal is the anglicized form of Banga or Bangala, a name which first makes its appearance in the work of the Delhi historian Zia al-Din Barani (d. 1357) in his *Tarikh-i-Firuz Shahi* (History of the Rule of Firuz Shah).[4] Abul Fazl (d. 1602), the official historian at Akbar's court, described Bangala, the easternmost province (*suba*) of the Mughal Empire, as bounded by hills in the north and south, by Suba Bihar in the west, and by a

---

2   J. Rennell, "An Account of the Ganges and the Burrampooter Rivers", Appendix to *Memoir of a Map of Hindoostan; or the Mogul Empire*, 3rd ed. (London, 1793), pp. 335-56.

3   *The Forests of Bengal* (Calcutta: Calcutta Revenue Department, Government of Bengal, 1935), p. 33.

4   Zia al-Din Barani, *Tarikh-i-Firuz Shahi*, ed. Saiyid Ahmad Khan (Calcutta, 1862), pp. 114-18; cited in Abdul Karim, *Banglar Itihash, Sultani Amol*, 2nd ed. (Dhaka, 1987), p. 2.

The Geography, History and Culture of Bengal

tract of land called Bhati (lowland) in the east. To the north is the country of Kuch, a very large principality that derives its name from Koch, the caste to which the ruling family belonged. It can be identified with the area between the upper reaches of the river Karatoya and the Brahmaputra before it turns south, of which Kamrup is a subject state, and next to it is Assam. In the southeast is Arakan with its port of Chittagong.[5] As long as it was a province of British India its boundaries remained unchanged, but with partition in 1947 it was split into two unequal parts; the smaller West Bengal became a province of India and the larger East Bengal a province of Pakistan. In 1971, the eastern province broke away to become the independent nation of Bangladesh.

Sources for the history of pre-Mughal Bengal include Arabic and Persian historical texts written on the Indian subcontinent, especially in Delhi; biographies, letters, Sufi discourses, inscriptions and coins, travellers' accounts, and contemporary Bengali poetry written by both Hindus and Muslims.[6] No histories written during the Sultanate period in Bengal have yet been discovered, though there are references to a few lost Persian manuscripts in the *Riyazu-s-Salatin*, a history written in Bengal by Ghulam Husain Salim (d. 1817), an employee of the East India Company, at the behest of the commercial resident of the company's factory in Malda in 1786.

The Turkish Conquest

In 1204 Ikhtiyar al-Din Muhammad Bakhtiyar (d. 1206), originally of Garamsir in northern Afghanistan, a Turkoman of the Khalji tribe, and a soldier of fortune, defeated the Hindu ruler Lakshmansena (ca. 1179-1205) at Nadiya, a city that is now identified with the village of Naoda, in western Rajshahi District (and not to be confused with the city of Nadiya in West Bengal[7]). At that time Bangala was not a unified country with a single ruler. In addition to Lakshmansena ruling from Gaur (also known as Lakshmanavati, Lakhnawti to the Muslims), there were a number of small independent kingdoms. Several of the Muslim rulers of Lakhnawti, as well as the Hindu rulers before them, had jurisdiction over Bihar.

From pre-Islamic times up to the middle of the fourteenth century, when Ibn Battuta visited the area, Bangala or Banga was the name applied only to south and east Bengal; its people were called Bangali. Abu Minhaj al-Din Usman ibn Siraj al-Din al-Juzjani, also known as Minhaj al-Siraj (ca.1193-ca.1260), the author of the *Tabaqat-i-Nasiri* and the first Delhi historian to write on the establishment of Muslim rule in Bengal, visited the area when Malik Yuz al-Din Tughral was the governor of Lakhnawti (1233-44). He does not mention Bangala by name in his history, but he describes the territory of

---

[5] Abul Fazl Allami, *Ain-i-Akbari*, trans. H. S. Jarrett, 3 vols. (rpt. Calcutta, 1993), vol. 2, pp. 130-32.
[6] Karim, *Banglar Itihash*, pp. 14-27.
[7] A. K. M. Zakariah, "Muhammad Bakhtiyar's Conquest of Nudiah", *Journal of the Varendra Research Museum* 6 (1980-81): 57-72.

Lakhnawti as divided in two by the river Ganges: Rarh (Ral) to the west roughly corresponds to West Bengal and Varendra (Barind) to the east roughly corresponds to north Bengal. The areas surrounding Lakhnawti were Banga (Bang), Kamrud, and Tirhut.[8] Gaur, the most important city in the area, was located in Varendra and was to eastern India what Delhi was to the north. In pre-Islamic times, the rulers of the smaller principalities were constantly trying to occupy it.

When the Turks attacked in 1204, Lakshmansena, along with his courtiers and several Brahmans, fled to the east, and Bakhtiyar established his kingdom of Lakhnawti, which in the early thirteenth century consisted only of a small area in Varendra. He ruled the area as a deputy of Sultan Muiz al-Din Muhammad Ghuri of Delhi (r. 1192-1206). All of east, south and west Bengal, and parts of the north remained outside his control. Beginning with Ali Mardan Khalji (d. 1212),[9] independent governors ruled Lakhnawti before the death of Sultan Ghiyath al-Din Iwaz Khalji in 1227. After that, Delhi seized control of Lakhnawti and governors administered it as a province until the death of Sultan Ghiyath al-Din Balban of Delhi in 1287.

Within these sixty years, two of the governors declared their independence, but their autonomy was shortlived. Zia al-Din Barani, in his *Tarikh-i Firuz Shahi*, writes that Bengal was known in Delhi as Bulghampur (land of rebels). As it was one of the farthest provinces from Delhi and because its forested riverine terrain and heavy monsoon climate set it apart from other places in north India, the central government could not keep a strict eye on its affairs, nor could it send forces quickly enough to quell incipient rebellions. As a result, whenever a new governor was sent, the courtiers and officials would incite him to revolt against the sultan, and if he did not comply they would arrange his downfall. The governors therefore had little choice but to join the rebels against Delhi.[10] This state of affairs prevailed throughout the thirteenth century when governors sent from Delhi would try to throw off their allegiance and assume the title of sultan. Thus internal intrigues, bloodshed, and military offensives from Delhi were the order of the day. From 1290 to 1324, corresponding to the era of Khalji rule in Delhi, Bengal was ruled independently.

By the turn of the century the kingdom had expanded to Bihar in the west, Devkot in Dinajpur district in the north, and Satgaon and parts of Banga in the south. During the reign of Sultan Shams al-Din Firuz Shah (r. 1301-22), Mymensingh, Sylhet, Satgaon and Banga were permanently annexed and a mint established in Sonargaon. Thus almost the whole of Bengal except some outlying territories were brought under Muslim rule.[11] It

---

8   Maulana Minhaj-ud-Din Abu-Umar-i-Usman, *Tabakat-i-Nasiri: A General History of the Muhammadan Dynasties of Asia, Including Hindustan from 810 A.D. to 1260 A.D.*, trans. Major H. Raverty, 2 vols, (rpt. Calcutta, 1995), vol. 1, pp. 584-88.
9   *Ibid.*, 1: 578. None of his coins have yet been discovered.
10 Zia al-Din Barani, *Tarikh-i Firuz Shahi*, ed. Saiyid Ahmed Khan (Calcutta, 1862), p. 82; cited by Karim, *Banglar Itihash*, p. 101.
11 *Ibid.*, pp. 125-28.

had taken more than a century, in contrast to north India where the Muslims had established their kingdom within a decade.

The death of Sultan Shams al-Din Firuz Shah in 1322 and the accession of his son Ghiyath al-Din Bahadur began a period of disorder that led the nobles of Lakhnawti to call upon Sultan Ghiyath al-Din Tughluq of Delhi (r. 1320-25) to intervene. The Tughluq sultan marched to Lakhnawti in 1324, conquered it after fierce fighting, and divided the country into three administrative units, Lakhnawti, Satgaon, and Sonargaon. He appointed a governor for each unit, and the area passed into the control of Delhi where it remained until 1338. Then the weak rule of Muhammad bin Tughluq over a disintegrating Sultanate in Delhi allowed Bengal once more to assert its independence with virtually no opposition, and this time it lasted for two hundred years.

The Independent Sultanate

In 1338, Fakhra, the armour bearer (*silahdar*) of the recently deceased Delhi-appointed governor of Sonargaon, assumed the title Sultan Fakhr al-Din Mubarak Shah and declared Sonargaon independent. Immediately the governors of Lakhnawti, Satgaon, and Kara attacked Sonargaon, but Fakhr al-Din was ready for battle. Qadr Khan, the governor of Lakhnawti, was killed; the fate of the other two is not known. When news of Qadr Khan's death reached Lakhnawti, Ali Mubarak, the paymaster (*ariz*) of Qadr Khan's army, seized the throne of Lakhnawti, and, assuming the name Sultan Ala al-Din Ali Shah, moved the capital to Firuzabad (Pandua), which was about twenty miles further north. The reason for this shift was probably defensive—located away from the river, Firuzabad was not vulnerable to attacks by Fakhr al-Din's navy which could sail up to Lakhnawti from Sonargaon. It was also perhaps a symbolic break with the Delhi Sultanate of which Lakhnawti was the provincial capital. Sultan Fakhr al-Din Mubarak Shah (r. 1338-49) failed to take either Lakhnawti or Satgaon, but was able to add Chittagong to his kingdom, bringing it under Muslim rule for the first time.[12]

As the affairs of the country stabilized in the fourteenth century, Muslims began immigrating to Bengal from north India and beyond in large numbers. Among them were Sufi shaykhs (leaders of mystical orders), who attached themselves to various courts, as well as charismatic holy men-cum-warriors who both conquered and proselytized. One of these was Shah Badr Alam, locally known as Pir Badr, who seems to have lived during the time when Chittagong was first brought into the Bengal Sultanate by Fakhr al-Din Mubarak Shah, and is credited with furthering the spread of Islam in Chittagong.[13] According to local tradition he arrived in Chittagong when the area was

12 N. K. Bhattasali, *Coins and Chronology of the Early Independent Sultans of Bengal* (Cambridge, 1922), pp. 14-17; Abdul Karim, *Corpus of the Muslim Coins of Bengal* (Dacca, 1960), pp. 40-41, 47-48; Karim, *Banglar Itihash*, pp. 145-52.

13 Abdul Karim, *Social History of the Muslims in Bengal*, 3rd ed. (Dhaka, 2001), pp. 135-36; Muhammad Enamul Haq, *A History of Sufism in Bengal* (Dacca, 1975), pp. 235-38.

still uninhabited by humans but infested with fairies and spirits. The holy man (*pir*) begged for a space for his lamp, which when lit, drove away the spirits by its magical power. In the local dialect *chati* means lamp, and this story is believed to be the origin of the name Chatigram (village of the lamp), later Chittagong. There is a tomb in Chittagong of an unknown pir which local people associate with Pir Badr and with the clearing and settling of this frontier.

Another pir was Shah Jalal (d. 1346), the most famous Muslim saint of Bengal. According to his biography, which was compiled in the sixteenth century by Shaykh Ali, a descendant of one of Shah Jalal's companions, the saint was born and raised in Turkestan from where his spiritual guide, Saiyid Ahmad Yasavi, sent him to India with 700 *ghazis* (warriors of the Faith) to bring the unbelievers under the mantle of Islam. Only 313 of them still survived by the time they reached Sylhet in the far eastern limits of India. After defeating the local Hindu ruler in battle and occupying the land, he distributed booty among his companions and allowed his followers to settle there as community leaders and householders. An inscription from Sylhet town, however, ascribes the date and conquest of Sylhet town to one Sikandar Khan Ghazi in 1303-4.[14]

When the famous Moroccan traveller Ibn Battuta visited Shah Jalal in his cave in 1345, Shah Jalal was an old man and so well known that Ibn Battuta had made a detour in his journey in order to visit him. After praising the unique personality and miracles of the shaykh, Ibn Battuta wrote, "It was by his labours that the people of these mountains became converted to Islam, and that was the reason for his settling amongst them."[15] According to local legend Shah Jalal came from Yemen, not Turkestan, and had come to Sylhet when a divine command had ordered him to preach in a land whose soil matched that of Yemen.[16] The story showed that rural people associated him with earth and settlement, and that is how the ghazis became linked with agriculture and the conversion of agricultural communities. A Chinese source of the mid-fourteenth century remarks on the prosperity and tranquillity of the Bengali people; its "source lies in their devotion to agriculture, whereby a land originally covered with jungle has been reclaimed by their unremitting toil in tilling and planting".[17] Men like Shah Jalal not only fought wars but also settled the land and converted many to Islam. Conversion to Islam was nothing new, however; it had been going on gradually over a long period of time, and is aptly described by Eaton as "creative adaptation" rather than spiritual conversion.[18]

Although the ruling dynasties occasionally changed—from the Ilyas Shahis (1342-1415), Raja Ganesh's dynasty (1415-33), the Restored Ilyas Shahis (1433-86), the

---

14   Richard Eaton, *The Rise of Islam and the Bengal Frontier 1204-1760* (Berkeley, 1993), pp. 73-76; Shamsud-din Ahmed, *Inscriptions of Bengal* (Rajshahi, 1960), vol. 4 pp. 24-25.

15   H. A. R. Gibb, *The Travels of Ibn Battuta* (rpt. New Delhi, 2001), pp. 268-69.

16   Haq, *A History of Sufism in Bengal*, pp. 218-19.

17   P. C. Bagchi, "Political Relations between Bengal and China in the Pathan Period", *Visva-Bharati Annals* 1 (1945): 99.

18   Eaton, *The Rise of Islam*, pp. 268-303.

Abyssinians (1486-93), and then the Husayn Shahis (1493-1538), the independence of Bengal remained firm, even though invasions from outside persisted. Two families of Afghans ruled Bengal for the next twenty-seven years, until 1576, when their last ruler was defeated by Khan Jahan, the Mughal General. The Surs (1538-64) the first of these, made Bengal a dependency of the Empire of Delhi for thirteen years when they also occupied the Delhi throne. But after 1553, the Sur viceroy of Bengal declared independence and the status was maintained through the rule of the next Afghan dynasty, the Karrani (1564-76) until the Mughals came in 1576. In that year the Mughal Emperor Akbar's (r. 1556-1605) general Khan Jahan defeated Daud Khan Karrani, the last Afghan sultan of Bengal. Although Emperor Jahangir's (r. 1605-27) general Islam Khan entered Dhaka and made it the capital in 1610 the Mughals were not granted peaceful possession of Bengal, because powerful local landlords continued to resist until 1612 when firm Mughal rule was established.

Ilyas Shahi Dynasty (1342-1415). In 1342 Shams al-Din Ilyas Shah, a new and significant name in Bengal, became sultan. Little is known about him. A coin from the Firuzabad mint dated 1342 shows him as the new monarch of north Bengal. One from 1346 struck at the Satgaon mint and one from 1352 from the Sonargaon mint tell us that he had become the overlord of those two regions as well, making him the first ruler of a consolidated Bengal.[19] The Delhi historian Shams-i-Siraj Afif refers to him as King of Bengal (Shah-i Bangala),[20] King of the Bengalis (*Shah-i Bangaliyan*), and Sultan of Bengal (*Sultan-i Bangala*). He extended his domain in every direction by defeating the local Hindu *rajas* (kings)—in the south to Jajnagar (Orissa), in the north and northeast to Kathmandu (Nepal) and Kamrup (Assam), and westwards to include the entire territory of Tirhut (north Bihar) up to Champaran and Benaras. Some of these territories were lost in 1353 to Sultan Firuz Shah Tughluq of Delhi, when he attacked Bengal, but he was unable to conquer the province itself.

Firuz Shah Tughluq made a second unsuccessful attempt to conquer Bengal during the reign of Ilyas's son Sikandar Shah (r. 1357-89). His success and sense of power at being able to turn back the huge Delhi army is projected in the size of the mosque that he built in Pandua, the largest ever built in India. In the inscription he calls himself "the greatest, the most learned, the most liberal, and the most perfect of the Kings of Arabia and Persia...".[21] On his coins Sultan Sikandar boldly called himself *imam al-azam* (great imam) and even *khalifa* (successor of the Prophet), terms traditionally used on the coins of Bengal to refer to the Abbasid caliph.[22]

Sikandar's son Ghiyath al-Din Azam Shah (r. 1389-1410), the third Ilyas Shahi ruler, was the first to establish links with the outside world; he sent ambassadors to Jaunpur, Iran, Arabia, and China, established madrasas in both Makka (Mecca) and Madina, and

---

19   Karim, *Corpus of Coins*, pp. 42-47.
20   Quoted in Karim, *Banglar Itihash*, p. 154.
21   Abdul Karim, *Corpus of the Arab and Persian Inscriptions of Bengal* (Dhaka, 1992), p. 89.
22   *Ibid.*, pp. 90-93.

even tried, though unsuccessfully, to pursuade Hafiz, the great poet of Shiraz, to come to his court in Pandua.[23] Thus it seems clear that for the early Ilyas Shahi rulers the sources of legitimacy were further to the west, even outside India.

In spite of the extraterritorial affiliations of the sultans, the relationship with the Hindus improved considerably with the establishment of the Independent Sultanate, the reason being that the number of Muslims who had come from Delhi was too small to fill the entire administration, so local people had to be recruited as officials. In addition, the sultans had to nurture local support in order to maintain their independence. The interaction between the ruling elite and Hindu Bengali society often raised the ire of the Sufis who were very influential at the royal court. In 1397 Mawlana Muzaffar Shams Balkhi, a Sufi of the Firdawsi order, expressed his regrets in a letter to Sultan Ghiyath al-Din Azam Shah that unbelievers had "been appointed officers over the Muslims in the lands of Islam" and desired that things should be different.[24] Another measure taken to nurture local support was the court's support of Bengali literature alongside Arabic and Persian. Baru Chandidas's *Sri Krishna-Kirtan* (Songs in Praise of Lord Krishna), written sometime in the fifteenth century, ended a hiatus of 300 years in Bengali literature: after the *Charyapadas*, short songs by Buddhist teachers—which are the earliest extant literary works—from the twelfth century, there was no known literary activity in Bengali until the fifteenth century, when several works were written on both Hindu and Muslim themes.[25]

Conspiracy and partisanship among his courtiers ended in the murder of the last powerful Ilyas Shahi sultan, Ghiyath al-Din in 1410, and ultimately to the downfall of the dynasty after the brief reign of his weak son.

Raja Ganesh Dynasty (1415-33). During the time of turmoil that followed Ghiyath al-Din's assassination, Raja Ganesh, a powerful and aristocratic Hindu landlord (*zamindar*) from north Bengal, became the real ruler, first by manipulating a line of puppet kings, and then in 1415 by placing his own twelve-year-old son Jadu on the throne and ruling as regent.[26] Upon his accession in 1415, Jadu had coins struck bearing his new Muslim name Jalal al-Din Muhammad (r. 1415-32). The conversion was apparently an attempt to ease the tension between the Bengali and Turkish elite, but the Sufis were shocked by the sham conversion. One of them, Shaykh Nur Qutb Alam, the leading Chishti saint of Pandua, wrote to a friend describing the reign of the infidel's son who sat on the throne wearing the

23 Karim, *Banglar Itihash*, pp. 181-82.
24 S. H. Askari, "The Correspondence of Two 14th-Century Sufi Saints of Bihar with the Contemporary Sovereigns of Delhi and Bengal", *Journal of the Bihar Research Society* 42, pt. 2 (1956): 187; Eaton, *The Rise of Islam*, p. 50.
25 Dusan Zbavitel, *Bengali Literature* (Wiesbaden, 1976), pp. 123, 148-49. For greater detail see Ahmed Sharif, *Bangla Sahitya* (Dacca, 1978), vol. 1, pp. 297-476.
26 There is disagreement among historians regarding the kind of power that Ganesh wielded at this time. See Eaton, *The Rise of Islam*, pp. 50-52. Karim is of the opinion that Ganesh actually reigned for a few years before giving up the throne to his son; *Banglar Itihash*, pp. 209-13.

guise of a Muslim. He also wrote to Sultan Ibrahim Sharqi of the neighbouring kingdom of Jaunpur imploring him to invade Bengal and rid them of Raja Ganesh, but the Raja was able to deal successfully with the invader.[27]

By an ironic turn of events Sultan Jalal al-Din Muhammad Shah became a spiritual disciple of Nur Qutb Alam and sought to legitimize his status as a devout Muslim by adopting the Hanafi legal tradition, building mosques at home and a madrasa in Makka, and establishing ties with Sultan Ashraf Barsbay, the Mamluk ruler of Egypt. He also struck coins bearing the Muslim confession of faith, a practice in abeyance for nearly 200 years, and took the bold step of proclaiming himself *khalifat Allah* (viceregent of God) on his coins. Coins issued from Fathabad (modern Faridpur) show that the sultan extended his jurisdiction to south Bengal.[28] He established diplomatic relations with the Chinese emperor and in 1430 helped to reinstate an Arakanese king who had been dispossessed of his throne by the king of Burma. This was a significant period in the history of Bengal because Jalal al-Din was the first Muslim ruler of Bengali origin to attempt to forge a Bengali Muslim identity that was firmly grounded in the local culture. Jalal al-Din's son Shams al-Din Ahmad Shah ascended the throne in 1432-33 and ruled for a short while, but left no accounts of his reign.

Restored Ilyas Shahi Dynasty (1433-86). According to the historians Firishta, who wrote in Bijapur during the reign of Ibrahim Adil Shah in the early sixteenth century, and Khwaja Nizam al-Din Ahmad, who wrote in Delhi at the end of the sixteenth century during the reign of Emperor Akbar, as well as the *Riyazu-s-Salatin*,[29] the next sultan of Gaur, Nasir al-Din Mahmud Shah (1433-59), was a descendant of Ilyas Shah. As a result this new line of kings came to be known as the "Restored" or "Later" Ilyas Shahis. During the reign of Sultan Nasir al-Din, his general Khan Jahan conquered the Khulna-Jessore area. The mosque inscription at Masjidbari indicates that by the time his son Rukn al-Din Barbak Shah (1459-74) ascended the throne, areas in what is today the Patuakhali district had been brought under Muslim control, giving the realm a continuous southern frontier up to the Bay of Bengal. Barbak Shah was also known as a patron of poets and learned men, both Hindus and Muslims. He inducted several Abyssinian (*habshi*) slaves from East Africa into both civil and military service, and his army also included a large number of Afghans.

27 Abdul Karim, "Nur Qutb Alam's Letter on the Ascendancy of Ganesa", *Abdul Karim Sahitya Bisarad Commemoration Volume*, ed. Muhammad Enamul Haq (Dacca, 1972), p. 338; Syed Hasan Askari, "New Light on Rajah Ganesh and Sultan Ibrahim Sharqi of Jaunpur from Contemporary Correspondence of Two Muslim Saints", *Bengal Past and Present* 67 (1948): 32-39; and Ghulam Hussain Salim, *Riyazu-s-Salatin: A History of Bengal*, trans. Abdus Salam (rpt. Delhi, 1975), pp. 114-15.
28 Karim, *Corpus of Coins*, p. 76; and Eaton, *The Rise of Islam*, pp. 54-63.
29 Muhammad Qasim Firishta, *Tarikh-i-Firishta*, quoted from Karim, *Banglar Itihash*, p. 243, note 3; Khwaja Nizam al-Din Ahmad, *Tabaqat-i-Akbari*, trans. Brajendranath De, 3 vols. (rpt. Calcutta, 1996), vol. 3, p. 434; Salim, *Riyazus Salatin*, p. 119.

Of Khan Jahan (d. 1459) we know little beyond what is inscribed on his tomb in Bagerhat, where he is identified as "Ulugh Khan-i Azam Khan Jahan",[30] denoting that he was a high ranking officer of Turkic origin. But locally Khan Jahan is remembered as the person who not only converted the population to Islam, but also laboured himself to clear the forest for settlement and drain the swamps for agriculture. He built a capital at Khalifatabad (probably the town of Bagerhat) with several large mosques and tanks, including the Shaitgumbad, the largest mosque in Bangladesh. He also built roads, mosques and tanks in Barobazar, a site northwest of Bagerhat in the Jhenaidah district, which some now identify with Mahmudabad of Sultanate times.[31] Buildings dating to his time have a distinctive style that is known as the Khan Jahan style.

The Restored Ilyas Shahi sultans went a step further than the converted Jalal al-Din Muhammad Shah, who had called himself *khalifat Allah* and sought greater legitimacy by assuming the even more grandiose title of *khalifat Allah bil hujjat wal burhan* (the vice-regent of Allah by proof and testimony). The Restored Ilyas Shahi rule ended in 1486 when Jalal al-Din Fath Shah was assassinated in a coup d'etat staged by the Abyssinian palace guards.

Abyssinians (1486-93). As their numbers increased, the Abyssinian slaves who had been recruited into military and civil service in the 1460s and 1470s, became very powerful, and played a decisive role in the palace intrigues that had started even before the death of the last Restored Ilyas Shahi king. The seven years following the death of Fath Shah were turbulent, rife with palace intrigues and assassinations as slave after slave conspired for power, and four Abyssinian kings succeeded one another on the throne of Bengal.[32]

Husayn Shahi Dynasty (1493-1538). In 1493, Ala al-Din Husayn Shah, who had served as chief minister under the last Abyssinian sultan, Shams al-Din Muzaffar Shah (1490-93), led a palace coup in the course of which the sultan was killed and Husayn placed himself on the throne. The reigns of Ala al-Din Husayn (1493-1519) and his son Nusrat Shah (1519-32) are often termed "the golden age" of the Bengal sultanate. We gather from literary sources that Husayn was of Arab origin, but had lived in Bengal for many years before he came to court.[33] As sultan, he occupied every part of the country, pushing its western frontier past Bihar up to Saran in Jaunpur and reduced the kingdoms of Orissa in the southwest, Arakan in the southeast, and Tripura in the east to vassalage. In 1494, when Sultan Husayn Shah Sharqi of Jaunpur fled to Bengal after being

---

30   Ahmed, *Inscriptions of Bengal*, vol. 4, pp. 64-66; Karim, *Corpus of Inscriptions*, p. 138.

31   A. B. M. Husain, "Baro Bazar: Was it the Mahmudabad of Sultani Bangla?", *Essays in Memory of Momtazur Rahman Tarafdar*, ed. Perween Hasan and Mufakharul Islam (Dhaka, 1999), pp. 228-36.

32   Eaton, *The Rise of Islam*, p. 63; Karim, *Banglar Itihash*, pp. 264-80.

33   The most comprehensive study of this period is M. R. Tarafdar, *Husain Shahi Bengal, 1494-1538 A.D.: A Socio-Political Study*, 2nd rev. ed. (Dhaka, 1999).

defeated in battle by Sultan Sikandar Lodhi of Delhi, the latter attacked Bengal in pursuit of the Jaunpur ruler. Unable to make any gains, Sikandar Lodhi returned home after concluding a peace treaty with the Bengal sultan. A pious Muslim, Sultan Husayn Shah was also very liberal toward the Hindus and appointed them to important positions. Two prominent Vaishnava Brahmans, Rup and Sanatan were appointed to his council of ministers, the former being also his private secretary (*dabir-i-khas*). Still others held important posts such as chief of his bodyguards, master of the mint, and governor of Chittagong, and another was his private physician. Hindu poets showed their appreciation of his liberal policy by calling him the *tilak* (the auspicious mark on the forehead) of kings.[34]

The disintegration of Husayn Shahi power started with its second ruler Nusrat Shah (r. 1519-32). A new influx of foreigners was making inroads into northern India including Bengal. In 1526 the Mughals established themselves in Delhi by defeating the Afghans, who arrived in large numbers to seek refuge in Bengal. In 1529 the army of the Mughal emperor Babur (r. 1526-30) defeated the Bengal army posted in Bihar and reached the outskirts of Tirhut, the gateway to Bengal. By the time of the last Husayn Shahi king, Ghiyath al-Din Mahmud Shah (r. 1532-38), the Portugese had also got permission to trade in Bengal. In 1538, the independent sultanate of Bengal under the Husayn Shahis came to an end when Gaur fell to Sher Shah Sur, the Afghan ruler of Bihar.

Sher Shah Sur and Succesors (1538-64). Sher Khan Sur, (later Sher Shah) was an Afghan chief who challenged Mughal authority from his *jagir* (revenue assignment) in Bihar. He occupied Bengal in 1538 and proclaimed his sovereignty. Pursuing his ambitions further he drove the Mughal emperor Humayun (r. 1530-40, and 1555-56) out of India and set himself up as emperor in Delhi (1540-45) where his family ruled until the Mughals regained the throne again. In the new Afghan empire Bengal became a dependency of Delhi, but only for thirteen years. At the death in 1553 of Islam Shah, Sher Shah's son, anarchy broke out and the empire dissolved. Bengal was one of the first limbs to break off, and Shams al-Din Muhammad Shah (1553-55), the Sur viceroy of Bengal declared independence. The last independent Sur ruler of Bengal was murdered after only a year on the throne by Taj Khan Karrani, another Afghan who set up his own dynasty in 1564.

Karrani Dynasty (1564-75). Taj Khan Karrani was one of the chief officers of Sher Shah who, during the anarchy that followed the death of Islam Shah fled first to Bihar and then to Bengal. There, both he and his brother Sulayman became very powerful by exploiting the situation of internecine warfare among the Afghan chiefs. When Taj Khan died in 1565, only after a year of assuming power, his brother Sulayman succeeded

---

34 Cited in Tarafdar, *Husain Shahi Bengal*, p. 68.

him. During Sultan Sulayman's reign from 1565 to 1572 Bengal became the dominant power in eastern India and the sultan ruled over all the territories east of the Son River, and southwards up to Puri in Orissa. He diplomatically kept the Mughal emperor Akbar placated by reading his name from the pulpit on Fridays (*khutba*), and never striking his own coins. At this powerful monarch's death a political void was created by the fratricide that broke out, a situation which the Mughals were ready to exploit. Moreover, when Daud, Sulayman's son took over he started striking his own coins and had his own name read in the khutba, acts tantamount to official declaration of independence. Although Mughal campaigns against Bengal started in 1574, Daud Khan Karrani was defeated and killed in Rajmahal in 1576, ending the Afghan Sultanate in Bengal. However, the zamindars of East Bengal, known as the Baro Bhuiyans, were able to operate as local chieftains, enjoying freedom in their own territories and continuing to defy the Mughals. It was only in 1612, after the defeat of the last Baro Bhuiyan, that all of Bengal was firmly integrated as a Mughal province and was administered by viceroys appointed by Delhi. Subsequently, it lost much of its regional character and began to resemble other Mughal provinces.

The spread of Islam in Bengal between the thirteenth and sixteenth centuries through pioneering heroes like Badr Alam, Shah Jalal, and Khan Jahan, many of whom still live on among the rural folk as immortal saints or pirs, parallels the spread of Hinduism in Bengal between the fifth and the twelfth century when Brahman settlers from north India were given land grants there.[35] The arrival of Islam coincided with major ecological changes, for it was in these same centuries that the entire riverine system of Bengal changed course. The most significant change was the gradual eastward shift of the Ganges from the Bhagirathi-Hughly channel in West Bengal to the channel of the Padma that now runs through the heartland of present-day Bangladesh. Since agriculture was the mainstay of the economy of deltaic Bengal and the best agricultural land is found in areas where the rivers are most dangerously active, the shifting of the river system also meant the shifting of economic centres. Old cities on the banks of the dried-up riverbed such as Lakhnawti and Satgaon were abandoned.

The sacredness the Hindus attached to the river Ganges was still retained by the old stream that flowed to the sea, but the Muslim pioneers took the opportunity to tackle the newly formed fertile areas and settled there. Many of the pioneers enjoyed the financial and political backing of the Muslim state, but in the absence of institutions like an organized church, there was little religious instruction after the initial conversion of the masses; consequently in their ways and manner of conducting their lives, these Muslims differed little from their Hindu brethren.

That conversion was mainly carried out among the rural population was still evident as late as 1872, when the first census of Bengal found that nearly 48 per cent of the total population of Bengal proper were Muslims, but that the majority of them lived in the

---

35 Radhagovinda Basak, "Tipperah Copper-Plate Grant of Lokanatha: The 44th Year", *Epigraphia Indica* 15, (1919-20): 301-15.

low-lying areas of eastern Bengal. The largest concentrations were in areas east, north, and south of the Hughly River. In some of the western and northern districts, where formerly the Muslim capitals were located, the percentage of Muslims had declined dramatically, and in the new urban centres of Dhaka and Chittagong, although also located in predominantly Muslim districts, Muslims were in the minority.[36]

In the earlier capital cities of Gaur, Satgaon, and Sonargaon, an urban culture had flourished. In their madrasas and mosques, some known only through literary sources, were resident Sufis of great learning, who often mediated in political affairs and were patronized by the sultans.[37] The massive conversions were not in these cities, but in the rural areas where the folk-hero pirs operated.

In the early sixteenth century a powerful Vaishnavite devotional movement spread through Bengal led by the great saint Chaitanya (1486-1533), according to whom the love of Radha for Krishna was seen as a microcosm of the love of a devotee for God.[38] This movement appealed to the same rural classes who were the targets of Islam, and were opposed by the conservative Brahmans, who emphasized Sanskrit over Bengali and the exclusiveness of the high caste. Chaitanya, the founder of the cult, was regarded as an avatar (incarnation) of God by his followers in eastern India, and was allowed to let his movement grow and flourish. It is significant that the Muslim court not only patronized Vaishnavite literature, but also appointed Vaishnavites to important positions in the court.

This kind of cultural accommodation is very boldly reflected in both the literature and architecture of the period. A Chinese traveller who visited Pandua in 1433 observed that, although Persian was spoken by some in the Muslim court, "the language in universal use is Bengali".[39] For the first time in Bengal, the rulers were encouraging the use of Bengali instead of Sanskrit. This is particularly true of the Husayn Shahi kings who, during the last quarter of the sixteenth century, sponsored translations by Kavindra Paramesvara from the *Mahabharata*, one of the most important Sanskrit epics. They also supported the writing of such important Bengali works as the *Manasa-Vijaya* (Victory of the Goddess Manasa), by Vipradas, *Manasa-Mangala* (In Praise of Manasa) by Vijaya Gupta, *Krishna-Mangala* (In Praise of Krishna) by Yasoraja Khan and *Sri Krishna-Vijaya* (Victories of Lord Krishna) by Maladhar Basu.[40]

From the fifteenth century onwards, Muslim poets wrote romances, epics, narratives, and devotional poems whose intention was to present Islam to the common people in familiar terms. The stated intention of all these writers to write in the vernacular language was to educate the masses of Bengali Muslims who were ignorant of their own religion and religious traditions, though they were well acquainted with the popular

---

36   Tables A and B in Rafiuddin Ahmed, *The Bengal Muslims 1871-1906: A Quest for Identity* (Delhi, 1981), pp. 2-3.
37   Askari, "The Correspondence of Two 14th-Century Sufi Saints", pp. 186-87.
38   Sushil Kumar De, *The Early History of the Vaisnava Faith and Movement in Bengal*, 2nd ed. (Calcutta, 1961), pp. 1-8.
39   Bagchi, "Political Relations between Bengal and China in the Pathan Period", p. 117.
40   Tarafdar, *Husain Shahi Bengal*, pp. 252-63.

non-Muslim lore of the exploits of Rama, Shiva, Manasa, Chandi, Dharma and other minor deities. Saiyid Sultan, a pioneering Muslim writer of the sixteenth century, regretfully writes that "Muslims as well as the Hindus in every home read Kavindra's version of the *Mahabharata*", and he was saddened to hear them recite stories of Rama and Krishna.[41] Several Muslim poets start off with an apology for writing religious stories in Bengali, but hope and pray for God's forgiveness because this is the only way that the faithful can understand what they write.

In their pioneering effort to use a language that would be understood by the people, the writers absorbed into their work all kinds of indigenous religious and cultural notions. The only works that did not deviate from the standard Islamic practices were of a liturgical nature, dealing with the rituals of fasting, funerals, prayers, baths and ablution, and the like, such as the *Bedaralgafelin* by Sekh Munshi Chamiruddin, a book listing heresies committed through negligence or carelessness.[42]

The extent to which Islam was reshaped to suit the Bengali environment can be gauged by the *Nabi Bangsha* (Genealogy of the Prophet) written by Saiyid Sultan. The poem begins with a creation myth and ends with the death of the Prophet Muhammad, with Brahma, Vishnu, Shiva, Rama, Krishna (Hari), Adam, Noah, Abraham, Moses and Jesus treated as successive prophets of God in between. The poet writes that under the influence of the devil the descendants of Qabil (Adam's son) became unbelievers, so God sent Krishna as a prophet to dissuade them from doing evil.[43] In a long description Krishna is seen in all his familiar images, as a cowherd, the slayer of the demon Kaliya, the lover of the milkmaids, and as the friend of Arjuna. Soon, a divine voice reminds him of his mission, and when Krishna goes into hiding to save himself from lovesick women, they make metal images of him to worship in every home. He leaves the country on his vehicle Garuda, accompanied by Arjuna. After travelling throughout the universe, he returns once more to reason with the people so that they can desist from worshipping idols. But they have already given up their souls to the devil and persist in their wrong ways.

Inspite of an Islamic worldview there is an attempt here to couch the Muslim concept of prophet in the Hindu concept of avatar. Each avatar/prophet received a scripture from God, which they preached. In course of time, when the religions that they taught became corrupt, Muhammad, the last and most perfect avatar/prophet, was sent with the Quran. In this way the new religion lost its foreignness and established roots in Bengali soil.

In the Sultanate period, the leaders of Muslim society were concerned with presenting Islam in an idiom that was within the experience of the common Bengali. This spirit is seen in all aspects of culture which, like the *Nabi Bangsha*, blended together the concept of prophet and avatar and gave the Prophet's adventures a setting

---

41   Saiyid Sultan, *Nabi Bangsha (Rasul Charit)*, ed. Ahmed Sharif (Dacca, 1965), vol. 1 p. vii, vol 2, p. 479.

42   Quoted by Q. A. Mannan, *The Emergence and Developement of Dobhasi Literature in Bengal up to 1855* (Dacca, 1966), pp. 152–71.

43   Saiyid Sultan, *Nabi Bangsha*, vol. 1, pp. 178–81 and vol 2, p. 467–500.

that made them readily understandable to the people of the delta. Even today, the rural Muslim, with limited knowledge of the finer points of his religion, is very emphatic about his identity as a Muslim. The cultural identity and the psychic mould of today's Bengali Muslim is rooted in the liberal attitudes of the Independent Sultans of Bengal who permitted Bengali culture to flourish and combined it with Islamic influences brought in from the central Islamic lands.

— 2 —

ORIGINS OF BENGALI MOSQUE ARCHITECTURE

Sultanate mosque architecture in Bengal showed the same spirit of adaptation to the old Hindu ways as did Sultanate life and culture. Indigenous forms were used to create a new type of building to meet the congregational needs of the Muslim community. The mosques were based on forms and concepts derived ultimately from the village hut, a small humble unit constructed of mud or woven bamboo with a thatched roof (*chala*) and curved cornice (fig. 2). Paintings of temples from Buddhist manuscripts of the eleventh century (fig. 3) as well as extant temples from neighbouring Burma (Myanmar) dating from the eighth to twelfth centuries (fig. 4), when Bengal had strong cultural and religious ties with it, indicate that these too had the same prototype. Unfortunately none of these huts has survived from Sultanate times, because of the ephemeral nature of their construction; through the centuries, the basic design of the hut has remained the

Fig. 2. Bagerhat, a do-chala thatched hut

Fig. 3. Shikhara-shirsha bhadra temple in Ashta Sahasrika Prajnaparamita

Fig. 4. Hmawza (Burma), Bebe Paya Temple, eighth century

Fig. 5. A chau-chala thatched hut

same: there has been no great demand for innovation, only corrugated iron sheets often replace the mud and bamboo building material if the villager sees better days.

A Bengali village homestead consists of a group of huts usually clustered around a courtyard. Each hut is a single-room rectangular or square structure with walls of woven bamboo, reed matting, or mud on a framework of bamboo or wooden posts. The roof, generally *do-chala* (two segments; fig. 2) or *chau-chala* (four segments; fig. 5), is most often made of thatch over bamboo framing. The *do-chala* roof of a hut slopes down in two directions away from the centre of the room. The ridge at the top formed by the meeting of the two slopes is curved because of the nature of the roofing material of bamboo and reed. The curvature of the thatched *chala* roof and the cornice is the result of using bamboo, which is extremely strong but very flexible; if the bamboo members are laid horizontally in the roof framing, they sag between the vertical supports. To prevent this, a slight upward curvature is given to bamboo roofing by increasing the height of the supporting bamboo or wooden posts towards the centre (fig. 6). As a result the frame for the roof which is placed over these posts is highest at the tallest centre pole. The curvature is not for drainage, since the slopes of the *chala* perform that function.

A *chau-chala* roof is constructed of the same material as the *do-chala*, but it slopes down in four directions; the end slopes are triangular in shape. A second, duplicate, roof in diminished scale is added if there is a central chamber surrounded by a *chala* verandah. Even today, when village houses are built of brick, roofs are not flat constructions in concrete, but *do-chala* or *chau-chala*, made of corrugated iron sheeting or clay tiles. Evidence from manuscript painting suggests that even palaces were sometimes based on the hut prototype; only the scale was larger and the building material and decoration used were more expensive and elaborate. One such palace is illustrated

Fig. 6. Sonargaon, bamboo frame for a do-chala hut

in the *Iskandar Nama* made for Sultan Nusrat Shah of Bengal in 1531-32, which, in the absence of extant examples, gives us an idea of what a grand residence looked like. Its miniature painting of Alexander receiving Dara's daughter Roshanak (fig. 7) shows the king sitting in the square chamber of a brick house decorated with terracotta and

Fig. 7. "Alexander Receiving Dara's Daughter Roshanak" from Iskandar Nama of Sultan Nusrat Shah, 1531-32

tiles.[1] The building has a triangular *chala*-roofed pavilion on the upper level and a projecting verandah with curved eave and roof supported by brackets. Although shown on the left of the picture, the verandah was properly situated in front of the building from where two women are approaching the king. The red border of the verandah with designs of a darker colour indicates that it is also of brick and terracotta. The square brick building with a verandah in front and decorated with terracotta plaques is common to mosques as well as contemporary residential buildings.

PRE-ISLAMIC TEMPLE ARCHITECTURE

In the pre-Islamic culture of Bengal, two types of temple—the *shikhara* (tower) and the *bhadra* (horizontal platform-like divisions of the superstructure)—were used interchangeably regardless of the religion of the user. By their structure and appearance it was impossible to tell whether a temple was Hindu, Buddhist, or Jain. A deity inside, or sometimes a specific iconographic symbol on the outside, was the only indication of its religious denomination. The *shikhara* was modelled after the north Indian *nagara* type of temple, characterized by a cruciform ground plan and a high curvilinear tower on which the projections of the sanctuary were continued. The tower had crowning elements such as the *amalaka* (a round fluted cushion-shaped element resembling a fruit of the same

Fig. 8. Votive shikhara temple from Dinajpur, ca. tenth century

---

1 Robert Skelton, "The Iskandar Nama of Nusrat Shah", *Indian Painting*, exhibition catalogue (London, 1978), pp. 135-52; illustration facing p. 140.

Fig. 9. Ashrafpur bronze stupa with bhadra temple in front, ca. seventh century

Fig. 10. Dhyani Buddha Amitabha seated inside a shikhara-shirsha bhadra temple, Dhaka, ca. eleventh century

name). The cruciform plan was achieved by projecting each side of the square chamber on the exterior only; the interior of the sanctuary retained its square shape. A few temples of this type are still extant in West Bengal, but in Bangladesh they are only seen in temple representations on votive offerings and stone sculptures (fig. 8).

The *bhadra* type had a tiered roof over the sanctuary, and consisted of a number of receding tiered stages surmounted by finials. Though the form of the *bhadra* was derived from rural hut construction, at least some were built in stone. Extant examples of *bhadra* temples in stone are found in the district of Bankura in West Bengal. In a Cambridge University Library manuscript (Add. 1643) of the *Ashta Sahasrika Prajnaparamita* (Eight Thousand Forms of the Goddess of Wisdom), copied in Nepal in 1015, many Buddhist shrines are represented. Among them as many as fourteen temples are of this type, and of those six were located in eastern India, including three in Bengal. Representations of this type of temple are also found in a number of relief sculptures of the Pala era in Bengal, mainly from areas that are now in Bangladesh. The shrine in relief on the Ashrafpur bronze votive *stupa* (a dome-shaped structure that contains the relic of a Buddha or other honoured individual) from around the seventh century is perhaps one of the earliest examples (fig. 9) of this

Fig. 11. Hmawza, Lemyethna Temple, eighth century

bhadra type of temple.[2] Evidence suggests that the type was well known in this area from ancient times. The Cambridge University Library manuscript lists similar temples in Nepal, Sri Lanka, and Cambodia. In Burma, the early type of plain palace building (*pyatthat, prasada*) represented by the tiered palaces of Prince Siddhartha among the sculptures of the Ananda Temple at Pagan also resemble the *bhadra* type.[3]

The basic *bhadra* type comes in two variations. In the *stupa-shirsha bhadra*, the superstructure of a succession of tiered roofs is surmounted by a stupa. Of the eight temples of this type illustrated in the Cambridge University manuscript, four are in Bangladesh. Of these, the shrine of Yajnapindi Lokanatha in Dand-Bhukti (southwest Bengal) represents its most primitive form, with the superstructure consisting of a roof of a single sloping tier surmounted by a stupa,[4] again closely linked to the design of the thatched hut in bamboo and wood. There are no extant examples of this type in India, but two temples in Pagan, the Abeyadana and Patothamya, display its most prominent features, thus providing evidence of a type common to both Pagan and Bengal.

The *shikhara-shirsha bhadra* has a succession of tiered roofs surmounted by a tower instead of a stupa. The monumental brick temples in the monastic complexes at Mainamati and Paharpur (seventh to thirteenth centuries) in Bangladesh belonged to this group, but they had cruciform plans with a central square core. None of the small

2   Published in S.K. Saraswati, *Architecture of Bengal* (Calcutta, 1976), bk. 1, pl. 1:1.
3   *Ibid.*, pp. 71-78; Perween Hasan, "Reflections on Early Temple Forms of Eastern India", in *Journal of Bengal Art* 2 (1997): 216-18.
4   Saraswati, *Architecture of Bengal*, bk. 1, pp. 72-73; Alfred Foucher, *Etudes sur l'iconographie bouddhique de l'Inde d'après des documents nouveaux* (Paris: Ernest Leroux, 1905), cat. 1, no. 36.

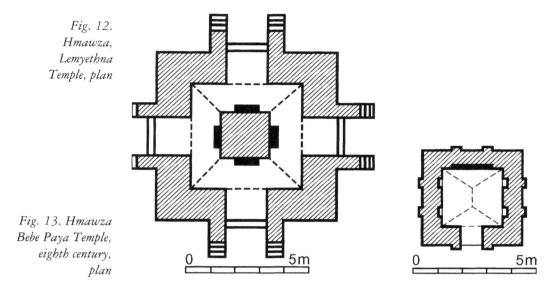

Fig. 12. Hmawza, Lemyethna Temple, plan

Fig. 13. Hmawza Bebe Paya Temple, eighth century, plan

temples of this type have survived in Bengal, but proof that they were common throughout the country is found both in manuscript illustrations and sculptures where the deity sits inside a temple (fig. 10). The Cambridge University manuscript illustrates ten examples of this type of temple, of which seven are in north and west Bengal. The simplest one in the group is in Varendra in north Bengal (fig. 3). It is a shrine on a high plinth approached by a staircase, with a single-tiered sloping roof surmounted by a *shikhara* with *amalaka*. Up to the tiered roof, it is clear once more that the prototype was the village hut. Several relief sculptures from pre-Islamic times are evidence of its popularity in east Bengal.

In the early medieval period, eastern India was an active centre of Buddhism, and Buddhist thought and ideas travelled from there to centres outside India. In the process, ideas concerning religious buildings were also transmitted. Religious and cultural contacts and a contiguous land mass probably account for the common traits in the architecture of Bengal and Burma (Myanmar). The resemblance in ground plan and elevation between the Ananda Temple at Pagan (eleventh century) and the utterly ruined temple in the Somapura monastery at Paharpur (eighth century) is remarkable.[5] In fact, the elevation and plan of the former, which is very well preserved, have helped scholars to reconstruct the plan of the earlier Paharpur temple. Climate and history have been kinder to Burma than to Bengal in the preservation of ancient monuments, but existing evidence strongly suggests that the models for the early Burmese temples must have come from Bengal.

Early prototypes of the temples of Pagan may be recognized at Hmawza, the site of Thayethettaya (Srikshetra), the capital of the Pyus, who were rice growers. The present

---

5   Saraswati, *Architecture of Bengal*, bk. 1, p. 80, fig. 9; p. 128, fig. 11, pls. 18 and 20.

village of Hmawza is near the old city of Prome, which was destroyed at the end of the eighth century. The Lemyethna Temple at Hmawza (figs. 11 and 12) is a simple square building of brick with entrances on all four sides, each with two flanking buttresses. In the centre of the chamber is a square solid masonry obelisk with sculpted Buddhas on four sides, each in an axial line with the entrance doorway on that side. Between the obelisk and the walls is a barrel-vaulted space. The roof is composed of three sloping tiers placed one above the other in a diminishing scale. The topmost one, corresponding to the top of the obelisk, is flat. The final *shikhara* is missing.

Another example at Hmawza is the Bebe Paya Temple (figs. 4 and 13) which is also of brick, and consists of a groin-vaulted cella with an altar at the far end. Externally, there are three stepped tiers on a diminishing scale surmounted by a *shikhara*. The sanctuary has a single entrance and the three sides are blind with false doors. Burmese chronicles say that during the tenth century, pagodas were built in Pagan after consultations with monks regarding the pagodas in old Prome, then known as Yathepyi.[6] Elaborate versions of the temples of Hmawza built in Pagan in the eleventh century are still in use today. In both elevation and ground plan the brick temples at Hmawza closely resemble the square, single-domed mosques of Bengal.

The Ananda Temple and its similarity with the earlier temple at Paharpur strengthen this argument. The excavations at Hmawza have produced terracotta votive tablets with representations of temples[7] that are similar to those in the stone-sculpture reliefs of Bengal or illustrated in manuscript paintings. That temples similar to those at Hmawza existed in Bengal during pre-Islamic times establishes a link between this "lost" type and the square, brick mosques of the Sultanate period.

Unfortunately, no early brick temples of the *bhadra* type exist in Bengal today. But the Hmawza temples, together with the numerous representations in sculpture and manuscript painting, suffice to demonstrate that the type was common in Bengal throughout the pre-Islamic period. The design and manner of execution that links the Bengali monuments with the Hmawza temples, in spite of the difference in roofing, is so close that it makes the Central Asian connection regarding the origin of the square-domed type of building tenuous.[8] The study of Sultanate mosques therefore has the added advantage of allowing us to document a period of building in Hindu/Buddhist architecture, for which we have no extant example.

---

6   Pe Maung Tin and G. H. Luce, *The Glass Palace Chronicle of the Kings of Burma* (London, 1923), p. 59; also cited in Saraswati, *Architecture of Bengal*, bk. 1, p. 144.

7   *Annual Report of the Archaeological Survey of India*, (1927-28): 131-32, pl. LV; Saraswati, *Architecture of Bengal*, bk. 1, pp. 147-48.

8   The kiosk mosque theory of André Godard, "Les anciennes mosquées de l'Iran", *Athar-e-Iran* 1 (1936): 187-210.

THE SULTANATE MOSQUES
(May be read as Conclusion)

Of the corpus of nineteen dated mosques in this study, seventeen were built between 1450 and 1550. The comparatively small number of monuments from the earlier period could be attributed in part simply to their being earlier—fewer have survived. But there was almost certainly some building in the early days even as the Muslim conquerors were busy coping with internal dissension as well as hostile forces at the frontiers.

The most active building period coincides with the rule of the Restored Ilyas Shahi dynasty (1433-86) and the Husayn Shahi dynasty (1493-1538). There are no dated mosques from the brief Abyssinian interregnum (1486-93). The rest of the mosques in the group all date from the early fifteenth to the mid-sixteenth centuries. This flurry of building activity indicates a rapid growth in the size of the Muslim community, as the countryside became dotted with the small mosques required for a growing and mainly rural population. With their low domes and low facades, and curved cornices, they fit nicely into the local cultural milieu. The lack of monumentality suggests that the immigrant Muslims were not concerned with projecting the majesty of religion or the power of the state. They felt little need to impress the conquered people with imposing architecture; they could concentrate instead on meeting their ritual needs by building small practical buildings.

Anyone familiar with the monsoon climate and countryside of Bengal crisscrossed by rivers knows the difficulty of overland communication. It was more practical to have small mosques sufficient for a population living in a confined area, than large ones for a congregation, some of whose members would have had to travel some distance. The resulting distinctly regional style had wide popular appeal. The immigrant Muslims fused their own methods and techniques of construction with a form that already existed and was well known in Bengal and its neighbouring areas. A new life was given to pre-existing forms, and the result was so close to the Bengali spirit that Sultanate mosques in their turn influenced sixteenth- to nineteenth-century *bangla* (*do-chala*), *chala* (four or more *chalas*), and *ratna* (single or multiple towers) temples (fig. 14).[9] In this post-Muslim tradition, very often the *chala* or *ratna* roof was an external shell hiding the dome inside.

Although there are no extant examples of these temples before the sixteenth century, their forms are so well developed that it is hard to believe that some equivalent did not exist earlier. Throughout the Islamic period, whenever temples were built, they assimilated the changes that were brought about by the Muslim rulers in their mosque construction, an unusual example of cultural and architectural accommodation. The brick mosque also faithfully followed its unpretentious model of the hut and reproduced the form inherent in bamboo and thatch construction. The addition of a dome and the square floor plan needed for dome construction were its only major formal modifications. The

---

9 As classified by David McCutchion, *Brick Temples of Bengal*, ed. George Michell (Princeton: Princeton University Press, 1983), pp. 36-43.

Fig. 14. Puthia, chala Govinda Temple, eighteenth century

importation of new technology by the Muslims made it easy to build domed structures, and the dome also had symbolic value in that it clearly differentiated the mosques from the places of worship of the other religions. The Muslims adopted a pre-existing form, adapted it to their needs, enriched it, and then shared it with the culture from which it had originally come. The non-Muslim culture also readily accepted it.

Characteristics of Sultanate Mosques

The Sultanate mosques could be small or large, square or oblong, with or without verandahs in front, plain or profusely decorated, but they all had in common a remarkable uniformity of design and a set of characteristics that identified them as belonging to the same group. Several features familiar from the Islamic architecture of the central Islamic lands and north India reappear here; others are totally new.

Brick construction. Brick is the dominant building material, as is to be expected in a region like Bengal where clay is readily available. Buildings of the Buddhist and Hindu cultures from very early times—e.g., the well-known Paharpur and Mainamati monastery complexes dating from the seventh to the thirteenth centuries—are already of brick.[10] Stone was not readily available and was used only sparingly: unless quarried from older buildings, it had to be transported from the Rajmahal hills or the Munghyr area of Bihar.[11] Generally, only the two outer sides of the brick walls were of dressed masonry with lime mortar; the core was of less careful brickwork and mud mortar.

The wall surfaces of Sultanate mosques were left unplastered but filled with brick designs and terracotta decoration, in contrast to the less adorned exteriors of buildings of the corresponding period in north India. Lime was used both in mortar and as plaster on the parapet, roof, and domes to make them water resistant.[12]

Fig. 15. Shankarpasha, thatched hut-mosque

10   M. H. Rashid, *Paharpur* (Dacca, 1980), and M. A. Qadir, "Recent Excavations", *Mainamati-Devaparvata* (Dhaka, 1997), pp. 93-124.
11   Frederick M. Asher, "Ancient Slate Quarry Revisited: A Source Located", *Journal of Bengal Art* 4, (1999): 263-65.
12   Chemical analysis of a sample obtained from Baba Adam's Mosque, Munshiganj, shows its composition to be 32% lime and limestone, about 46% clay, the rest sand and powdered brick.

Origins of Bengali Mosque Architecture

A brick mosque with terracotta decoration would have been very special in Sultanate Bengal, where most construction was of mud and thatch. Perhaps it belonged to a wealthy person; it certainly represented an extraordinary effort and was not the everyday utilitarian structure found in Muslim communities and neighbourhoods. The everyday places of worship were probably just like any hut, except that they were reserved for prayer. In the typical Bengali village, the rooms in each hut had specialized functions such as bedroom, store, kitchen, cattle pen, etc., so it would only have been natural to erect one more hut to provide a space for worship. Such hut-mosques are common even today in rural areas; one was found (fig. 15) not far from the Shankarpasha Mosque in Habiganj, where a simple mihrab projection on the west side is the only external expression of the building's function. Otherwise, it is entirely indistinguishable from the other structures in the village.

Domes and the square domed unit. Usually the dome is considered the best way to cover a large space without the use of columns. The square unit was necessary because the dome was considered indispensable in Muslim buildings, especially religious ones, and the base of a dome must be inscribed within a square. Domes were ubiquitous; they were used in mosques, tombs, and sometimes even gateways. Since temple roofs were pitched, tiered or spired, it was the dome that signalled that a building was a mosque. Otherwise, in plan and much of the external elevation particularly, the small mosques

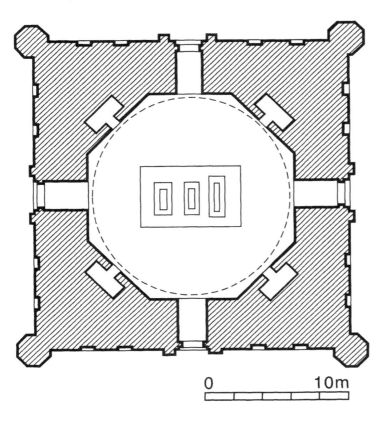

Fig. 16. Pandua, West Bengal (India), Eklakhi Tomb, early fifteenth century, plan

Fig. 17. Pandua, Eklakhi Tomb

closely resembled the temples of the Hindu/Buddhist tradition. The square-domed unit became the basic module for all Sultanate mosques, regardless of whether they had one dome or nine or were multi-domed rectangles.

There is some uncertainty regarding the earliest domed square building built by the Muslims in Bengal, but the earliest firmly dated one is Binat Bibi's Mosque in Narinda, Dhaka (1456-57). There is also, however, a small single-domed mosque in Molla Simla in the Hughly district of West Bengal (India) that has been tentatively dated even earlier; an inscription tablet recording the building of a mosque in 1375 was found affixed to the wall of a nearby tomb. Since this was the only old mosque in the village, it seemed possible to assign the inscription to it.[13] The mosque has been completely rebuilt, but if the 1375 date is accepted, then it, not Binat Bibi, would be the first extant mosque of this type in Bengal.

The Eklakhi Tomb in Pandua, Malda district of West Bengal (India) is more universally accepted as the earliest example of the square single-domed type of building (figs. 16-17).[14] The tomb is not dated by inscription, but gives an early fifteenth-century date on the basis of the primitive solution to the transition zone between square sides and round dome. To minimize the size of the squinches that comprise the zone of transition, the interior was made octagonal in form with exceptionally thick walls (nearly four metres). Rudimentary squinches appear as the transition zone on each corner of the octagon. If the Molla Simla Mosque is accepted as having been built in 1375, however, then it would also preempt the introduction of the use of squinches.

13   A. H. Dani, *Muslim Architecture in Bengal* (Dacca, 1957), pp. 49-50; Shamsud-din Ahmed, *Inscriptions of Bengal* (Rajshahi, 1950), vol. 4, pp. 38-40; Catherine B. Asher, "Inventory of Key Monuments", *The Islamic Heritage of Bengal*, ed. G. Michell (Paris, 1984), p. 86.

14   Dani, *Muslim Architecture in Bengal*, pp. 76-83; Asher, "Inventory of Key Monuments", p. 113.

The grandness of the Eklakhi Tomb has also led scholars to assign it as the final resting place for the family of Sultan Jalal al-Din Muhammad Shah, the converted son of Raja Ganesh and the last sultan who ruled from Pandua. The building is a landmark in Bengal architecture, as it establishes a style that became the hallmark of this area during the entire Sultanate period, and even beyond. Among its typical features are a gently curved cornice, engaged corner towers, and terracotta decoration on the walls. As the first Muslim king of native Bengali origin, it would seem natural for Jalal al-Din to model his family tomb after sacred and domestic buildings with which he was familiar and which also emphasized his local roots. Possible sources of inspiration are the indigenous *chala* hut and the pre-Islamic brick temples discussed earlier.

On the subcontinent as a whole, the earliest extant square building with a dome is the tomb of Iltutmish in Delhi, dated about 1235.[15] The dome has since collapsed. Its plan became the model for gateways such as the Alai Darwaza (1311) as well as tombs (e.g., the tomb of Ghiyath al-Din Tughluq of a few years later) in Delhi, but it was never used for mosques. The Delhi buildings also differ from those in Bengal in plan and elevation. They sometimes have battered walls, may or may not have corner towers, but never have curved cornices. These differences rule out a strong Delhi influence in Bengal, except perhaps in the buildings in the Khan Jahan style, whose stark exteriors and circular corner towers seem to have been Tughluq inspired.

In searching for prototypes to the square, domed buildings of Bengal, some have cited earlier buildings in Islam,[16] particularly the tenth-century Samanid Tomb in Bukhara. The so-called kiosk mosques of Iran, thought to be derived from the Sasanian *chahar taq* fire temples, have also been cited as a possible source.[17] The square, single-domed Bengali mosque and the Samanid Tomb are similar to the extent that they are both square buildings with domes; otherwise, they represent two different worlds. The Central Asian building tapers upwards, has a very refined and intricate brickwork pattern on all four sides which is integral to the design, has doors on all four sides, and is surmounted by a blind gallery. The brick construction and the plaque-covered walls of the Bengal buildings give a greater impression of massiveness, but they are more crudely executed than the Central Asian monuments. As for the "kiosk mosque" theory of André Godard, which hypothesizes the existence of a single domical room type of early Iranian mosque, it has by now been entirely discounted.[18]

15 P. Brown, *Indian Architecture (Islamic Period)* (Bombay, 1968), pp. 14-15; R. Nath, *History of Sultanate Architecture* (Delhi, 1978), p. 39.
16 Syed Mahmudul Hasan, *Mosque Architecture of Pre-Mughal Bengal* (Dacca, 1979), p. 113.
17 M. A. Bari, "Khalifatabad and its Monuments", M. Phil thesis, Rajshahi University, 1980, p. 89.
18 For kiosk mosque theory, see Godard, "Les anciennes mosquées de l'Iran", *Athar-e-Iran* 1 (1936): 187-210. For arguments against it, see Oleg Grabar, "The Visual Arts", *Cambridge History of Iran* (Cambridge, 1975) vol. 4, pp. 338-39; Jean Sauvaget, "Observation sur quelques mosquées seljoukides", *Annales de l'Institut d'Etudes Orientales, Université d'Alger* 4 (1938): 81-120; Janine Sourdel, "Inscriptions seljoukides et salle à coupoles de Qazvin en Iran", *Revue des Etudes Islamiques* 42 (1974): 3-43.

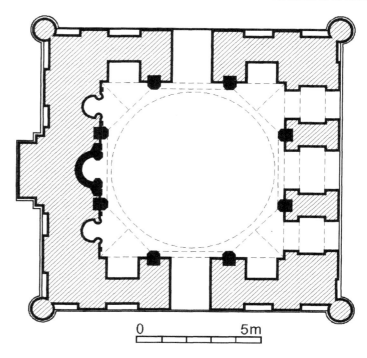

Fig. 18. Sonargaon, Goaldi Mosque, 1519, plan

In its simplest and most common form in Bengal, the mosque was a small building consisting of a single square chamber with a dome. Binat Bibi's Mosque has the smallest interior (3.20 m sq.). Large mosques, such as the Ranbijoypur Mosque in Bagerhat with an interior of 10.80 m sq., were rare. The single square chamber had three doors in front exactly opposite the three mihrabs in the qibla wall. Side entrances were also exactly

Fig. 19. Sonargaon, Goaldi Mosque, southwest view

opposite each other on the north and south sides. Sometimes a verandah was added to the front of a single-domed mosque just as it would be in front of a hut, or even a palatial building. The small square building with a dome was most popular for mosques in Bengal, and numerous examples can be cited from all over Bangla-

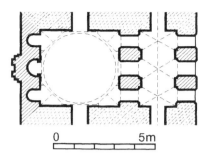

Fig. 20. Dinajpur, Gopalganj Mosque, 1460, plan

desh. A typical one is the Goaldi Mosque of 1519 (figs. 18-19) in Sonargaon. Eight square single-domed mosques, e.g., the Gopalganj Mosque, Dinajpur, of 1460 (figs. 20-21) have verandahs in front. The only large rectangular mosque with a verandah is the Darasbari Mosque of 1479-80 (figs. 22-23) in Gaur. Mosque verandahs are either divided into small bays and covered by small *chau-chala* vaults and domes or one large *chau-chala* as in the Masjidbari Mosque of 1465-74 (fig. 24) in Patuakhali. They provide additional space to accommodate the congregation when the interior room is filled.

To form a large mosque with a central aisle (for the central mihrab) and equal number of aisles on either side, the basic square module was simply multiplied: this made either a larger square with an equal number of bays and aisles for a nine-domed mosque, or a rectangular mosque if aisles and bays were unequal in number. In these large mosques the symbolic value of the domes is emphasized, as several small domes are used. Each dome roofs a square bay formed by four columns.

Fig. 21. Dinajpur, Gopalganj Mosque, cross-vaulted verandah

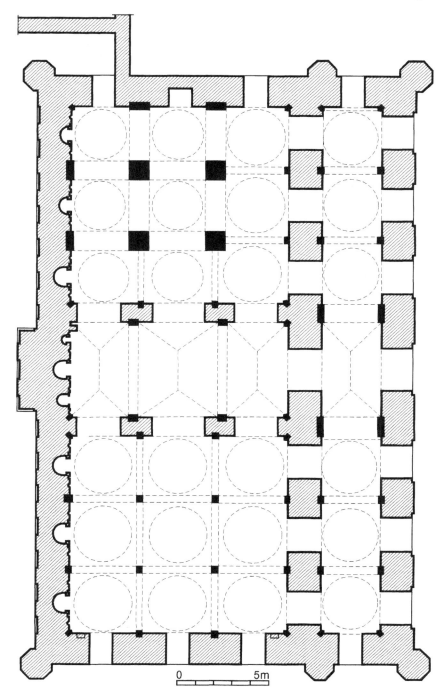

Fig. 22. Gaur, Darasbari Mosque, 1479-80, plan

ORIGINS OF BENGALI MOSQUE ARCHITECTURE

Fig. 23. Gaur, Darasbari Mosque, southeast view

Nine-domed mosque. To retain the basic unit of a single-domed square, the simplest way to enlarge a mosque and still keep a central mihrab and an equal number of smaller mihrabs on either side was to build a nine-domed structure. This made the interior area larger, while retaining the symmetry of the square, single-domed mosque. The next enlargement using the same principles would produce an extremely large square building with twenty-five bays. But the Bengali Muslims seem not to have been much concerned with projecting the majesty of state or the power of Islam by building huge mosques; the Adina Mosque in Pandua in Malda district of West Bengal is only one of a few exceptions. Once the Muslims had overcome the initial resistance of the local population, they were satisfied with building small mosques that fulfilled their ritual needs.

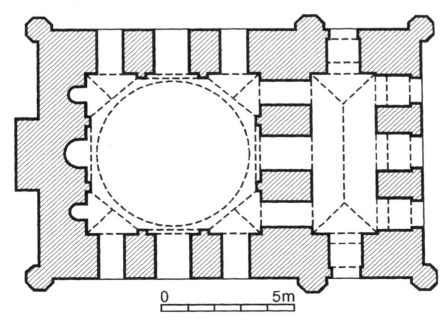

Fig. 24. Patuakhali, Masjidbari Mosque, 1465-74, plan

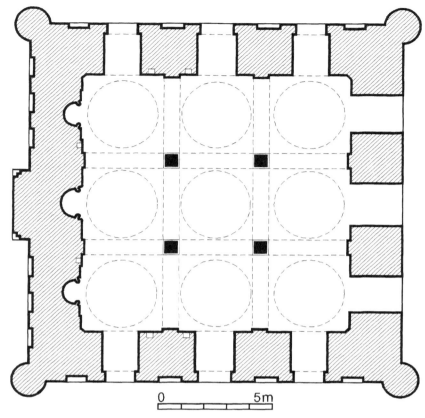

Fig. 25. Bagerhat, Nine-domed Mosque, mid-fifteenth century, plan

Fig. 26. Bagerhat, Nine-domed Mosque, southwest view

Compared to the typical Bengal single-domed mosque, however, the nine-bayed mosques were large and certainly built for the Friday congregation. There are four mosques of this type in Bangladesh, but none in West Bengal or Delhi; the four can be dated stylistically to the fifteenth and sixteenth centuries. They are the Nine-domed Mosque, Bagerhat (figs. 25-26); the Masjidkur Mosque, Khulna; the Kasba Mosque, Barisal; and the Shatoir Mosque, Faridpur. They range in size from 11.60 m sq. (Kasba Mosque) to 13.70 m sq. (Shatoir Mosque).

In the nine-domed mosques, four pillars in the centre of the square chamber divide the interior into nine equal square bays, each of which is covered by a dome. In addition to the three entrances in front, there are entrances on the north and south sides. The Kasba Mosque is the exception—it has only two side entrances. The three mihrabs in the west wall are on an axis with the front entrances.

One building with this plan that is not a mosque is the structure attached to the exterior west wall of the Adina Mosque in West Bengal. It is popularly believed to be the tomb of Sultan Sikandar Shah. Considering the location, the position of the four interior pillars, and the absence of any trace of a sarcophagus, the building was more likely used as a resting and meeting place for the king and his company before they entered the *maqsura* of the mosque.[19] If that is the case it would be the only nine-domed building with a non-religious function.

In Delhi the mosque of Jahanpanah (Begumpur Mosque, 1343) has a nine-bayed maqsura projecting off the north end of the prayer wall; the Khirki Mosque (ca. 1375) incorporates a nine-domed scheme into the plan of a larger square mosque with four enclosed courtyards. The Khirki is almost contemporary to the Adina Mosque, and is believed to be one of the seven mosques built by Khan-i-Jahan Junan Shah, prime minister of Firuz Shah Tughluq (1351-88). Its plan is a symmetrical arrangement of twenty-five squares, of which four are open courts, nine are nine-bayed with domes, and the remaining twelve are also nine-bayed but with flat roofs.[20]

The nine-bayed mosque is known to have been imported from the central Islamic lands, as is clear from the predominance of Arab examples among the earliest of them.[21] The type became popular in Bengal, probably because it was an entirely covered building that suited the need of the Bengalis for a covered space to shelter the assembly from the heat and rain. Nowhere else do we find such a concentration of nine-domed

---

19 C. Asher, "Inventory of Key Monuments", p. 111.
20 Anthony Welch and Howard Crane, "The Tughluqs: Master Builders of the Delhi Sultanate", *Muqarnas* 1 (1983): 130, 138.
21 Lisa Golombek, "Abbasid Mosque at Balkh", *Oriental Art* 15, no. 3 (1969): 188. For the mosque at Kura along the Darb Zubaydah, a pilgrimage road with accommodations en route built by Zubaydah, wife of the Abbasid caliph, Harun al-Rashid (787-809) that connected the holy places of Arabia with southern Iraq, see Saudi Arabia, Department of Antiquities, *An Introduction to Saudi Arabian Antiquities* (Riyadh, 1975), pp. 13, 29. For an excavation report, see K. al-Dayel et al., "Preliminary Report on the Third Season of Darb Zubaydah Survey 1978", *Atlal* 3 (1979): 46.

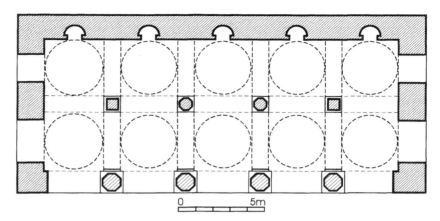

Fig. 27. Tribeni, West Bengal (India), Zafar Khan Ghazi's Mosque, 1298, plan

buildings. We know of no pre-Islamic examples of nine-bayed buildings in Bengal, which also supports the hypothesis that it was an imported type that became thoroughly Bengalized with use. Because the local single-domed square unit had simply been multiplied, it made it appear to belong to the local tradition. Although nine-bayed mosques were not built in Bengal after the Sultanate period, the Mughals built tombs containing nine rooms of different sizes, and the plan was followed in several late medieval and early modern Hindu temples.[22]

Rectangular mosques. Occasionally the basic square domed unit was multiplied to form an unequal number of bays and aisles resulting in an oblong building, with the longer sides on the west (qibla) and east to accommodate the long prayer rows. In the process of enlargement, columns replaced interior walls, and domes covered each four-columned bay. The result is a hypostyle mosque that from outside appears as clusters of single-domed square units. Hypostyle mosques of oblong shape where the interior columns divide the space into square bays, each covered by a dome, seem to have been popular in Bengal from very early times. The earliest extant dated example is Zafar Khan Ghazi's Mosque (1298) in Tribeni, in Hughly district of West Bengal (figs. 27-28). It has been restored, but with no change to the ground plan. This type of rectangular mosque where a dome covers each bay pre-dates similar mosques built in Delhi. Sultan Firuz Shah Tughluq built the earliest example of the type, the Kotla Mosque in Delhi,[23] immediately

---

[22] The tombs of Shah Niamatullah Wali at Gaur and Bibi Pari in Dhaka, modelled after tombs with similar plans in Delhi and Agra, have large central rooms and four corner rooms with vaulted passages in between (Dani, *Muslim Architecture in Bengal*, pp. 256-58 and 212-15). Plans of Sonarang Temple, Munshiganj; Dolmancha, Shiva, and Govinda temples in Puthia; Kantanagar Temple, Dinajpur; and Shashana Temple in Gazipur are also very similar. See Saif Ul Haque et al., *Pundranagar to Sherebanglanagar: Architecture in Bangladesh* (Dhaka, 1997), figs. 59, 73-81.

[23] J. A. Page, *A Memoir on Kotlah Firoz Shah* (Delhi, 1937), p. 1.

ORIGINS OF BENGALI MOSQUE ARCHITECTURE

Fig. 28. Tribeni, Zafar Khan Ghazi's Mosque

after his return from his first Bengal expedition in 1354. Each aisle in the rectangular covered prayer chamber terminates on the west with a mihrab and on the east with an entrance. Generally the end bays running north to south also terminate in entrances, but occasionally they are replaced by recesses, as in the north and south walls of Baba Adam's Mosque, Munshiganj of 1483 (figs. 29-30). The number of domes that cover the

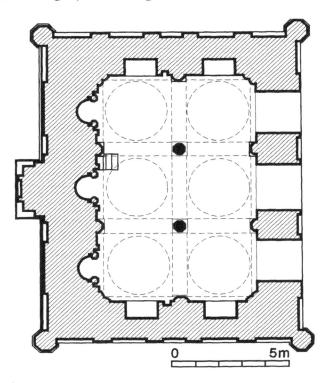

Fig. 29. Munshiganj, Baba Adam's Mosque, 1483, plan

Fig. 30. Munshiganj, Baba Adam's Mosque, reccesses in the exterior south wall

building is determined by multiplying the number of eastern entrances by the number of northern or southern ones.

The courtyard with surrounding porticoes, ablution fountain, and the minaret that are always present in the mosques of West Asia and North Africa are absent in Bengal. The heavy monsoon rains make a courtyard useless. The rectangular shape could be an adaptation of the Quwwat al-Islam Mosque at Delhi where the western portico was turned into an independent building, and each bay was roofed with a dome. The Delhi mosque, in turn, had as its prototype the oblong, covered *zulla* (shaded area of a mosque; sanctuary) of the early mosques of Islam.[24] (Several rectangular mosques with uniform bays are included in the catalogue; Baba Adam's Mosque is a good example.)

In a few of the large rectangular mosques, for example, the Adina Mosque of West Bengal (1375), an emphasized nave-like central aisle divided the zulla into two equal wings. The Adina's long barrel vault has by now completely collapsed (figs. 31-32). In Sultanate Bengal, with the exception of the Gunmant Mosque in Gaur of Malda district of West Bengal, where the central aisle is a smaller version of that the Adina, such aisles are always divided into small rectangular units, each one covered by a *chau-chala* vault. This innovation proved to be longer lasting than the single, large barrel vault. Three mosques of different sizes are of this type: the Shaitgumbad Mosque in Bagerhat (mid-fifteenth century, figs. 33-34); the Darasbari Mosque, which also has a verandah in front (1479), and the Chhota Sona Mosque (1493-1519), both in Gaur of Bangladesh.

---

24 Dani, *Muslim Architecture in Bengal*, p. 51. For drawing of the Quwwat al-Islam Mosque, see C. Asher, *The Architecture of Mughal India* (Cambridge, 1992), p. 3, fig. 1. Richard Ettinghausen and Oleg Grabar, *The Art and Architecture of Islam, 650-1250* (Harmondsworth, 1987), pp. 20-21, and 35-45.

ORIGINS OF BENGALI MOSQUE ARCHITECTURE

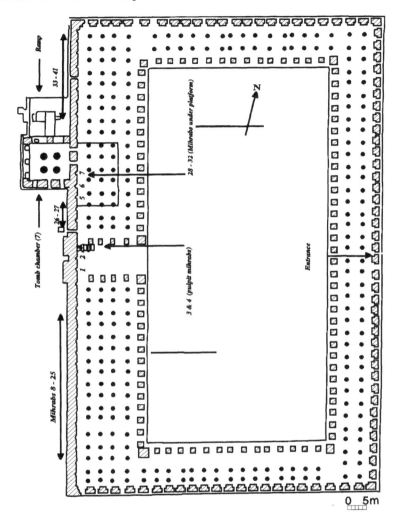

Fig. 31. Pandua, West Bengal, Adina Mosque, 1375, plan

Fig. 32. Pandua, Adina Mosque, central aisle with collapsed vault

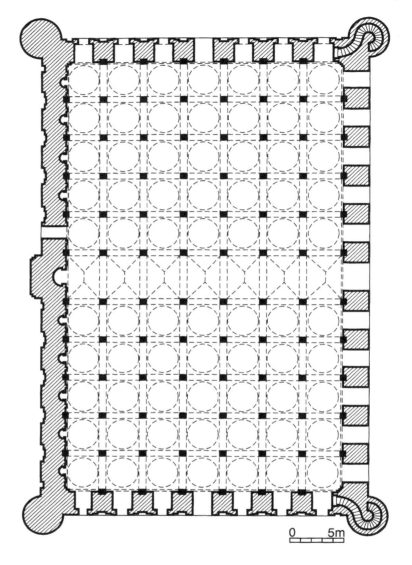

Fig. 33. Shaitgumbad Mosque, Bagerhat, mid-fifteenth century, plan

Two of the rectangular mosques—Fath Shah's Mosque, Sonargaon (1484) and the Badr Awlia Dargah Jami Mosque, Chittagong (late fifteenth century)—have only single domes. In these mosques, the domes rest on squares formed by the east and west walls and two wide vault-like transverse arches on the north and south sides (fig. 35-36). This was probably an attempt to enlarge the more conventional single-domed square space, but it resulted in two flat sections of roof over the transverse arches and was not very popular.

The most developed form of this type is Qutb Shah's Mosque in Kishoreganj (late sixteenth century), where a balance was sought by placing smaller domes in the four corners of the roof (figs. 37-38). Its plan is a combination of a single-domed square structure with a rectangular structure of three bays and two aisles. The two side entrances in the north and south and the corner domes reinforce a sense of linearity in the interior

Fig. 34. Bagerhat, Shaitgumbad Mosque

space. The plan resembles the Jamatkhana Mosque of Delhi of the early fourteenth century where, according to some scholars, the side wings are later additions.[25]

Curved cornice. The curved cornice of a brick mosque was a decorative element; it was not, of course, the result of using bamboo as in a thatched hut. It did not exist in pre-Islamic temples of wood or brick, or in sculpture where such temples are carved in relief. The very gently curved cornice in brick appears for the first time in the Eklakhi Tomb of West Bengal (early fifteenth century; fig. 17), and only after that did it become a characteristic feature of all Sultanate buildings.

Engaged corner towers. Engaged corner towers are another feature common to all Sultanate mosques. They are more often associated with the architecture of large fortified buildings, and are not generally found in small brick structures. But in rural hut construction corner posts are an essential part of the framework on which the fabric of the hut stands. With the exception of the Shaitgumbad Mosque in Bagerhat (figs. 33-34), where the two front towers have staircases inside and functioned as minarets, these towers are solidly built forms. In the Adina Mosque rudimentary corner towers are still confined within the rectangular plan (fig. 31). They are prominently featured for the first time in the Eklakhi Tomb, the first building in the true Bengal style (figs. 16-17).

In northern India, corner towers appear as early as the Arhai-din-ka-Jhompra Mosque of circa 1205 in Ajmer and in the tomb of Sultan Ghari (1231) in Delhi. They reappear later in the Tughluq mosques of Delhi, and in the regional styles of Jaunpur, Gujarat and

---

25 Nath, *History of Sultanate Architecture*, pp. 49-50.

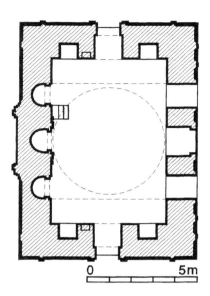

Fig. 35. Sonargaon, Fath Shah's Mosque, 1484, plan

the Deccan. Their source need not be Muslim. The Great Mosque of Damascus (706), the first mosque with corner towers, took the feature from a pre-Islamic tradition and used it for the *azan*, the Islamic ritual call to prayer. In Bengal, however, they were not used for that purpose. Nor were there many minarets. Although the minaret is elsewhere an architectural feature traditionally associated with a mosque, it is conspicuously absent from the mosques of Bengal, at least the smaller ones. The call to prayer was probably given from the forecourt or from inside the prayer chamber whenever weather conditions did not permit one to go outside. Since the majority of mosques served small rural communities in clusters of huts, hearing the call was not a problem.

On the Indian subcontinent as a whole, the vast majority of mosques also lacked minarets, leading some scholars to conclude that Indian rulers rejected their use because the first mosque, the Mosque of the Prophet in Madina, did not have one.[26] While a few examples can be found in Bengal, there are none in the neighbouring eastern Indian state of Jaunpur. The Shaitgumbad Mosque in Bagerhat is the only example of a mosque with minarets in Bangladesh (fig. 34). It is believed to have been built in the tradition of the Tughluq mosques of Delhi like the Khirki and Kalan (both ca. 1375), and the minarets are explained as part of the overall Tughluq influence on the Khan Jahan style of Bengal in the fifteenth century.[27]

In West Bengal (India) there are two examples of minarets that are detached from mosques—the minaret of the Adina Mosque in Pandua, Malda, and that of the Bari Masjid in Chhota Pandua, Hughly, both of the fourteenth century. Minarets are therefore only associated with the three largest mosques in Bengal, all located in cities that were well known in Muslim times. The Adina minaret, built strategically behind the mosque to face a highway, and the Chhota Pandua minaret, a monumental structure of over thirty-eight metres, show that the call to prayer was not their primary function. They functioned in the first place as powerful symbols of the presence of Islam[28] and to

---

26   A. B. M. Husain, *The Manara in Indo-Muslim Architecture* (Dacca, 1970), p. 16.
27   Dani, *Muslim Architecture in Bengal*, pp. 141-52; Husain, *The Manara in Indo-Muslim Architecture*, pp. 51-63, 91.
28   Oleg Grabar, *The Formation of Islamic Art* (New Haven, 1973), p. 120.

embellish the few large cities in a predominantly rural country. The countryside was so flat and vegetation so thick that a minaret would not have been visible from a distance in any case. Moreover, if it is true that entire communities were converted by pirs and charismatic leaders then the need to have these monumental symbols of Islam would not have been felt at all. As men like Khan Jahan of Bagerhat cleared the forests for agriculture and brought the peasants within the fold of Islam, there was virtually no non-Muslim population left in the countryside to be impressed with any symbols of power directed to them.[29]

Mihrabs, doors and other openings. No matter where one stands inside a Bengal mosque, beyond the columns one always sees an entrance on the east, doors or windows on the south and north, and a mihrab on the west. All over the Islamic world mosques traditionally have a single mihrab in the form of a niche in the qibla wall, and it is considered the only indispensable part of the building. During congregational prayer, when everyone stands in straight lines facing the qibla, the prayer leader (*imam*) positions himself just before the mihrab. The mihrab is an indicator of the direction of prayer, but it is also regarded as both a symbolic doorway to Paradise and a memorial to the Prophet as the first imam in Islam.[30] Because of its importance, it is often the most decorated element in the mosque.

In Bengal, mosques have an unusual feature in the articulation of the qibla wall: from the earliest times, regardless of the size of the mosque, there are as many mihrabs as there are entrances on the eastern (the opposite) side (fig. 33). Sometimes, as in the mosque adjoining Khan Jahan's Tomb, the Shingra, and Zinda Pir's Mosques in Bagerhat, there is a single large mihrab in the centre with small niches on either side instead of side mihrabs. The multiple mihrabs are in axial alignment, as if the entrances generated the niches. This feature, found only rarely in the monuments of Delhi and the other provinces of India, is seen in the Jamatkhana Mosque and the tomb of Iltutmish in Delhi and in the Jami Mosque of Mandu. The Atala and Jami Mosques of Jaunpur and the Jami Mosque of Champanir have as many mihrabs as doorways but they are not all of equal prominence.[31] The same feature occurs regularly in the mosques of Bengal.

The practice may have originated in the pre-Islamic temple. Generally, temples have images of deities on the same axis as the entrances, as can be seen in the temples of Hmawza, Burma (figs. 12 and 13). The temples of Bengal, which are considered to be the prototypes of the Burmese ones, must have followed the same convention. In the

29   Richard Eaton, "Islam in Bengal", *Islamic Heritage of Bengal*, ed. George Michell (Paris, 1984), pp. 26-27; idem, *The Rise of Islam and the Bengal Frontier, 1204-1760* (Berkeley, 1993), pp. 207-19.
30   Ettinghausen and Grabar, *Art and Architecture of Islam 650-1250*, p. 40; Perween Hasan, "Rugs, Niches and Prayer", *Journal of Bengal Art* 1 (1996): 241-44.
31   Nath, *History of Sultanate Architecture*, figs. 17, 20; Brown, *Indian Architecture (Islamic Period)*, pl. XLII, fig. 2; and Satish Grover, *The Architecture of India, Islamic* (New Delhi, 1981), figs. on pp. 54, 56, 102.

Fig. 36. Sonargaon, Fath Shah's Mosque

Bebe Paya Temple of Hmawza, which has a single entrance, the altar is on the wall exactly opposite the entrance. Where there are four doorways on four sides like the Lemyethna, there are correspondingly four images on the four sides of a central obelisk inside the chamber. Therefore there is a strong convention of a door corresponding to an image niche in the temples. Because they were congregational mosques, multiple doorways were needed; the multiple mihrabs seem to have resulted from retaining the idea of a matching doorway opposite found in temples.

The most important place in a temple is the image niche. The devotional rites (*puja*) are performed by, and usually restricted to, the officiating Brahman priest who alone enters the sanctuary. In contrast, a ritual requirement of congregational prayer in Islam is that all worshippers take part. The worshippers form straight lines facing the qibla; when one row is completed the next one is begun. A row of mihrabs on the qibla wall aligned to a row of entrances on the east, as well as the real and blind doorways opposite each other on the north and south sides, give a horizontal, linear emphasis to the internal space. This is especially significant to centrally planned buildings of square shape, like the numerous single-domed mosques of Bengal.

In the mind of the newly converted Muslim, the niche associated with the worship of deities had specific religious connotations. In temples, even when minor deities were placed in niches outside, the interior always had a niche reserved for the major deity. A single mihrab in the west wall of mosques would appear to be a direct transplant of the niche from its sacred position in the temple, where the main deity to whom the temple was dedicated stood. The multiple mihrabs in mosques not only took up that concept, but also helped to emphasize the importance of the whole qibla wall, not just a single niche. Several niches along the qibla wall also helped make clear which was the proper orientation for prayer. Nevertheless, the universal

Origins of Bengali Mosque Architecture

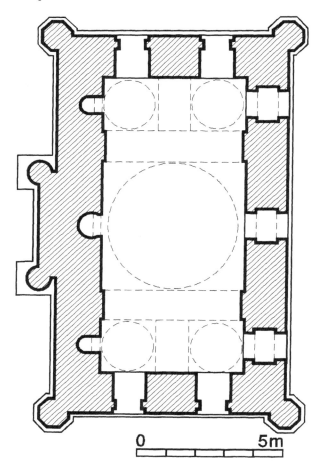

Fig. 37. Kishoreganj, Qutb Shah's Mosque, late sixteenth century, plan

Fig. 38. Kishoreganj, Qutb Shah's Mosque, southeast view

Fig. 39. Sonargaon, Muazzampur Shahi Jami Mosque, 1432-33, mihrab motif on exterior west wall

significance of an ornamented mihrab singled out from the row and emphasized by size and decoration is recognizable even in the multiple mihrab mosques of Bengal. In several of the mosques that were visited, devotees anointed the central mihrab, lit votive candles, and placed incense in it, because they considered the spot a special source of blessing (*baraka*).

The importance attached to the central mihrab is further corroborated by its vivid external manifestation in the Muazzampur Shahi Jami Mosque, Sonargaon, Baba Adam's Mosque in Munshiganj, Shankarpasha Mosque in Habiganj, Majlis Awlia's Mosque in Faridpur, and the Shubhorara Mosque in Jessore.[32] Here a single mihrab motif, as in Muazzampur (fig. 39) or Baba Adam's, or several as in Shankarpasha (fig. 40) is framed in a sunken rectangular panel in the central offset of the western wall. Its

32   See Catalogue, below.

Fig. 40. Habiganj, Shankarpasha Mosque, 1493-1519, mihrab motifs on exterior west wall

prototype can be found in the central *rathas* (projections) of *shikhara* temples that usually had a recessed niche for exterior images on three sides and the doorway on the fourth.[33] Some of the larger mosques, e.g., the Shaitgumbad, had an entrance on the qibla side at the end of the bay just south of the central one used only by the imam or administrator.

Ponds. Like village dwellings, rural mosques always have a pond or a large tank nearby. The pond is excavated because earth is needed to raise the building site above flood level. It also supplies the house with water; and in the case of a mosque a place for ritual cleansing in lieu of the traditional ablution fountain.

Whenever a large mosque with a pond was built, it also affected the planning of the rest of the settlement. Often the house of the ruler, governor, or administrator was built either behind the congregational mosque, as in the Adina or Shaitgumbad, or to one side of it, as in the Darasbari or Chhota Sona Mosques, depending on where the ceremonial entrance reserved for royalty was located. Houses for the officials and nobility were then laid out around it according to their social status.

Fig. 41. Narasimha Vishnu from Rajshahi, seventh-eighth century

Terracotta decoration. The ornamental style of pre-Islamic stone sculpture of the twelfth century is marked by a linearity and sharpness that are not present in earlier

---

33 P. Hasan, "Temple Niches and Mihrabs in Bengal", in *Islam and Indian Regions*, ed. A. L. Dallapiccola and S. Z. Lallemant, 2 vols. (Stuttgart, 1993), vol. 1. p. 94.

Fig. 42. Vishnu from Dhaka, twelfth century

sculpture (figs. 41-42). Not only are the deities themselves profusely ornamented and bejewelled, but the settings are also elaborate and overwrought. A kind of nervous fussiness replaced the earlier composure. The Muslims arrived at the opportune moment when art in Bengal was going through this phase. The ornamental tradition was rejuvenated when the medium was translated from stone to clay, a medium so flexible that it gave new life to an art form that had become as hard and sharp as the stone on which it was carved. Marshall comments that "the mural ornaments which the mason would ordinarily have cut out of stone facings were imitated in the softer material of brick and tiles, often with great skill. As a rule, these brick decorations were not moulded, but were actually cut out with a chisel, and workmen trained in this art are still to be had...."[34] The extensive use of geometric and vegetal designs by Muslim artisans was responsible for a flowering of decorative art in terracotta. The earliest extant examples are in the mihrabs of the Bari Masjid of Chhota Pandua,[35] and the Adina Mosque in Pandua (fig. 43), both in West Bengal. Although Zafar Khan Ghazi's Mosque in Tribeni is the earliest extant mosque in Bengal, its present terracotta decoration is datable to the fifteenth and early sixteenth centuries. Some of the terracotta surfaces (as in Majlis Awlia's Mosque in Faridpur of the early sixteenth century) still have vestiges of a thin lime wash that suggests the designs in relief may have been painted.[36]

---

34 Cited by Naseem Ahmed Banerji, *The Architecture of the Adina Mosque in Pandua, India: Medieval Tradition and Innovation* (Lewiston, 2002), p. 100, from John Marshall in the *Annual Report of the Archaeological Survey of India Annual Report 1902-3*, p. 51.

35 Dani, *Muslim Architecture in Bengal*, p. 48; H. Blochman, "Notes on Places of Historical Interest in the District of Hughli", *Proceedings of the Asian Society of Bengal* 4 (April 1870): 122; Alexander Cunningham, "Report of a Tour in Bihar and Bengal in 1879-80 from Patna to Sunargaon", *Archaeological Survey of India, Report* (1882), vol. 15, p. 125; Asher, "Inventory of Key Monuments", p. 52.

36 For lime wash and painted designs in the Adina Mosque, see Banerji, *The Architecture of the Adina Mosque*, pp. 102-3.

Fig. 43. Pandua, Adina Mosque, terracotta decoration on tympanum above mihrab

Pointed arches. The two-centred pointed arch is common to all the mosques. There are no surviving pre-Islamic specimens of the pointed arch in Bengal, but they were used in Buddhist temples at Bodhgaya and Nalanda in the nearby state of Bihar in India. Pointed brick arches and vaults with radiating voussoirs are also found in the temples of Hmawza and Pagan in Burma (fig. 11).[37] It is possible, therefore, that the form and technology of the voussoired arch were already known in Bengal in pre-Islamic times, but

37 Benjamin Rowland, *Art and Architecture of India* (Harmondsworth, 1977), pl. 109; Gordon H. Luce, *Old Burma–Early Pagan* (Locust Valley, 1969), vol. 1, p. 62, and vol. 3, pl. 190 b, c. Luce claims that the true pointed arch with voussoirs as it appears in Bodhagaya is part of the Burmese reconstruction of the late eleventh century because it resembles the arch of the Nagayon Temple of early Pagan.

only after the Muslim conquest were such arches widely used. In north India pointed arches turn up in the earliest buildings starting from the screens of the Quwwat al-Islam Mosque in Delhi (1199) and the Arhai-din-ka-Jhompra Mosque in Ajmer (1205).

Arched facade. The arched facade is a regular feature of all mosques, whether they are small with only three entrances, or large with several. The piers that bear the arches of the facade in later mosques are rectangular. Arches on hexagonal piers appear in Zafar Khan Ghazi's Mosque (1298) in Tribeni, West Bengal (figs. 27-28) and could have had prototypes in earlier mosques of Bengal which have now disappeared. It is also possible that Persia, where brick mosques had developed arcaded facades much earlier, had its influence through the immigration of artisans to Bengal.

Corbelled pendentive. Brick set cornerwise is a very simple decorative motif in the repertoire of almost any brick mason. In Bengal this cornerwise setting of brick in overlapping courses appears in the zone of transition of every square bay (fig. 44). Earlier in Delhi, stone beams were used to construct similar corbelled pendentives in the complex of buildings in the southwest corner of the Quwwat al-Islam Mosque.[38]

Inscriptions. Where they are present, inscriptions, in addition to giving the date of construction, indicate whether the mosque is a *masjid* or a *jami*, and sometimes provide information about the patron. The Darasbari and the Bagha Mosques were built under the patronage of sultans. Eleven other inscriptions give the names of other donors, generally following the name of the ruling king, but occasionally, as in Baba Adam's Mosque and the Bandar Shahi Mosque, appearing before it. With three exceptions, the rest of the donors have titles identifying them as officials of the sultan. The exceptions are Binat Bibi, the only woman sponsor, a *mulla* (religious scholar) named Hizbar Khan, sponsor of the Goaldi Mosque, and Sulayman, donor of the Kusumba Mosque, Naogaon, whom local tradition identifies as a converted landlord. The inscription on Binat Bibi's Mosque does not mention the reigning king, nor does it have any Quranic verse or *Hadith*. The donor simply describes herself as Musammat Bakht Binat, daughter of Marhamat.

Inscription slabs of stone and one of terracotta (in Jorbangla Mosque, Barobazar) have been found on nineteen mosques, of which thirteen can be clearly read. The other six, on the Muazzampur Shahi Jami Mosque, Masjidbari Mosque, Faqir's Mosque, Shankarpasha Mosque, Jorbangla Mosque and Hammad's Mosque, are only partly legible. Of the thirteen legible inscriptions five belong to large rectangular mosques (Darasbari, Baba Adam, Chhota Sona, Bagha and Kusumba), and all except the last are identified as *masjid al-jami*. Among the legible words and phrases on the Muazzampur Shahi Jami Mosque is the word *kabir* (great or large). If this refers to the size of the mosque, then one may assume that it too was a Friday

---

38 Nath, *History of Sultanate Architecture*, p. 13 and fig. 5.

mosque. None of the inscriptions on the square, single-domed mosques, with or without verandahs, identify them as Friday mosques, although some may have functioned as such.

Most of the inscriptions are in Arabic, with sometimes a few Persian words interspersed in between. The exception is Binat Bibi's Mosque where, except for the *Bismillah* and the *azan*, the inscription is in the form of a Persian couplet. Although the pattern is not always strictly followed, the texts usually have six elements: the *Bismillah*, a Quranic verse, a quotation from the Hadith, the name of the reigning king, the donor, and the date.

Only three inscriptions, those of Binat Bibi's Mosque, the Gopalganj Mosque, and the Chhota Sona Mosque, start with the *Bismillah*. In the Gopalganj and the Chhota Sona Mosques, the Quranic verses follow the *Bismillah*; in the other six, the Darasbari, Baba Adam's Mosque, the Bandar Shahi Mosque, Fath Shah's Mosque, Baba Saleh's Mosque, and the Goaldi Mosque, the inscription begins with a quotation from the Quran. The most commonly quoted text is 57:18: "And the places of worship are for Allah (alone): so invoke not anyone along with Allah." In north India this verse is found in the mosque attached to the tomb of Sultan Ghari (1232) and the Alai Darwaza (1311) in Delhi, and in the Great Mosque of Cambay (1325), Gujarat, all of them dating from a fairly early period of Muslim settlement in India.[39] It was not as commonly used in the rest of India, but is often seen over doorways in the rest of the Islamic world, separating as it does believers from non-believers. The message appears to have had particular relevance for the newly converted Muslims of the time. Dissemination of Islamic learning and culture was slow in those early days of Islam in Bengal, and the new Muslims differed little from the others in their daily activities except for the ritual of prayer. For those living in the midst of an idolatrous culture, this particular text served to remind them of their duty.

The inscription on the Gopalganj Mosque has two verses: "Help from Allah and a speedy victory: so give the glad tidings to the believers" (61:13); and "But Allah is the best to take care (of him), and He is the Most Merciful of those who show mercy" (12:64). The first is also found in Delhi in the Bara Khan ka Gumbad (sixteenth century) and is quite commonly used elsewhere in the Islamic world. The second is used in the Baghi-Alam ka Gumbad (1501) and Bara Khan ka Gumbad both in Delhi, but not much used elsewhere.

The Chhota Sona Mosque uses verse 9:18: "The mosques of Allah shall be visited and maintained by such as believe in Allah and the Last Day, establish regular prayers, and practice regular charity, and fear none (at all) except Allah. It is they who are expected to

---

39 For the inscriptions in Delhi and Cambay, see Erica C. Dodd and Shereen Khairallah, *The Image of the Word*, 2 vols. (Beirut, 1981), vol. 2, pp. 139-40, 132, 63, 42-53; also vol. 1, p. 63.

Fig. 44. Rajshahi, Bagha Mosque, 1523-24, corbelled brick pendentive in interior

be on true guidance." Although this is the most common Quranic text used in the decoration of mosques all over the Islamic world, it is the only example so far found in Bengal.

"Whoever built a mosque, Allah will build for him a similar place in Paradise"[40] is the Hadith, or tradition of the Prophet, used most often ("place" is sometimes replaced by "palace", "castle" or "seventy castles"). In the Sultanate mosques of Bangladesh it appears in twelve inscriptions, in six of them (Darasbari, Bandar Shahi Mosque, Baba

---

40   The translation is from Muhammad Muhsin Khan, *Sahih Al-Bukhari*, 9 vols. (Ankara, 1976), vol. 1, p. 26.

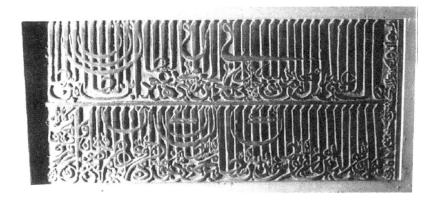

Fig. 45. Tughra inscription of Sultan Shams al-Din Yusuf Shah dated 879/ 1474-75

Adam's, Fath Shah's, Chhota Sona and Goaldi Mosques) following a Quranic verse and in six (Masjidbari, Aroshnagar, Bagha, Jorbangla, Nabagram, and Kusumba) appearing independently.

In the mosque inscriptions all the sultans, except Ahmad Shah (where they may just be missing) have eulogistic titles like "Sun of the World and the Faith" (*Shams al-Dunya wal-Din*), "Pillar of the World and the Faith" (*Rukn al-Dunya wal-Din*), "Splendour of the World and the Faith" (*Jalal al-Dunya wal-Din*), "Most Exalted in the World and the Faith" (*Ala al-Dunya wal-Din*), "Helper of the World and the Faith" (*Nasir al-Dunya wal-Din* and *Ghiyath al-Dunya wal-Din*).

The inscriptions also provide a list of official titles of those who served under the sultan. These are *jangdar* (soldier, or one who attained prominence by his bravery), *shiqdar* (head of an administrative unit known as a *shiq*, which was like a district of today), *wazir* (vizier; minister who performed multiple functions and worked in various capacities), *sar-i-lashkar* (commander of an army; officers with this title are always called *wazir*), *malik* (lord), *malik al-muazzam* (exalted lord), *muqarrab al-dawla* (an adherent of the state, i.e. "a great noble". Siddiq translates the title as "favourite of the government"), *jamdar ghayr mahalli* (superintendent of royal robes), *majlis al-majalis majlis mansur* (a great noble attached to the royal court), *mir bahr* (admiral of the fleet), *nazir* (an officer of the revenue department).[41] The holders of these titles were not always the sponsors, but are mentioned in the inscriptions because of their connections with them.

The calligraphic style of Bengal inscriptions is also unique, being a combination of *naskh* and *tughra*, but most often described as *tughra* because of the stylization (fig. 45). The vertical shafts of the letters were raised upwards, and arranged in rows, and the curves rendered in a manner that has led them to be likened to marching soldiers, bows and arrows, or boat and oars. Although this style is found from the fourteenth century, it reached a climax in the Husayn Shahi period in the early sixteenth century.[42]

---

41 Karim, *Corpus of Inscriptions*, pp. 109, 119, 148, and 343; and Mohammad Yusuf Siddiq, *Arabic and Persian Texts of the Islamic Inscriptions of Bengal* (Watertown, 1992), p. 108.

42 Karim, *Corpus of Inscriptions*, pp. 13-14.

Stylistic Evolution

Although individuals or groups are often responsible for introducing changes to suit their tastes, architectural styles do not automatically change with each dynasty. Therefore, classifying the Sultanate mosques dynastically as Ilyas Shahi, Raja Ganesh, Restored Ilyas Shahi, Abyssinian, Husayn Shahi, Sur and Karrani seems less useful than dividing them according to periods that show easily perceivable changes in style. Each of these periods covers roughly a century. The period of Turkish governors precedes the Sultanate; the Early, Middle, and Late Sultanate periods correspond to the fourteenth, fifteenth, and sixteenth centuries. The Khan Jahan group of monuments is the exception; it represents a homogeneous style of much briefer duration. Sultanate mosques are scattered all over Bangladesh, but are more concentrated in four areas: Gaur, Barobazar, Bagerhat, and Sonargaon.

Period of Turkish governors (1204-1338). From the thirteenth century, which coincides with the rule of the Turkish governors and is the earliest period of Muslim domination, extant monuments are few. The period is sometimes called "Mamluk", though the term is not entirely applicable, as only ten out of the fifteen governors were really *mamluk*s or soldier-slaves. The only firmly dated mosque from this period is the ruined Zafar Khan Ghazi's Mosque of 1298 in Tribeni, Hughly district in southwest (Indian) Bengal.[43] As the inscription on the central mihrab describes this building as a madrasa it is assumed that it functioned both as a madrasa and a mosque. We know from texts that there were other mosques: Ikhtiyar al-Din Muhammad ibn Bakhtiyar Khalji, who established Muslim rule in Bengal, constructed several mosques, as well as madrasas and *khanqas*, in or around the city of Lakhnawti.[44] As there are no mosques left from this time, the best we can do is obtain some idea of the thirteenth-century style by extrapolating from what Zafar Khan Ghazi's Mosque looks like (figs. 27-28).

Zafar Khan Ghazi's Mosque is a large multi-domed rectangular building. During the early years of Muslim occupation, it was important to assert the authority of the conquerors, and large rectangular mosques built chiefly with plundered material would have projected an image of power and superiority. In addition, as the Muslims were still few in number, a single Friday mosque had to serve Muslims converging from a large area. Later, as their numbers increased, local groups could support neighbourhood mosques.

Zafar Khan Ghazi's Mosque was built of brick and stone. The stone, taken from pre-existing temples, was used as a veneer. The rectangular-cut stones were laid one upon

---

[43] Dani, *Muslim Architecture in Bengal*, pp. 38-43; Asher, "Inventory of Key Monuments", p. 135.

[44] Maulana Minhaj-ud-Din Abu-Umar-i-Usman, *Tabakat-i-Nasiri: A General History of the Muhammadan Dynasties of Asia, Including Hindustan from 810 A.D. to 1260 A.D.*, trans. Major H. Raverty, 2 vols. (Calcutta, 1995), vol. 1, pp. 559-60.

the other without mortar, using a traditional Indian technique. The pointed arches of the facade spring directly from huge piers giving the mosque a squat appearance. A row of stone columns divides the interior into five aisles and two bays, a total of ten squares, each one covered by a small dome. In front of each aisle is an entrance, opposite which is a mihrab in the qibla wall. Side entrances correspond to the two end bays on each side of the mosque. The domes are supported by corbelled pendentives; the cornice is straight, and there are no engaged corner towers. Ornamentation is both stone and terracotta carved with vegetal and geometric motifs.

Early Sultanate period. For the fourteenth century, roughly the time of the Ilyas Shahi rule, there are also no extant dated mosques in Bangladesh, aside from the totally ruined Mankalir Bhita Mosque in Mahasthan (Bogra district) of which only the foundation and the stumps of a few piers remain and which is conjecturally dated to the fourteenth century (figs. 47-48). In front are the remains of five massive brick piers which supported the entrance arches and two additional similar rows in the interior which divide the space into three aisles and five bays. The mosque must have had fifteen domes, but as there is no superstructure left at all, it is difficult to reconstruct the style with any accuracy. The early date is based on the massiveness of the brick piers; the facade, which is assumed to have had arches on piers similar to Zafar Khan Ghazi's Mosque; the absence of corner towers, and the large size and rectangular shape of the building.

The Adina Mosque (1375) of Pandua, West Bengal (India), is the only firmly dated mosque from this time, and also the only mosque of its type from medieval Bengal (figs. 31-32).[45] It is the largest mosque in the whole of India, and the only one in Bengal with an enclosed courtyard, a feature traditionally associated with the central Islamic lands of West Asia. Dating from the beginning of the Independent Sultanate, it was clearly conceived as a monumental expression of the glory of the new religion and the authority of the new rulers. Its enclosed courtyard and main prayer chamber with a great vaulted central aisle are reminiscent of the Great Mosque of Damascus, the earliest extant mosque in Islam, which was built by the Umayyad caliph al-Walid in 706. The early mosques of Delhi and Ajmer also have enclosed courtyards, but do not emphasize the central aisle in the main prayer area. Perhaps it was an intentional gesture on the part of Sikandar Shah, the patron of the Adina; he was the first Bengal sultan to style himself *khalifa* (successor of the Prophet) in an inscription and the only one to emphasize his affiliation to Arabia and Persia rather than to India. The design was never popular, and when it was used, it was done cautiously and with adaptations, perhaps because the soil, climate, and needs of the community did not make a building with a long vault suitable, and local craftsmen were not experienced in executing long barrel vaults of such proportions.

---

45 Karim, *Corpus of Inscriptions*, p. 89; Dani, *Muslim Architecture in Bengal*, pp. 58-72; Asher, "Inventory of Key Monuments", pp. 109-11; Banerji, *The Architecture of the Adina Mosque*, pp. 61-100.

Although the plan of the Adina Mosque was exceptional in its use of the central barrel vaulted aisle, all the other interior spaces of the sanctuary were like those in Zafar Khan Ghazi's Mosque. Columns formed numerous square bays, and a dome covered each square. The qibla wall of the western prayer area had a mihrab corresponding to the front entrance. The building has a staggering number of 306 domes and forty-one mihrab niches (figs. 31 and 32). It also shows that brick and stone continued to be used as building materials and that cornices were still straight. The carved stone minbar to the north of the central mihrab shows that, although much of the stone was taken from earlier temples, it was used with a good understanding of how it worked, in contrast to the helter-skelter manner in which plundered material had been used in the early Muslim architecture in both Bengal and elsewhere.

Mosques with emphasized central aisles were built later; the long barrel vault of the Adina was repeated only once, in the Gunmant Mosque of Gaur, West Bengal (sixteenth century) but there it is much smaller.[46] In other instances, such as the Shaitgumbad Mosque in Bagerhat, and the Darasbari and Chhota Sona Mosques in Gaur, the long central aisle was broken up into small oblong bays that could be covered by *chau-chala* vaults (fig. 33).

The building is also important for vestiges of coloured decoration that still remain, and which provide proof that the surfaces of the brick and terracotta mosques were probably once covered with colourful decoration.[47]

Two other mosques assigned to the fourteenth century are also in West Bengal, India.[48] One is the Bari Masjid in Chhota Pandua, considered to pre-date the Adina. It has a large rectangular plan of three bays, twenty-one aisles, and sixty-three domes, and its stone minbar is supposed to have been a precursor of the one in Adina. The second mosque, very small, located in Molla Simla in the Hughly district of West Bengal, is rather tenuously dated to 1375. An inscription that refers to the building of a mosque was found in a nearby *dargah* (tomb), and the assumption that it refers to this particular mosque is quite arbitrary. If the building does belong to the fourteenth century, then it is the earliest extant square mosque in Bengal, a type that became very popular later on. Apart from the plan, which shows the basic square single-domed unit, all other features have been remodelled so many times that it is impossible to draw any conclusions about its date based on style.

The sultans and their officials were constantly at war with each other as well as with Delhi during this period. Only after the middle of the fourteenth century did the Ilyas Shahi sultans finally rule over a consolidated Bengal. Threats from Delhi continued until much later, and the absence of security and stability may account for the scarcity of building activity.

---

46   Dani, *Muslim Architecture in Bengal*, pp. 133-36; Asher, "Inventory of Key Monuments", p. 75.
47   Banerji, *The Architecture of the Adina Mosque*, pp. 102-3.
48   *Ibid.*, pp. 48-50; 52, 86.

Middle Sultanate period. In the fifteenth century, which includes roughly the last part of the first Ilyas Shahi rule, Raja Ganesh's dynasty (1415-33), the Restored Ilyas Shahi dynasty (1433-86), and the period of the Abyssinian Sultans (1486-93), the most significant building is not a mosque but a tomb, the Eklakhi Tomb in Pandua in the Malda district of West Bengal in India (figs. 16-17), which is believed to contain the graves of Jalal al-Din, the converted son of Raja Ganesh, and his family.[49] It re-established unfaced brick as the primary building material, a tradition that went back to the Buddhist monuments of ancient times. Its form, a single-domed, square building with curved cornice, engaged corner towers, and terracotta ornamentation, influenced all subsequent buildings in Sultanate Bengal, particularly mosques, the only building type that has survived in large numbers. If the early fifteenth-century date is accepted, then credit for delineating the exact forms of a typical Bengal mosque, or for that matter of most buildings, goes to the first line of kings who were truly Bengali in origin. Even after Raja Ganesh's dynasty was overthrown, the architectural form of the Eklakhi Tomb was retained as a model for later buildings.

The first mosque listed in this group is dated to the period of Ahmad Shah, Jalal al-Din's son. But as the building is plastered and whitewashed on the exterior much of its original character has been obliterated. The mosques in Bangladesh that belong to this group are the Muazzampur Shahi Jami Mosque, Sonargaon (1432-33); Binat Bibi's Mosque, Dhaka (1456-57); Gopalganj Mosque, Dinajpur (1460); Makhdum Shah Awlia's Mosque, Shahzadpur (mid- to late fifteenth century); Bibi Chini's Mosque, Barguna (mid- to late fifteenth century); Faqir's Mosque, Chittagong (1474-81); Darasbari Mosque, Gaur (1479-80); Bandar Shahi Mosque, Narayanganj (1481); Baba Adam's Mosque, Munshiganj (1483); Fath Shah's Mosque, Sonargaon (1484); and Yusufganj Mosque, Sonargaon; Dhunichak Mosque, Gaur; Khania Dighi Mosque, Gaur; Badr Awlia Dargah Jami Mosque, Chittagong; and Shatoir Mosque, Faridpur – all of the late fifteenth century.

These buildings are all constructed of brick; the walls are very thick and left unplastered to be covered with ornamented brick or terracotta designs. Stocky, octagonal towers at the corners emphasize the solidity of the structure; the cornice and roof are curved; and the various parts of the building convey a sense of harmonious proportion. Several innovations were made in its design, which were later assimilated into the architectural vocabulary of the area. Among them are the addition of a verandah to both the single-domed square and the multi-domed rectangular mosques; three small domes, cross vaults, or a single large *chau-chala* covering the verandah; and additional engaged octagonal towers placed where the verandah joined the prayer chamber. When the central aisle of a large rectangular mosque was singled out for emphasis, it was broken up into rectangular bays and each bay covered with a small *chau-chala* vault.

This was a time of innovation. When Nasir al-Din Mahmud Shah (1433-59), the first ruler of the Restored Ilyas Shahi dynasty moved his capital from Pandua to Gaur, differences

---

49 Dani, *Muslim Architecture in Bengal*, pp. 76-85; Asher, "Inventory of Key Monuments", p. 113.

between the Pandua and Gaur buildings, and even among the Gaur buildings, are noticeable. One can see a progression of style from the Eklakhi Tomb in Pandua to the Dakhil Darwaza in Gaur, West Bengal, and then to the Darasbari Mosque (1479-80).[50] The earlier buildings give an impression of massive strength which, towards the end of the century, tends to give way to greater decorativeness. The Faqir's Mosque in Chittagong, a district in the southeast also has a distinctive style that sets it apart from the Gaur monuments.

The terracotta decoration is subordinated to the building design; there is no excess of ornamentation, but the large decorated panels stand out in high relief against the plain walls. The hanging lantern motif so often used in the Adina Mosque is transformed into a floriate design. Enamelled tiles, first introduced in the Eklakhi Tomb, are much used in the Gaur buildings in West Bengal as well, but rarely in other mosques in Bangladesh.

Khan Jahan style. In the middle of the fifteenth century a group of monuments in southern Bengal were built in a style associated with Khan Jahan, who in his tomb inscription in Bagerhat is identified as "Ulugh Khan-i Azam Khan Jahan," suggesting he was an ethnic Turk (*Ulugh*) and a high-ranking officer (*Khan-i Azam*) in the Bengal Sultanate.[51] The inscription also states that he was a good Muslim, a patron of other Muslims, a hater of infidels, and that he died in 1459. He is popularly thought to have been responsible for the Islamization of the area that now comprises the Bagerhat, Khulna, Satkhira, Jessore, Jhenaidah, Patuakhali, and Barisal districts of Bangladesh. He is said to have cleared the forests there, and founded Khalifatabad, of which the administrative centre was Haveli Khalifatabad, in the town of Bagerhat, where the majority of the Khan Jahan style mosques are located.

There are only two firmly dated monuments in this group, Khan Jahan's Tomb in Bagerhat (1459), and the Masjidbari Mosque in Patuakhali dated 1465-74, both built during the reign of Barbak Shah.[52] Based on his tomb inscription, and the absence of any coinage showing Khan Jahan as a ruler, it is probable that he never set himself up as an independent king. The Khan Jahan group consists of the Shaitgumbad Mosque, the mosque adjoining Khan Jahan's Tomb, the Ranbijoypur Mosque, Bibi Begni's Mosque, the Shingra Mosque, Nine-domed Mosque, and Chunakhola Mosque, all in Bagerhat; the Masjidkur Mosque in Khulna; Kasba Mosque, Barisal; the Shatgachhia and Galakata Mosques, Barobazar; Sailkupa Mosque, Jhenaidah; and the Masjidbari Mosque, Patuakhali (1465-74).

Although rooted in the fifteenth-century architectural tradition of Bengal, these buildings also show the influence of the Tughluq architecture of Delhi. They are stark and unadorned on the exterior. The engaged corner towers are circular instead of octagonal; the cornice is curved; the buildings have very thick walls and a massive quality. As

---

50   Asher, "Inventory of Key Monuments", pp. 70-71.
51   Dani, *Muslim Architecture in Bengal*, pp. 141-52; Karim, *Corpus of Inscriptions*, pp. 137-39; and Eaton, *The Rise of Islam and the Bengal Frontier*, pp. 209-11.
52   Karim, *Corpus of Inscriptions*, pp. 171-73.

the vaulting of the Adina Mosque was not very successful, a new type of vaulting was devised in which the central aisle was divided into a number of rectangular bays, each of them covered by a small *chau-chala*. The new system was first tried out in the Shaitgumbad Mosque in Bagerhat, the largest mosque in Bangladesh (fig. 33-34). A number of nine-domed mosques and some of the largest single-domed mosques of Bengal are in this style.

The late Sultanate period. The late Sultanate period (sixteenth century) includes the reign of the Husayn Shahi dynasty (1493-1538) and of the Sur (1538-64) and Karrani rulers (1564-75), before the takeover by the Mughals in 1576. The general peace and prosperity brought about by the Husayn Shahi rulers allowed the construction of a large number of buildings; they all have a more or less uniform style. The Bengal style of building spread to every nook and corner of the country as far as Bihar and Assam,[53] but none of the buildings was particularly outstanding or innovative in design. Instead, craftsmen occupied themselves with refining decoration and details.

The style is well represented in the Bagha Mosque in Rajshahi dating from 1523-24. Several buildings in Gaur, in both its West Bengal and Bangladesh parts, also display it.[54] Some, like the Gumti Gate and Lattan Mosque in West Bengal, have a profusion of glazed tiles; others, like the Chhota Sona Mosque in Bangladesh, were gilded. Tiles had already appeared in a restrained use in buildings of the Middle Sultanate Period such as the Eklakhi Tomb in Pandua and the floor of Khan Jahan's Tomb in Bagerhat.[55] Now stone is sometimes used to encase brick as in the Sura Mosque in Dinajpur and the Kusumba Mosque in Naogaon.

Firmly dated mosques of the early sixteenth century are: Chhota Sona Mosque, Gaur (1493-1519); Shankarpasha Mosque, Habiganj (1493-1519); Aroshnagar Mosque, Khulna (1501-2); Baba Saleh's Mosque Narayanganj (1505); Goaldi Mosque, Sonargaon (1519); Bagha Mosque, Rajshahi (1523-24); Nabagram Mosque, Sirajganj (1526); Jorbangla Mosque, Barobazar (1532-38); and Hammad's Mosque, Chittagong (1532-38). Other early sixteenth-century mosques are: Majlis Awlia's Mosque, Faridpur; Ten-domed Mosque and Rezai Khan's Mosque in Bagerhat; Gorar Mosque, Manohar Dighi Mosque, Pirpukur Mosque, Noongola Mosque, Pathagar Mosque and Shukur Mallik Mosque in Barobazar; and Parbajpur Mosque in Satkhira.

The Kusumba Mosque, Naogaon is dated to the middle of the century (1558). Others datable to this period are: Osmanpur Gayebi Mosque, Sylhet; Sura Mosque,

---

53 Pir Shah Nafa's tomb in Munghyr, Bihar, in M. H. Kuraishi, *List of Ancient Monuments Protected in Act VII of 1904 in Bihar and Orissa, Archaeological Survey of India* (Calcutta, 1931), pp. 213-15. For the gateway to Dimapur, Assam, see *Journal of the Asiatic Society of Bengal* (1874): 3-4 and pl. IV.
54 Dani, *Muslim Architecture in Bengal*, pp. 116-40; Asher, "Inventory of Key Monuments", pp. 65-70, 74-77, 80-81.
55 Dani, *Muslim Architecture in Bengal*, pp. 77 and 143.

Fig. 46.
*Naogaon,
Kusumba Mosque,
1558, mihrab*

Dinajpur; and Shialghuni Mosque, Barisal. Qutb Shah's Mosque, Kishoreganj, Zinda Pir's Mosque, Bagerhat; and Shubhorara Mosque, Jessore are datable to the late sixteenth century.

These buildings are all of brick or brick and stone. The structural features of the previous period are faithfully copied. The curved cornice and roof, the engaged octagonal corner towers, the drumless dome, and the corbelled pendentives all remain. No new forms are introduced. Decoration is often excessive. The entire wall surface is covered with terracotta or carved stone. The tendency to over-elaboration ultimately killed the form, as the lush, curving vine that was once so full of life became reduced to dry brittle stalks and dots. The resulting surface appears to be extremely overwrought and busy, as in the Kusumba Mosque (fig. 46). Stone carving is reintroduced, but continues to imitate the same terracotta designs.

After the Mughal conquest in the seventeenth century, the Sultanate style of mosque architecture disappeared, at least in the major buildings of the capitals, and was replaced by the imperial Mughal style of Delhi and Agra. It lived on in the Hindu temple architecture of Bengal, however, until in its turn it was replaced by British colonial influences. But the elements of the Bengal style, most particularly the curved *chala* roof, that had been exported to other parts of India, became prominent features of the seventeenth-century architecture of Delhi. From there, in the eighteenth century, the tradition passed into the palace balconies and garden pavilions of Rajasthan.

— 3 —

Catalogue of Sultanate Mosques in Bangladesh

Fifty-five mosques of the Sultanate period in Bengal, dating from the fourteenth to the sixteenth centuries, are catalogued here. Most of them are known by the name of the village where they are located, or by the name of a local saint whose tomb is in the precinct. In Bangladesh, a group of villages is under the control of a police station (Beng.: *thana*) that serves as a centre for administration. Locating a village accurately requires knowing which police station has jurisdiction over it, as sometimes there are villages of the same name in different thanas. These police stations are grouped under larger administrative units known as districts. The mosques are titled by the name of a saint, village, town or the general area, whichever is more commonly used. The exact location follows the title. The descriptions are organized under different headings to facilitate use by researchers looking for specific information.

All the mosques except the nine in Barobazar were surveyed by the author during 1981-82, and the descriptions are based on their condition at that time. The Barobazar mosques, surveyed and excavated by the Department of Archaeology and Museums of the Government of Bangladesh in the 1990s, are also included; however, the Department's reconstruction of these mosques has been quite heavy-handed.

The inscriptions have not been recorded in the original Arabic language (with the occasional Persian word or phrase) as they have all been translated and published. Abdul Karim's *Corpus of the Arabic and Persian Inscriptions of Bengal* (1992) is the source of most of the translations of the non-Quranic texts. Other translations are given only in the rare instances when Karim's translations were not available. The Quranic texts in the inscriptions are according to Abdullah Yusuf Ali's *The Holy Quran: Text, Translation and Commentary* (Lahore: Sh. Muhammad Ashraf, reprint, 1988), as this is most widely used in South Asia. The description of each monument is followed by a bibliography whenever available, and a list of abbreviations used in the catalogue bibliography follows the appendices.

The mosques of the Sultanate period in Bangladesh have been arranged chronologically so that an evolution in style can be perceived: the three sections are the Early, Middle, and Late Sultanate Periods, covering the mosques of the fourteenth, fifteenth, and sixteenth centuries respectively. The Middle Sultanate Period includes mosques in the distinctive Khan Jahan style under a separate heading.

AREAS WHERE MOSQUES ARE CONCENTRATED

Bagerhat.[1] The city of Bagerhat in the district of the same name has been identified as Khalifatabad, a mint town of the Bengal Sultanate. It is associated with the name of Ulugh Khan Jahan, whose tomb is located there and who is credited with building a large number of mosques, all in the same style. He is still venerated as a pir, and his tomb attracts swarms of devotees. The tomb inscription gives the date of his demise as 1459, so the buildings in the Khan Jahan style must date to around the mid fifteenth century. The ancient city of Khalifatabad stretched for about six kilometres along the former course of the Bhairab River. Ten mosques in this study, seven in the Khan Jahan style (Shaitgumbad, the mosque adjoining Khan Jahan's Tomb, Ranbijaypur, Bibi Begni, Shingra, Chunakhola, the Nine-domed Mosque) and three of later date (the Ten-domed Mosque, Rezai Khan, Zinda Pir) are located there. Khan Jahan is believed to have been an important adminstrator, although he did not issue any coins or assume any royal titles. His influence spread over a large area in south Bengal to the districts of Jhenaidah, Satkhira, Patuakhali, and Barisal, where buildings in the same style are found. It is said that Khalifatabad was also founded in honour of Sultan Nasir al-Din Mahmud Shah (1433-59) who had declared himself "khalifah of Allah with proof and testimony".[2]

Barobazar. The railway station of Barobazar in Jhenaidah district is about fifteen kilometres north of Jessore, beside the Jhenaidah-Jessore highway. In 1992-93 the Department of Archaeology excavated the remains of several monuments within an area of about 1 sq. km. Among them were ten mosques known as Shatgachhia, Gorar, Sadiqpur, Pirpukur, Manohar Dighi, Jorbangla, Galakata, Pathagar, Noongola, and Shukur Mallik, the first three of which were already known. Sadiqpur

---

[1] M. A. Bari, "Khalifatabad and its Monuments", M.Phil thesis, Rajshahi University, 1980; J. E. van Lohuizen de Leeuw, "The Early Muslim Monuments of Bagerhat", in *Islamic Heritage of Bengal*, ed. George Michell (Paris, 1984), pp. 166-78.
[2] Abdul Karim, *Corpus of the Arabic and Persian Inscriptions of Bengal* (Dhaka, 1992), p. 123.

CATALOGUE OF SULTANATE MOSQUES IN BANGLADESH

Mosque is not included in the catalogue as it is totally redone. Their period of construction seems to have been the fifteenth and early sixteenth centuries. Recently scholars have attempted to identify Barobazar as Mahmudabad or Muhammadabad, a city that was founded by Sultan Nasir al-Din Mahmud Shah (r. 1433-59), or even earlier.[3]

Gaur. Gaur is in northwestern Bangladesh at the junction of the Ganges and Mahananda rivers (the eastern part of the city is now in the Nawabganj district of Bangladesh, while the larger western part spreads into the district of Malda in West Bengal, India). Ancient Gaur, probably one of the royal capitals of the Pala and Sena kings, was renamed Lakshmanavati after Lakshmansena the last Hindu ruler; the name was later Persianized to Lakhnawti by the Muslims.[4] This fortified city of about 40 sq. km remained the capital of the Independent Sultanate, except for the ninety years between 1342 and 1432, when Sultan Shams al-Din Ilyas Shah and the rulers of the house of Raja Ganesh ruled from Pandua. Sultan Nasir al-Din Mahmud Shah of the Restored Ilyas Shahi dynasty re-transferred the capital back to Gaur. In 1538 the city began to decline after Sher Shah sacked and burned it. The Darasbari, Dhunichak, Khania Dighi, and Chhota Sona Mosques all dating from the late fifteenth to early sixteenth centuries, are located here.

Sonargaon. Today Sonargaon is the name of a police station (thana) in the Narayanganj district. The historical site of Sonargaon lies between the rivers Sitalakhya on the west and the Meghna on the east, and the confluence of the Sitalakhya, Dhaleswari, and Meghna on the south. Its northern border was probably the Brahmaputra, which runs from the north to the south-east before flowing further south near Muazzampur.

A flourishing centre of trade and commerce, Sonargaon was well known for the manufacture and export of muslin, and is mentioned in the travel accounts of Ibn Battuta (1346), Mahuan (early fifteenth century), Fei Sin (1415) and Ralph Fitch (1586). Known as Suvarnagram in pre-Muslim times, it became the capital of the region of Bang and had a mint by the end of the thirteenth century when Muslim rule was established there. The city lost its importance in the early seventeenth century when the Mughals shifted the provincial capital to Dhaka.[5] Today the boundaries of the ancient city of

---

3   A. B. M. Hussain, "Baro Bazar: Was it the Mahmudabad of Sultani Bangla?", in *Essays in Memory of Momtazur Rahman Tarafdar*, ed. P. Hasan and M. Islam (Dhaka, 1999), pp. 229-36; M. A. Qadir, "Eight Unpublished Sultanate Inscriptions of Bengal", *Journal of Bengal Art* 4 (1999): 250-54.

4   M. Abid Ali Khan, *Memoirs of Gaur and Pandua* (Calcutta, 1931), p. 15, A. B. M. Husain, *Gawr-Lakhnawti* (Dhaka: Asiatic Society of Bangladesh, 1997), pp. 1-28.

5   A. M. Chowdhury, "Site and Surroundings", in *Sonargaon-Panam*, ed. A. B. M. Husain (Dhaka: Asiatic Society of Bangladesh, 1997), pp. 1-32.

Sonargaon are unclear, but the remains of medieval buildings help us to identify the site, which is confined to the Sonargaon and Bandar police stations of the Narayanganj district. The mosques located there are the Muazzampur Shahi Jami, Bandar Shahi, Fath Shah, Yusufganj, Baba Saleh, and Goaldi.

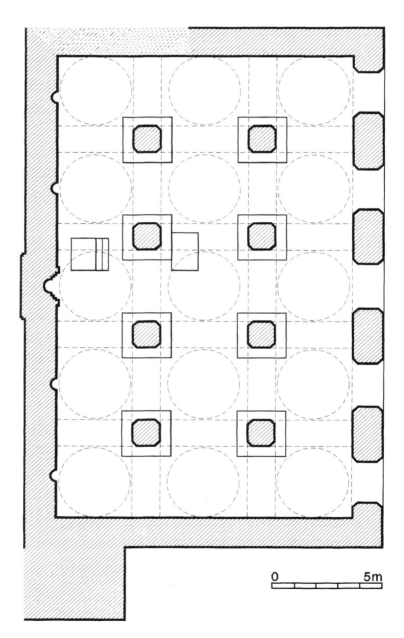

Fig. 47. Mahasthan, Mankalir Bhita Mosque, reconstructed plan

Early Sultanate Period

Mankalir Bhita Mosque, Mahasthan

Location: Police station, Shibganj; district, Bogra (Bogura). On a mound known as Mankalir Bhita (Cunningham calls it Mankali-ka Kundi) in Mahasthangarh (Mahasthan-gawr), identified as Pundranagar, the ancient capital city of Pundravardhana.

Date: There is no inscription, but the building is similar in plan to the two earliest extant mosques, both in West Bengal—the Zafar Khan Ghazi in Tribeni, dated by inscription to A.H. 696/1298 C.E., which has similar large piers, and the Bari Masjid in Chhota Pandua, datable to ca. 1300—and may therefore be tentatively ascribed to the early fourteenth century, making it possibly the earliest mosque in Bangladesh. An inscription recording the date for the building of a shrine for Mir Namwar Khan, a high-ranking officer of the Bengal Sultanate, in Mahasthangarh as 700/1300 is another indication of the presence of Muslims there from these early times.

The large rectangular plan, the massiveness of the piers in the interior and the absence of any indication of corner towers are evidence of an early date, probably earlier than the Adina Mosque in Pandua of 1375.

Condition: Almost completely ruined; aside from the bases of the piers and walls, the foundations of which have been partially excavated by the Department of Archaeology and Museums, Government of Bangladesh. Little of the structure remains; the plan was drawn on the basis of the foundation exposed after excavation.

Dimensions: The interior is 22.70 m x 13.70 m; the wall thickness is 1.50 m.

Material: Brick.

Plan and elevation (figs. 47-48): Eight piers divided the rectangular interior into five aisles and three bays, indicating that the roof had fifteen domes. The central bay, running from north to south, is slightly wider than the other two. Each one of its smaller bays measures 3.60 m x 4.00 m; the rest are 3.60 m square. This irregularity must have posed problems at the base of the dome. An awkward solution such as varying the width of the arches may have been used, or the shape of the dome may have been compromised. It is unlikely that, at this early date, the *chau-chala* vault or similar roof solutions were known.

There were five entrances on the east side. The number in the north cannot be determined. On the west wall opposite the five entrances were five semicircular mihrabs, of which the central niche is the largest. A three-stepped minbar slightly to the north of the central mihrab has been reconstructed. Aligned to the minbar is the base of a 1.85 m x 1.26 m platform between two rows of pillars. This may be the base of a seat used by a

Fig. 48. Mahasthan, Mankalir Bhita Mosque, ruined interior piers

teacher or savant during religious discussions, and the additional width of the central bay was probably linked to the function of this platform. The raised floor level suggests more than one major rebuilding.

The sections between the entrances in front are the remains of rectangular piers with chamfered edges. In the exterior west side there is a small projection for the central mihrab, but no sign of any engaged corner towers. In the southwest corner there seems to have been some construction, but its nature could not be determined.

The square piers in the interior are massive, have chamfered corners, and rest on square platform-like bases. Behind the dressed brick facing is a core of rubble masonry. The bases of the facade piers are slightly wider than the interior ones and are rectangular instead of square. The size of the piers indicates that the arches they supported were very wide.

Further excavation will reveal whether or not the mosque was built on an older foundation. The mound on which it sits certainly points to the existence of earlier structures on the site. Before its excavation, Cunningham assumed that the building was a temple, on the basis of some plaques belonging to a brick and terracotta temple that he had discovered there.

Decoration: The brick moulding around the pillars and the triangles at the chamfered corners are the only decoration that remain. The central mihrab projection had offsets on either side.

Bibliography: N. Ahmed, *Mahasthan*, pp. 42-43; S. Ahmed, *IB*, 4: 21-23; Asher, "Inventory of Key Monuments", p. 85; Cunningham, "Report of a Tour", 106, 108-9, pl. XXXI; Dani, *MAB*, pp. 40-43 and 48-49.

MIDDLE SULTANATE PERIOD

Muazzampur Shahi Jami Mosque, Sonargaon

Location: Police station, Sonargaon; district, Narayanganj, in the village of Majampur (Muazzampur), about 20 km south-east of Dhaka city. The area is included in the ancient and medieval city of Sonargaon. The Shahi Jami Mosque is in an enclosure, on one side of which is the tomb of a local pir, Shah Langar and a well whose water is said to have the same properties as the Zamzam in Makka (Mecca).

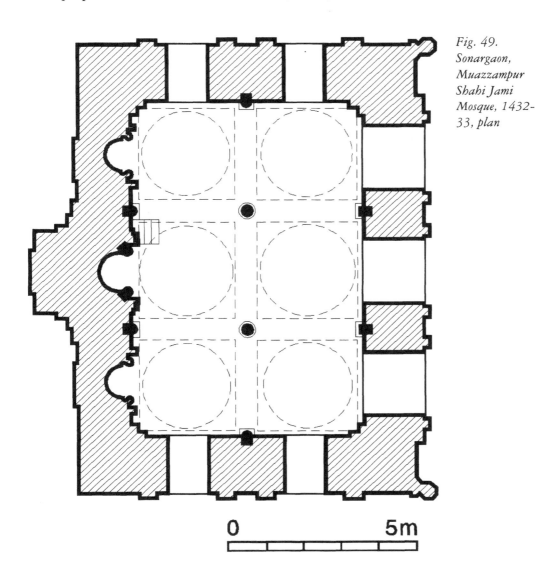

Fig. 49. Sonargaon, Muazzampur Shahi Jami Mosque, 1432-33, plan

Date: Reign of Shams al-Din Ahmad Shah (836-37/1432-33).

Condition: The mosque has been renovated and enlarged in modern times by adding a verandah in the front, the cornice straightened and the domes rebuilt. The west wall retains some original structures.

Dimensions: The interior is 9.50 m x 6.30 m; the wall thickness is 1.65 m.

Material: Mainly brick; the engaged pilasters (two each in the east and west walls, and one each in the north and south walls), two free-standing pillars in the prayer chamber, and the central mihrab are of rough stone. The front of the mihrab (the pillars and the arch) is of black basalt.

Plan (fig. 49) and elevation: The building is rectangular with three aisles and two bays covered by six domes. Three entrances are on the east; the central one is slightly larger (1.58 m wide) than the other two. Two entrances each on the north and south sides are 1.15 m wide. All but the one on the northwest have been turned into windows.

There are two engaged octagonal corner towers on the east, but the two on the west have disappeared. Recesses articulate the exterior surfaces of the walls; there is a prominent mihrab projection on the west.

The domes are carried on pendentives that are neither very deep nor large, because the wide arches supporting them are quite high. The mihrabs have half-domes. The two end mihrabs are now used as closets.

Two free-standing octagonal pillars in the interior have circular bases raised about 15 cm from the floor (fig. 50). The southern one has a bulbous capital with a square top and carved in one section; the northern one is stepped (square, circular, square, and bulbous), indicating that perhaps they were collected from different sources. The engaged pilasters

Fig. 50. Sonargaon, Muazzampur Shahi Jami Mosque, interior

have short square bases with projections, octagonal shafts, and wide square capitals. The southern pilaster in the east wall has a rectangular shaft. All the arches are pointed. The northern and southern entrances and the side mihrabs are set in rectangular recesses.

Decoration: In the interior, some original decoration remains over the entrances on the north and south sides. It consists of a band of terracotta on top of the recessed rectangular frame of the entrances and rosettes on the spandrels. Thick layers of paint blur their details. Most of the remaining original decoration is on the mihrabs. The central mihrab is entirely preserved, but it has been gaudily painted. The pillars have hanging chains carved on their shafts, and they support a large block of stone in which the trefoil-cusped arch of the mihrab has been carved. The northern pillar has a plain square base and appears to be unfinished; the base of the other pillar has a vegetal motif. The front of the mihrab is unadorned except for the large rosettes on the spandrels, and have the *kalasha* and *amalaka* (water pot and fluted fruit motifs that are usually the crowning emblems in a temple) as crowning elements. The hanging chain and lamp motif, now painted red and white, is the only decoration in the interior of the mihrab.

The side mihrabs are of brick and terracotta. The hanging motifs in their niches are not the conventional ornate lamp, but a loop formed by a hanging chain; the octagonal interior of the loop is filled with vegetal patterns. These too have rosettes in the spandrels and diamond and flower motifs at the apex. The tops of the recessed rectangles have bands of curving vines, beads and lozenges.

Part of the west wall is original. Its most striking feature is the mihrab projection, with a rectangular panel in the centre enclosing a mihrab motif (fig. 39), a feature which is also present in Baba Adam's and Shubhorara Mosques. This external mihrab is complete with elaborately ornamented pillars, trefoil-cusped arch and lotuses on the spandrels. An elaborate terracotta motif hangs by a chain from the apex of the arch. The motif is topped by a band of continuous six-pointed stars with flowers inside.

Inscription: In Arabic. The inscription stone that dated the mosque fell and shattered into small pieces; it was reconstructed with difficulty:

> "Firuz Khan ... Kabir (the Great), may God perpetuate his kingdom till the day of judgement ... during the occupation of the royal throne by Ahmed Shah ... Ali Musa Sultan hopeful of ..."

The ruling king is referred to as Ahmad Shah, and the names of two other persons, Firuz Khan, probably the patron, and Ali Musa Sultan are also mentioned. The last two are not known from any other source, but Shams al-Din Ahmad Shah, who reigned from 1432 to 1433, is the only sultan named Ahmad, so the mosque is assigned to his reign.

Bibliography: A. S. M. Ahmed, *Choto Sona Mosque*, p. 88; Eaton, *The Rise of Islam*, p. 324; P. Hasan, "Eight Sultanate Mosques", pp. 188-89; S. A. Hasan, *Notes*, pp. 54-55; S. M. Hasan, *MMB*, p. 126; Karim, *Corpus of Inscriptions*, pp. 110-11, Siddiq, *Islamic Inscriptions of Bengal*, p. 50.

Binat Bibi's Mosque, Dhaka

Location: Police station, Sutrapur; district, Dhaka. In Narinda area of Old Dhaka city on the bank of Dulai Khal, a canal, which has now been filled to make a wide road.

Date: Dated by inscription to 861 (1456-57). The inscription tablet is fixed above the central entrance of the original mosque, now the second entrance from the north. The only mosque known to have been sponsored by a woman, though we do not know who Binat Bibi was. The inscription unusually is in the form of a Persian couplet.

Condition: Completely renovated and enlarged in all directions except the north (fig. 51). The most recent expansion added two floors above the original one (fig. 52). It now functions as a Friday mosque.

Fig. 51. Dhaka, Binat Bibi's Mosque, 1456-57, exterior north wall

Dimensions: The original mosque interior measured 3.20 m sq.; the wall thickness is about 1 m.

Material: Brick. The mosaic on the north wall and the dome belong to the later construction.

Plan (fig. 53) and elevation: The dome, north wall with curved cornice, engaged octagonal corner towers on that side, parts of the east wall, and the upper portions of the south and west walls are all that remain of the original

Fig. 52. Dhaka, Binat Bibi's Mosque

structure. The first extension of the mosque, made in 1930, was on the south. To add it, the lower part of the south wall was removed and the original square chamber was duplicated on that side. Steel beams now support the remaining upper portions of the original wall. The second and larger extension was built on the western side later and pillars support the remaining upper part of the mihrab wall. A flat ceiling supported by concrete beams covers the entire western extension. A new verandah was added on the east.

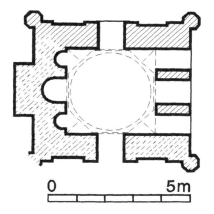

Fig. 53. Dhaka, Binat Bibi's Mosque, reconstructed plan

The remaining upper portions of the walls indicate their original thickness. The north wall is still intact (fig. 51). The reconstructed plan depends on the observation that mosques of this period were generally symmetrical. The three entrances on the east side were probably narrower than indicated in fig. 53, because the drawing uses the present dimensions. The blind-arch window on the north side was probably originally an entrance doorway which was later blocked. The blind alley on the north side is extremely narrow and leads to a congested residential quarter. The mihrabs in the west wall are conjectural, as almost nothing remains of the wall itself. The southeast and southwest corners probably also had engaged octagonal corner towers similar to the two existing ones at either end of the north wall.

The drumless dome is raised on squinches. In the interior, only the upper parts of these squinches with their recessed front arches are visible. The corbelling of the triangular pendentives between the squinches was transformed into horizontal courses. The dome can be seen both from the north side and by climbing up to the roof.

Decoration: The building is stripped of all original decoration. It is now plastered, whitewashed, and painted, and parts (e.g., the north wall and the dome) covered with mosaic.

Inscription: Written in Arabic and Persian, the text begins with the *shahada* (affirmation and creed fundamental to Islam):

> "In the name of Allah, the Merciful and Compassionate. There is no God except Allah and Muhammad is the Messenger of Allah,"

and then continues,

> "Adorned by the voice of *haiyya falah* [come to safety. It is part of the azan or ritual call to prayer] at night and morning in the mosque of this humble

person [erected by] Musammat Bakht Binat, daughter of Marhamat. In the year 861 [1456-57]."

Musammat Bakht Binat seems to be a pious lady about whom nothing else is known.

Bibliography: S. Ahmed, *IB*, 4: 57-58; Dani, *MAB*, p. 193; P. Hasan, "Eight Sultanate Mosques", pp. 180-81; S. A. Hasan, *Notes*, pp. 270; Karim, *Corpus of Inscriptions*, pp. 130-33; Siddiq, *Islamic Inscriptions of Bengal*, pp. 62-63.

Gopalganj Mosque, Dinajpur

Location: Police station, Kotwali; district, Dinajpur. The mosque adjoins the tomb of Chehel Ghazi (traditionally forty martyrs to the cause of Islam) and is on the western side of the Dhaka-Dinajpur road about 6 km from the town of Dinajpur.

Date: Dated by inscription to Safar 16, 865 (December 1, 1460).

Condition: Much of the building is in ruins. The dome has collapsed, and almost nothing remains of the exterior wall. The interior of the prayer chamber and the verandah retain most of the original features, although in a dilapidated state. The building is overgrown with vegetation and had to be cleared for measuring.

Dimensions: The interior of the prayer chamber is 4 m sq.; the interior of the verandah is 4 m x 1.8 m; the wall thickness is a little over 1 m.

Material: Brick; stone at the springing of the entrance and squinch arches. The walls are not faced with stone, contrary to Chakravarti's report.

Plan (fig. 20) and elevation: There are three entrances on the east and one each on the north and south sides of the verandah. The central entrance on the east side and the north and south entrances of the verandah are all 72 cm wide; the flanking entrances in the east are 54 cm wide. Three doors on the east corresponding to the outside verandah entrances and one each on the north and south sides (1 m wide) provide access to the square prayer chamber. There are three mihrabs on the west wall. The exterior walls are too dilapidated for any definite plan to be established; only the lower part of the central mihrab projection is still visible.

Intersecting barrel or cross vaults roof the verandah (fig. 21), a feature not seen in any other mosque of the period. All the arches are pointed. The dome of the prayer chamber was supported on squinches, which sprang from stone brackets on the walls. The brackets are positioned a little above the level of the springing of the entrance arches. On the eastern end of the north and south walls are small niches for lamps.

Decoration: Traces of thin plaster can be seen on the vaulted roof of the verandah. The base of the dome had rows of lozenge and merlon patterns. The mihrabs have cusped arches with a terracotta border and lotus plants on the spandrels. The lower half of the mihrabs are divided into three rectangular panels. The north and south mihrabs have cusped niches with hanging motifs in the panels. In the central mihrab the patterns in the niche are much abraded. Above the mihrab are horizontal rows of petals (turned both upwards and downwards), and interwined lotus vine, festoons and lozenges. The whole composition is capped with merlons with vegetal motifs inside. In the centre of this row is a very prominent *kalasha* motif.

Inscription: The text is in Arabic interspersed with Persian. It reads:

> "In the name of Allah the Merciful and the Compassionate. Help from Allah and a speedy victory: So give the glad tidings to the believers" [Quran 61:13].

> "But Allah is the best to take care [of him], and He is the Most Merciful of those who show mercy" [Quran 12: 64].

> "The construction of the mosque took place during the reign of the Sultan, son of Sultan Rukn al-Dunya wal-Din Abul Mujahid Barbak Shah, the Sultan, son of Mahmud Shah the Sultan, may Allah perpetuate his kingdom and sovereignty. [It was built] at the direction of the great Khan and the exalted Khaqan, the hero of the age and time, Ulugh Iqrar Khan, *Sar-i lashkar* and *Wazir*; the builder of this benevolent work, the said mosque and the repairer of the tomb is the great Khan and the exalted Khaqan Ulugh Nusrat Khan, *Jangdar* and *Shiqdar* of the affairs of Jor [place-name that cannot be identified] and Baror [an administrative unit in Purnia district of Bihar, India] and of other *mahals* [administrative units]. [Built on] the 16th of the month of Safar [1 December], may Allah bring it to a happy and successful end, in the year 865 [1460]".

The meaning of the inscription is unclear. Shamsuddin Ahmed interprets it as meaning that both the builder of the mosque and the repairer of the tomb was Ulugh Nusrat Khan, who was carrying out the orders of Ulugh Iqrar Khan. Abdul Karim's reading is that the mosque was built under orders of Ulugh Iqrar Khan who was his superior, and Ulugh Nusrat Khan carried out his orders and repaired the tomb.

Bibliography: A. S. M. Ahmed, *Choto Sona Mosque*, p. 123; S. Ahmed, *IB*, 4: 71-73; Blochmann, *Contributions*, pp. 67-70; Chakravarti, "Pre-Mughal Mosques", p. 26; Dani, *MAB*, p. 15; idem, *Bibliography*, p. 23; Karim, *Corpus of Inscriptions*, pp. 152-54; Saraswati, "Indo-Muslim Architecture", pp. 22-23; Siddiq, *Islamic Inscriptions of Bengal*, pp. 72-73.

Makhdum Shah's Mosque, Shahzadpur

Location: Police station, Shahzadpur (Shahjadpur); district: Sirajganj.

The mosque is named after Pir Makhdum Shah Dawlah Shahid, who according to tradition was a Sufi who came to Shahzadpur from Yemen in the thirteenth or early fourteenth century, and is buried on the south side of the courtyard. There is another tomb in the northeast corner and a mass grave on the south side. The river Karatoya (Korotoya) flows in front the mosque.

Fig. 54. Shahzadpur, Makhdum Shah's Mosque, mid- to late fifteenth century, minbar

Makhdum Shah's Mosque, Shahzadpur

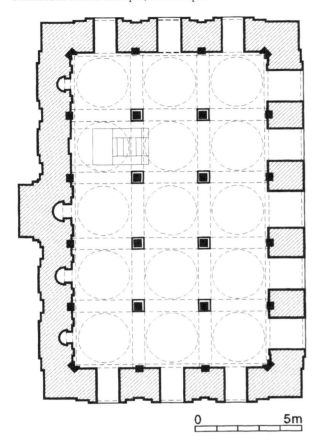

Fig. 55. Shahzadpur, Makhdum Shah's Mosque, plan and top view of minbar

Date: There is no inscription. Stylistic evidence, especially the close resemblance of the decoration on the east facade with the ornamentation of Baba Adam's Mosque in Munshiganj dated to 1483, suggests the mosque belongs to the mid- to late fifteenth century.

Condition: Renovated by local residents several times during the course of the last century. Both the interior and exterior are plastered, whitewashed, and painted. The stone pillars, regularly anointed with oil by the worshipers, have acquired a varnished look. The front of the minbar (fig. 54) has settled about 10 cm, so that it is now inclined towards the east. The exterior of the west wall bulges out at mid-height at the position of the mihrabs.

Dimensions: The interior is 15.8 m x 9.6 m; the wall thickness is 1.7 m.

Material: Brick; the interior pillars, engaged pilasters on the walls, a pair of half-pilasters in the corners and brackets at the springing of the entrance arches are of stone.

Fig. 56. Shahzadpur, Makhdum Shah's Mosque, northeast view

Plan and elevation (figs. 55-56): The interior space of the rectangular building is divided into five aisles and three bays by two rows of four pillars in the north/south direction. The roof has fifteen domes. There are five entrances on the east, the central one being the largest (1.87 m wide), the others diminish in size as one moves towards the corners. There are three entrances each on the north and south sides with the largest one in the centre (1.20 m wide). Corresponding to the five eastern entrances are five mihrabs in the west wall, with the largest in the centre and others diminishing in size towards the corners. All the mihrabs are semicircular and roofed with half-domes, except the second one from the north, which has a rectangular base and is a flat shallow niche in the wall. Corresponding to the stone pillars are engaged stone pilasters on each wall and a pair of half-pilasters in each corner.

Fig. 57. Shahzadpur, Makhdum Shah's Mosque, interior

Just in front of the rectangular mihrab, hiding it from view and occupying the entire bay, is an elevated minbar (fig. 54) covered by a cupola and mounted by a flight of seven steps; it appears to be contemporary with the mosque. This minbar is unique among Sultanate mosques in Bangladesh, but there are similar canopied, stepped minbars from the fourteenth century in the Bari Masjid in Chhota Pandua and the Adina Mosque in Pandua in West Bengal, India. The exterior wall is recessed on the south, west, and north sides, and there is a projection for the central mihrab in the west.

The cornice is very gently curved and the domes are so low that the parapet hides them; they are invisible from the front courtyard. All the entrance arches are set in rectangular recesses. The interior arches spring from the tops of the free-standing pillars and engaged pilasters (fig. 57), and pendentives support the domes. The columns in the middle of the prayer chamber are of varying dimensions, suggesting that they were culled from different sources. Five of these have hanging bell motifs on the shafts. All but one have square bases and capitals with octagonal shafts; the second one from the south in the front row has a circular base.

The canopied minbar has a pointed arch on each of its three sides and a blind niche on the fourth, the western side. Its cupola is supported on four brick pillars. A barrel vault, which on one side springs from the west wall and on the other side from the masonry work forming the steps, supports the minbar speaker's platform. The turrets in the roof corners are probably modern.

Decoration: Most of the original terracotta decoration is now lost. On the outside there are still terracotta mouldings on the tops of the rectangular recesses of doorways, and rosettes and lozenges on the spandrels of the entrance arches. Two rectangular panels, with small mihrabs on either side of the central entrance on the east, were reconstructed in modern times. An arcade of miniature niches on pillars runs all along the cornice of the building. These niches had discs with terracotta motifs inside, but most of them are either lost or have been replaced in recent times. Inside, the mihrabs have cusped arches and semi-domes and are set in large rectangular panels. Except for the rectangular motif that runs down the base of the semi-dome, everything is covered with paint. The minbar is also very gaudily painted.

Bibliography: A. S. M. Ahmed, *Chota Sona Mosque*, p. 88; Asher, "Inventory of Key Monuments", p. 130; Dani, *MAB*, pp. 160-61; Karim, *Social History*, pp. 121-90; Wali, "On the Antiquities and Traditions", pp. 262-71.

Bibi Chini's Mosque, Barguna

Location: Police station, Betagi; district, Barguna. The village and the mosque are named after Bibi Chini, a historically unknown woman, who is locally believed to be the mosque's patron. To reach it one takes a boat from Patuakhali to a village near Niamati

Fig. 58. Barguna, Bibi Chini's Mosque, mid- to late fifteenth century, ruined interior

(Niamoti), once an outpost marking the extent of settled areas before the Sundarban (Shundorbon) forest. The mosque is on a raised mound surrounded by flat land.

Date: There is no inscription, but it can probably be placed in the mid- to late fifteenth century, since the area came under Muslim control around that time, and the nearby mosque at Masjidbari was built in 1465. The building is too ruined to allow any accurate dating, but some Sultanate characteristics may be identified, e.g. pointed arches, squinches with frontal arches, and brick decoration at the base of the dome.

Condition: The building is completely ruined (fig. 58). The dome has collapsed on the east side. A crude attempt was made to rebuild the mosque, but was apparently abandoned.

Dimensions: The interior is 7.20 m sq; the wall thickness is 2.04 m.

Material: Brick.

Fig. 59. Barguna, Bibi Chini's Mosque, plan

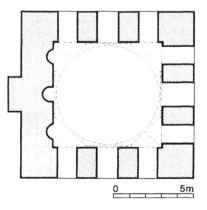

Plan (fig. 59) and elevation: The mosque is a square building with three entrances each on the north, east, and south sides. The central entrances on these sides are larger (the eastern one is 1.60 m wide, and the north and south 1.35 m wide) than the flanking ones (1.20 m wide). There were three mihrabs in the west; although none of them have survived, semi-circular impressions on the floor indicate where they were. On the exterior is a projection for the central mihrab. There is no trace of any corner tower.

All the arches are pointed. The dome was supported by squinches with wide frontal arches (fig. 58). There are remains of engaged brick pilasters in the brickwork, and two engaged brick pilasters on each wall.

Decoration: Traces of thin lime plaster can be seen in the interior. There is a moulding at the base of the dome, and above it a horizontal row of bricks with one corner exposed. Similar brickwork is seen in the oversailing courses of corbelled pendentives, but their use at the base of the dome is unique.

Bibliography: Beveridge, *District of Bakarganj*, p. 40.

Faqir's Mosque, Chittagong

Location: Police station, Hathazari; district, Chittagong (Chawttogram). Hathazari is about 16 km north of Chittagong proper. The mosque is in a busy marketplace that gives the locality its name (*hat*, market). It is known as Faqir's Mosque (*Phokirer Moshjid*), because it is said that when the mosque was overgrown with jungle, a *faqir* (pious ascetic, beggar) cleared it and made it suitable for prayers. It is on the bank of a large pond which has a north/south orientation.

Date: Dated by inscription to the reign of Sultan Shams al-Din Yusuf Shah, 879-86 (1474-81). The inscription stone, which is affixed over the central doorway on the east, is badly damaged.

Condition: The mosque has been renovated and enlarged in front in modern times by the addition of a verandah. The parapet has been straightened and the corner towers extended beyond it. Except for the verandah, the renovation probably dates to the seventeenth century, during Mughal rule, as suggested by the lotus finials over the domes, prominent merlon decoration on the parapet, and the shallow blind niches on each facet of the octagonal corner towers.

Dimensions: The interior is 11.50 m x 7.38 m; the wall thickness is 2.00 m.

Material: Brick; the two free-standing pillars and the central mihrab in the prayer chamber are of stone.

Plan and elevation (figs. 60-61): The stone pillars along the middle of the prayer chamber divide the building into three aisles and two bays covered by six domes. There are three entrances on the east and two each on the north and south sides. Of these, the central entrance on the east is the largest (1.70 m wide); the rest are all the same size (1.45 m wide). Corresponding to the three entrances on the east are three mihrabs in the west wall. The central one is larger and has a semicircular niche; the flanking ones have

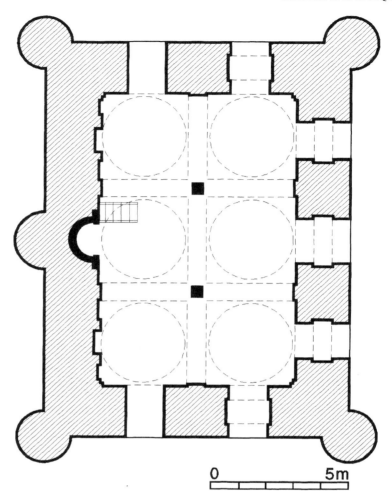

Fig. 60. Chittagong, Faqir's Mosque, 1474-81, plan

rectangular niches. There are engaged brick pilasters, two each in the east and west walls, and one each in the north and south walls. The edges of a pair of half-pilasters in the corner are exposed.

On the outside are four circular engaged corner towers, and a semicircular projection for the mihrab. The towers are circular as in the Khan Jahan style. The three entrances in front and the northeast and southeast entrances have front and rear arches with *chauchala* vaulted spaces in between (fig. 62).

The domes are very low, as are the pointed entrance arches set in rectangular recesses. The arches for the domes spring from the tops of the stone pillars in the centre of the prayer chamber and the engaged brick pilasters. The domes are carried on pendentives. The stone pillars are identical, with square bases and stepped square capitals on octagonal shafts. On each side of the pilasters in the wall are small lamp niches.

Faqir's Mosque, Chittagong

Fig. 61.
Chittagong,
Faqir's Mosque

Decoration: Some of the original decoration remains in the interior. The central mihrab of stone has a cusped arch with a lotus plant motif and full-blown lotuses on the spandrels. A large rectangular motif on a chain descends down the base of the semi-dome. The mihrab is set in a rectangular stone frame inscribed with almost obliterated Quranic verses. Above the crowning merlons of the rectangular frame is a full-blown large rosette. The side mihrabs of brick also have cusped arches with rosettes on the spandrels and hanging rectangular motifs in the niches.

The rectangular recesses of the mihrabs have mouldings on the top. Their frames are crowned with an arcade of miniature niches, a band of moulding and merlons. Above all this is a cluster of five full-blown rosettes similar to those seen in some of the Khan Jahan

Fig. 62.
Chittagong,
Faqir's Mosque,
chau-chala
entrance vault

style monuments of Bagerhat. These clusters are also seen above the rectangular recesses of the entrance arches, which have mouldings on top and rosettes in the spandrels. Their apexes have lozenge motifs. The bases of domes also have a band of miniature niches running around them.

The *chau-chala* vaulted spaces in the entrances have emphasized purlins and rafters in imitation of the bamboo frame of huts, with rosettes at the intersections (fig. 62).

Inscription: The inscription is in Arabic; it reads:

"The Sultan Shams al ... Abul Muzaffar Yu ... Ba ... bak Shah."

This was reconstructed by Karim as:

"The Sultan Shams al-Dunya wal-Din Abul Muzaffar Yusuf Shah son of Barbak Shah."

So he concludes that the mosque was built during the reign of Sultan Shams al-Din Yusuf Shah whose regnal dates are 879-86 (1474-81).

Bibliography: A. S. M. Ahmed, *Choto Sona Mosque*, p. 122; Eaton, *The Rise of Islam*, p. 325; S. M. Hasan, *MMB*, p. 38; Karim, "Two Unnoticed Sultanate Mosques", pp. 321-31; *idem*, *Corpus of Inscriptions*, pp. 194-96; Siddiq, *Islamic Inscriptions of Bengal*, p. 103.

Darasbari Mosque, Gaur

Location: Police station, Shibganj; district, Nawabganj. The mosque is less than a quarter of a kilometre from the border between India and Bangladesh; to its east is a large pond. The Kotwali Gate, on the other side of the border, can be seen as one goes to the Darasbari Mosque from the Chhota Sona Mosque. The ancient name of the locality is Umarpur. The name Darasbari (lit., school) comes from a madrasa that once adjoined the mosque and whose foundations were excavated by the Department of Archaeology and Museums.

Date: Dated by inscription to 884 (1479-80), and built according to the inscription by Shams al-Din Yusuf Shah bin Barbak Shah. The inscription tablet was found under a heap of rubble, when the jungle around the mosque was being cleared. It is now in the Indian Museum, Calcutta. This is one of the two Sultanate mosques in Bangladesh known by inscription to have been built by a sultan, the other being the Bagha Mosque in Rajshahi.

Condition: The mosque is in ruins; the roof and verandah facade have collapsed. The bases of the corner towers remain, but there is enough of the fabric remaining to enable a reconstruction. The Department of Archaeology and Museums has done some reconstruction work, and has repaired the west and south walls.

Dimensions: The interior of the prayer chamber is 30.32 m x 11.81 m; the interior of the verandah is 30.32 m x 3.27 m; the wall thickness is 1.82 m.

Darasbari Mosque, Gaur

Material: Brick, except for the pillars, engaged pilasters, and string courses in the walls, which are of stone.

Plan and elevation (figs. 22-23): Because of its ruined state the mosque has to be reconstructed from the remains. It is a rectangular building with a verandah in front. The prayer chamber is composed of three bays and seven aisles of which the central aisle is the widest (11.81 m x 5.41 m). It divides the interior into northern and southern wings, each nearly 11.81 m sq. Four stone pillars in the centre divided each wing into nine square bays; those in the northern wing were short and massive having rubble cores and stone facing. The walls as well as the central aisle have engaged stone pilasters from which the arches of the interior sprang.

The central aisle has four mihrabs of different sizes, the largest one in the centre and the smallest two, one above the other in the northern end (fig. 63). This suggests that there was a minbar against the northern section of the west wall whose steps would hide the lower mihrab from view. The upper mihrab would be above the steps probably under a domed canopy.

In the northern wing, there is a similar multiplicity of mihrabs in the last two bays (fig. 64), suggesting additional construction in that corner. The south wing follows the convention of three mihrabs opposite three entrance doorways.

The prayer chamber had seven entrances in the east (the central one being the largest), four in the south and five in the north including the north and south verandah entrances. The arrangement of the northern entrances is relatively complex. There is a regular entrance in the northeastern bay and three others in the central and northwestern bays, which together with a deep blind niche are arranged in two rows, one above the other (fig. 64). Traces of construction which remain on the exterior northwestern side, the multiple entrances and mihrabs, massiveness of the pillars and pilasters inside strongly suggest that there was a platform in this corner which was approached by

Fig. 63. Gaur, Darasbari Mosque, 1479-80, central aisle

Fig. 64. Gaur, Darasbari Mosque, interior northwest

a flight of steps from the outside. Entry to the area underneath the platform was possible through the lower doorway, which probably had an exit outside through a tunnel-vaulted passage underneath the staircase platform as in the Chhota Sona Mosque.

In the south wing, the stone pillars are not identical: one of them has a chain and bell motif on the shaft, which suggests that it was collected from an older building. The verandah had a central *chau-chala* vault, and three side bays with small hemispherical domes on pendentives. Only the bases of the verandah piers which carried the entrance arches remain, but they indicate that there were seven entrances from the outside similar in width to the entrances into the prayer chamber.

Oversailing courses of brick in the corners confirm that each wing had nine hemispherical domes supported on corbelled pendentives. The central aisle was a single hall with three arched openings each on the north and south sides. There were no oversailing courses of brick here; instead, there are traces of lateral arches, indicating that the central aisle was covered neither by hemispherical domes, nor by a long barrel vault as in the Adina Mosque in Pandua of West Bengal. Similar lateral arches are seen in the central aisle of the Chhota Sona Mosque nearby and the Shaitgumbad Mosque in Bagerhat, both of which have a *chau-chala* vault over each rectangular bay of the central aisle. The three bays of the central aisle in this mosque must have had similar vaults, with an additional one to cover the central bay of the verandah.

On the outside, the wall has shallow recesses and the remains of six octagonal towers, four at the corners of the building and two where the verandah joins the prayer chamber. The west wall has a projection for the central aisle. There is a gently curved cornice over the south and parts of the west wall. A string course of stone ran along the middle of the prayer chamber walls at the level of the springing of the entrance arches which were set within rectangular recesses.

Decoration: Some decoration still remains on the exterior west wall, the bases of the octagonal corner towers and the wall recesses, which had rows of moulding. A prominent horizontal moulding just above the string course divides the wall into two zones. Above are rectangular panels with niches and hanging motifs; on the projections of the upper zone the panels have bold, decorative frames and *kalashas* with banners on top. Below the cornice are two arcades of miniature niches.

Inside, the mihrabs are set in rectangular frames and their tympana are filled with terracotta designs (fig. 63) as in the Adina Mosque of Pandua. Each has a different design, e.g., a grid pattern with rosettes, or a flowering tree; they are remarkable for their liveliness and high relief.

Inscription: The text is in Arabic; it reads:

"Allah the most High has said, 'And the places of worship are for Allah [alone], so invoke not anyone along with Allah' [Quran 72]. And the Prophet, peace and blessings of Allah be upon him, has said, 'Whoever builds a mosque for Allah, Allah will build for him a palace in Paradise' [Hadith]. This Jami mosque was built by the great and just Sultan, master of the *necks* [people] and nations, the Sultan, son of the Sultan, son of the Sultan Shams al-Dunya wal-Din Abul Muzaffar Yusuf Shah the Sultan, son of Barbak Shah the Sultan, son of Mahmud Shah the Sultan, may Allah perpetuate his kingdom and sovereignty, and make his bounty and gift universal, in the Hijri year 884 [1479-80]."

Bibliography: A. S. M. Ahmed, *Choto Sona Mosque*, pp.107-9; S. Ahmed, *IB*, 4:104-6; M. A. A. Khan, *Memoirs*, pp. 76-77, 111; Asher, "Inventory of Key Monuments", p. 71; Beveridge, "Notes on the Khurshid-i Jahan Numa", p. 222; Cunningham, "Report of a Tour", p. 76; Dani, *Bibliography*, p. 49; idem, *MAB*, pp. 108-12, and pls. 13-16. S. M. Hasan, *Mosque Architecture*, pp. 155-60; Karim, *Corpus of Inscriptions*, pp. 186-88; Saraswati, "Indo-Muslim Architecture", p.19; Siddiq, *Islamic Inscriptions of Bengal*, pp. 94-95.

Bandar Shahi Mosque, Narayanganj

Location: Police station, Bandar (Bawndor); district, Narayanganj. In Khondkartola, a residential area in Bandar, the river port for Dhaka just across the Sitalakhya (Shitalakkha) River from Narayanganj, 17 km southeast of Dhaka city, and about half a kilometre from the mosque and tomb of Haji Baba Saleh.

Date: Dated by inscription to 1 Zul Qada 886 (22 December 1481). The stone inscription tablet is fixed above the central doorway in the east.

Condition: The exterior of the mosque was renovated and plastered in the early twentieth century, and later a verandah with a roof of corrugated-iron sheeting was added in front. The dome raised on a drum crowned with a band of merlons, the elevated corner towers, and their crowning with *chhatris* is evidence of renovation in Mughal times, probably the seventeenth century when Dhaka was the capital of Bengal province (*suba*), and there was a spate of local construction. The interior of the mosque, although plastered and painted, retains most of its original features.

Dimensions: The interior is 6.00 m sq.; the wall thickness is 1.70 m.

Material: Brick; the engaged pilasters are of stone, two in each wall, as are the stone imposts at the springing of the doorway arches.

Plan and elevation (figs. 65-66): The mosque is a square building with three entrances in the east, and one each on the north and south sides. The three front entrances have pointed barrel vaults framed by front and rear arches. The central entrance is 1.70 m wide; the two entrances in the north and south are 1.50 m wide. Engaged octagonal towers and recesses articulate the exterior surface of the walls.

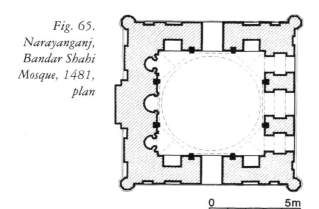

Fig. 65. Narayanganj, Bandar Shahi Mosque, 1481, plan

Inside, the north and south walls have deep recesses, one on either side of each of the entrances, which are almost equal in width to the side entrances in the east. There are three semicircular mihrab niches in the west wall.

The mosque has a large hemispherical dome that is carried on squinches. The squinch arches spring from the tops of the two engaged stone pillars in each wall (fig. 67). The mihrabs have half-domes. The straight cornice is probably a later addition.

Decoration: All the ornamentation is terracotta. Some original decoration is retained in the mihrabs in spite of several layers of paint (fig. 67). Each mihrab has a rectangular frame with floral vines and a miniature colonnade with floral discs in the interstices just above the arch. A similar ornamental colonnade also appears in the exterior of the Goaldi Mosque in a continuous band along the cornice and corner towers. In the niches of the north and south mihrabs are rectangular hanging motifs with ornate lamps carved on them. The central mihrab niche has three cusped arches, from the apexes of which rectangular plaques are suspended by chains. The plaque on the right is decorated with an ornate lamp; the other two with rosettes; the spandrels of the arches with kalashas and foliage. The deep niches on either side of the north and south entrances are now used for storage. The engaged stone pillars have square bases and capitals and octagonal shafts.

Bandar Shahi Mosque, Narayanganj

Fig. 66. Narayanganj, Bandar Shahi Mosque, north view

Inscription: The inscription is in Arabic. The text reads:

> "Allah the most High, says, 'And the places of worship are for Allah [alone]. So invoke not anyone along with Allah' [Quran 72:18]. The Prophet, peace and blessings of Allah be upon him, says, 'He who builds a mosque, Allah will build for him a palace in Paradise' [Hadith]. This blessed mosque was built by the great Malik [lord] Baba Saleh, in the reign of the Sultan, son of the Sultan, Jalal al-Dunya wal-Din, Abul Muzaffar Fath Shah the Sultan, son of Mahmud Shah the Sultan, may Allah perpetuate his kingdom and sovereignty; on the 1st of the month of Dhul Qada, in the Hijri year of the Prophet 886 [22 December 1481]."

Fig. 67. Narayanganj, Bandar Shahi Mosque, interior northwest

It should be noted that Baba Saleh uses the title of *malik* here instead of *haji*, as in the inscription on the mosque of Haji Baba Salih built in 911 (1505-6), indicating that he had not performed the *haj* (annual pilgrimage to Makka) yet.

Bibliography: A. S. M. Ahmed, *Choto Sona Mosque*, pp. 118-19; S. Ahmed, *IB*, 4: 113-14; Blochmann, *Contributions*, pp. 77-78; S. M. Hasan, *MMB*, p. 105: Karim, *Corpus of Inscriptions*, pp. 196-98; Siddiq, *Islamic Inscriptions of Bengal*, pp. 103-4.

Baba Adam's Mosque, Munshiganj

Location: Police station and district, Munshiganj; in the village of Dargapara, which derives its name from the tomb (*dargah*) of Baba Adam Shahid, who is traditionally known to be a Sufi who came to Bengal before the Muslim conquest and was martyred. The area is also known as Rampal, traditionally a capital of the Hindu kings before the thirteenth century.

Date: Dated by inscription to middle of Rajab 888 (August 1483); the inscription is in situ fixed over the central doorway in the east.

Condition: Protected and restored by the Department of Archaeology.

Dimensions: The interior is 10.96 m x 6.93 m; the wall thickness is 1.70 m.

Material: Brick; two free-standing pillars in the prayer chamber, imposts in the walls at the base of the springing of the arches and a slab about 15 cm thick at the base of the mihrab pillars are all of stone.

Plan and elevation (figs. 29-30): The mosque is a rectangular building with three aisles and two bays covered by six domes. There are three entrances in the east, the central one (2.15 m wide) is a little larger than the other two (1.90 m). On the north and south sides the entrances have been replaced by blind arched niches, 75 cm deep, two each in the north and south walls. In the west wall are three semicircular mihrabs opposite the front entrances. Engaged brick pilasters, two each, are in the east and west walls, and one each in the north and south; a pair of engaged brick pilasters is in each corner.

Outside are four octagonal engaged corner towers, a prominent recessed mihrab projection in the west wall, and shallow recesses all along the exterior surface of the walls. The very low domes are borne on corbelled pendentives. The cornice is curved.

The arches in the interior spring from the tops of stone imposts placed on top of the engaged brick pilasters and the tops of the square capitals of the free-standing pillars. These two pillars have low, square, recessed bases about 15 cm high and their shafts are first octagonal, then sixteen-sided. All the arches are pointed and set in recessed rectangles.

Decoration: The mihrabs are all about the same size, but the central one is slightly larger. They have half-domes and rectangular hanging motifs. In the southern mihrab, this

Baba Adam's Mosque, Munshiganj

Fig. 68.
Munshiganj,
Baba Adam's
Mosque, 1483,
mihrab pillar

motif is still quite clear with its traditional chain and ornate lantern and rosettes in the spandrels of the arches. A miniature arcade with floral discs inside adorns both the base of the half-dome and the tops of the recessed rectangle of the central mihrab. The shafts of the mihrab pillars have bells hanging from chains and strings of beads terminated by a flat leaf-like motif on both sides (fig. 68).

Outside are rectangular panels with miniature mihrab motifs on both sides of the central entrance; and mouldings above the plinth around the corner towers and the corners of the mihrab projection. The central mihrab projection on the back wall has a mihrab motif in a recessed rectangular panel in the centre (fig. 69), similar to the decoration seen in the Muazzampur Mosque in Sonargaon dated to around 1432-33. The later, ruined mosque at Shubhorara seems to have had a much larger external mihrab; it occupied the entire length of the projection. The miniature arcade with colonnettes is used as a decorative motif all along the cornice, the top and middle of the corner towers, and above the rectangular recesses of the doorways and blind arches. The domes are capped

Fig. 69. Munshiganj, Baba Adam's Mosque, exterior mihrab projection

with nipple pinnacles. Except for the external octagonal corner towers and low domes, the style of this mosque recalls the Goaldi Mosque in Sonargaon.

Inscription: The inscription is in Arabic. The stone inscription tablet is affixed over the central doorway in the east. It reads:

"Allah, the Most High says, 'And the places of worship are for Allah [alone]: So invoke not anyone along with Allah' [Quran 72: 18]. The Prophet, peace and blessings of Allah be upon him has said, 'He who builds a mosque in the world,

Allah builds for him a palace in Heaven' [Hadith]. This Jami mosque was built by the great *malik*, Malik Kafur, in the time of the Sultan, son of the Sultan Jalal al-Dunya wal-Din Abul Muzaffar Fath Shah, the Sultan, son of Mahmud Shah the Sultan, on a date in the middle of Rajab in 888 [August 1483]."

Bibliography: S. Ahmed, *IB*, 4: 118-20; Asher, "Inventory of Key Monuments", p. 128; Blochmann, *Contributions*, pp. 79-80; Chakravarti, "Pre-Mughal Mosques", p. 2; Cunningham, "Report of a Tour", pp. 134-35; Dani, *MAB*, pp. 154-56; S. A. Hasan, *Notes*, pp. 67-68; S. M. Hasan, *MMB*, pp. 131-33; Karim, *Corpus of Inscriptions*, pp. 201-3; Saraswati, "Indo-Muslim Architecture," p. 25; Siddiq, *Islamic Inscriptions of Bengal*, pp. 106-7; Wise, "Notes on Sonargaon", pp. 284-85.

Fath Shah's Mosque, Sonargaon

Location: Police station, Sonargaon; district, Narayanganj. Near the market in the village of Mograpara, which was a part of the ancient capital of Sonargaon (Shonargaon). It is locally known as Dargabari Shahi Jami Masjid, and is situated on the north side of the tombs of Pir Manna Shah Darvesh and Shaykh Muhammad Yusuf.

Date: There are two inscriptions: one dates the building to Muharram, 889 (February, 1484), the other to 1112 (1700-1). The inscription of 1700-1 is over the entrance, while the earlier one is plastered into the enclosure wall of the graveyard opposite the mosque.

Condition: The two inscriptions suggest that the original mosque was built during Sultanate times and later renovated. The exterior was plastered and the wall surface divided into rectangular panels as in Mughal buildings (fig. 36). The dome was heightened and raised on a drum. The central opening on the east side is adorned with elaborate cusping. All sides display the curved cornice over which a parapet with a level top has been added. The corner towers have disappeared. The interior has been plastered, whitewashed and painted.

Dimensions: The interior is 5.20 m x 7.70 m; the wall thickness is 1.60 m.

Material: Brick, except for the central mihrab which is of stone.

Plan and elevation (figs. 35-36): The mosque is a rectangular building with three entrances on the east, and one each on the north and south. The entrance on the north side has been blocked. The central east entrance is 1.40 m wide; the other two 1.20 m wide; and the north and south entrances 1.30 m wide. The openings have been reduced in size on the outside by a smaller arch set inside the entrance arch. On either side of the north and south entrances are deep arched recesses (85 cm wide x 70 cm deep). On the west wall are three semicircular mihrabs; the central one is the largest. Two short barrel vaults or wide arches on the north and south of the dome, spanning the whole width of the prayer chamber in the east-west direction, add 1.20 m on each side and turn the square into a rectangle.

The large hemispherical dome is supported on pendentives that are high up on the wall. The mihrabs are covered with half-domes. The pointed barrel vaults on the north and south sides (fig. 70), which are like wide arches, appear also in Badr Awlia Dargah Jami Mosque in Chittagong and in a more developed form in Qutb Shah's Mosque in Kishoreganj. Such transverse arches are common in Mughal mosques, where they are used to separate one bay from another. In this mosque, they appear to be part of the original design and not Mughal renovation work because the curved cornice of the original structure continues around the two arched areas. It would hardly be worthwhile to demolish the end walls for the sake of such a small increase in space, in any case, and in Mughal times construction techniques would not have been sufficiently advanced to do away with the entire load-bearing wall. Examples of these arches outside Bengal can be found in the Jamatkhana Mosque of Delhi, and the mosque of Orhan Ghazi in Bilecik, Anatolia, both from the fourteenth century.

Decoration: The general features of the central mihrab, that is, trefoil-cusped arch, pillars, and rosettes on the spandrels, are reminiscent of the central mihrab of the Goaldi Mosque (fig. 124) also in Sonargaon. A vine motif accentuating the arch and a hanging bell motif on the mihrab pillars, although indistinct, are still distinguishable underneath the heavy lime wash.

Inscription: The inscription is in Arabic. General Cunningham first found the stone inscription in 1879 affixed to the enclosure wall of the mosque. The villagers regarded it as miraculous—if someone was robbed, all he had to do was apply a coat of lime to the stone and the thief would break out with blisters, so whatever he had stolen could be recovered. When the *List of Ancient Monuments* was compiled in 1895, the stone was found on the enclosure wall of the graveyard opposite the mosque. The lime was scraped off and the inscription read; it is still there and continues to be subjected to the same use.

Fig. 70. Sonargaon, Fath Shah's Mosque, 1484, interior, arched vault on south side

The text of the first inscription reads as follows:

"Allah the Most High says, 'And the places of worship are for Allah [alone]. So invoke not anyone along with Allah' [Quran 72: 18]. And the Prophet, the peace and blessings of Allah be upon him, has said, 'He who builds a mosque, Allah will build for him seventy palaces in Heaven' [Hadith]. This mosque was built during the time of the great and exalted Sultan Jalal al-Dunya wal Din Abul Muzaffar Fath Shah, the Sultan, son of Mahmud Shah, the Sultan, may Allah perpetuate his kingdom and sovereignity. The builder of the mosque is Muqarrab al-Daulat (favourite of the government) Malik ... al-Din, the governor, the extraordinary keeper of the wardrobe, and Sar-i-lashkar and Wazir of Iqlim [region] Muazzamabad, also known as Mahmudabad, and Sar-i-lashkar of Thana Laud. This [i.e., the construction of the mosque] took place in the month of Muharram of the year 889 [February 1484]."

The second inscription reads:

"O God bless the untaught Prophet Muhammad, and his descendants and his Companions and his saints, and beautify and give him peace. Peace be upon you, O leader of saints, Commander of the Faithful, Ali, son of Abi Talib; the year 1112 [1700-1]."

Bibliography: S. Ahmed, *IB*, 4: 121-22; Cunningham, "Report of a Tour", p. 141; P. Hasan, "Eight Sultanate Mosques", pp. 183-84; *idem*, "Muslim Architecture", pp. 68-69; S. A. Hasan, *Notes*, p. 48; Karim, *Corpus of Inscriptions*, pp. 203-4, and 483; *List of Ancient Monuments*, p. 212; Siddiq, *Islamic Inscriptions of Bengal*, pp. 107-8 and 285-86.

Yusufganj Mosque, Sonargaon

Location: Police station, Sonargaon; district, Narayanganj. It is on the north side of the road to Mograpara, within the area of the ancient capital of Sonargaon.

Date: There is no inscription, and insufficient original features preclude accurate dating. It does retain some of the general characteristics of Sultanate-period mosques, however, so it can be assigned generally to the late fifteenth century.

Condition: Renovated, plastered, limewashed and painted both outside and in, but not enlarged. The cornice has been straightened and turrets erected on the roof. There are no corner towers.

Dimensions: The interior is 5.40 m sq.; the wall thickness is 1.80 m.

Material: Brick.

Plan and elevation (figs. 71-72): A square building with three entrances on the east side. The central opening with a width of 1.25 m is larger than the other two, which are 1.00 m across. The entrances on the north and south sides are 1.35 m wide. Inside, small niches flank the entrances. The central mihrab in the west is semicircular and covered with a half-dome; it is projected on the exterior.

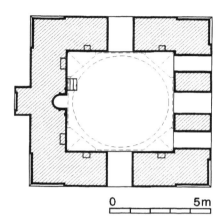

Fig. 71. Sonargaon, Yusufganj Mosque, late fifteenth century, plan

The dome is very low, and squinches are used in the transition zone. All the arches are pointed. Below the now-straightened cornice, the curve of the original one is still visible. All the entrances are set in recessed rectangles. The entrance on the south side has been turned into a window.

Decoration: No original decoration remains.

Fig. 72. Sonargaon, Yusufganj Mosque

Bibliography: P. Hasan, "Eight Sultanate Mosques", p. 187; *idem*, "Muslim Monuments", pp. 70-71; *List of Ancient Monuments*, p. 214.

Dhunichak Mosque, Gaur

Location: Police station, Shibganj; district, Nawabganj. The name of the mosque probably derives from the cotton carders (*dhuni-chak*) who once plied their trade there.

Date: No inscription remains. The decorative style is similar to the Tantipara Mosque at Gaur in West Bengal, which is dated by inscription to 1480. A late fifteenth-century date is also in line with its decoration and the six-bay plan popular at that time.

Condition: The building is in ruins. Only the north and west walls, foundations of the south and east walls, and two pillars in the middle of the prayer chamber remain (fig. 73). The Department of Archaeology and Museums protects what remains.

Dimensions: The interior is 13.61 m x 8.89 m; the wall thickness is 1.67 m.

Material: Brick; the two pillars, engaged pilasters, and the string course in the wall are of stone.

Plan (fig. 74) and elevation: A rectangular building that had six square bays, two running east-west and three north-south. Each bay was covered with a dome. Corresponding to the stone pillars in the middle are two stone pilasters in the west wall and one in the north, all that remains of the pillars of the fallen walls. The central entrance on the east was probably larger than the other two. Corresponding to these entrances are semicircular mihrabs in the west. The north wall has two arched niches, 1.42 m deep, instead of entrances. The south wall was similarly arranged.

Outside is a mihrab projection on the west. All that remains of the corner towers are their foundations. In the north wall, shallow recesses indicate the locations of the two deep interior niches.

Fig. 73. Gaur, Dhunichak Mosque, late fifteenth century, northwest view of ruined interior

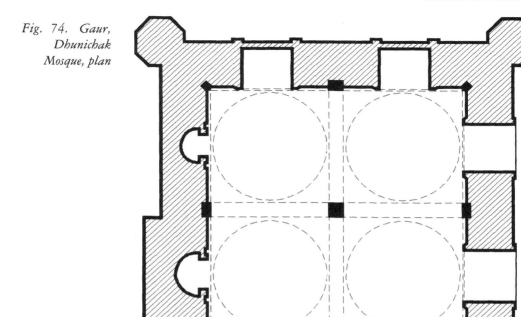

Fig. 74. Gaur, Dhunichak Mosque, plan

Oversailing courses of brick at the top of the walls confirm that the building was covered by six domes carried on corbelled pendentives. The two columns in the middle of the chamber have square bases, octagonal shafts with two rows of mouldings, and capitals with crenellation. The engaged pilasters are of similar design. The arches supporting the dome sprang from the tops of the columns and the engaged pilasters.

Decoration: Some terracotta decoration still remains on the mihrab wall and on the interior and exterior of the north wall. The mihrab arches are cusped and set in rectangular frames decorated with bands of vines and rosettes. The decoration inside the mihrabs has disappeared, but their spandrels are filled with a flowering vine with tendrils in relief that emerges from a *kalasha*. The spaces around the mihrabs are filled with rows of rectangular panels with niches and hanging motifs. The arched niches on the north side have rosettes in the spandrels and banners on each side. The exterior recesses corresponding to these niches are decorated in relief. There is an arch imitating a doorway, rosettes in spandrels, and a decorated rectangular frame with cusped niches and rosettes. The ornamental cusped niches with hanging motifs as well as the rosettes are similar in style to those found in the Tantipara Mosque just over the nearby border in India.

Bibliography: A. S. M. Ahmed, *Choto Sona Mosque*, pp. 93-94; Asher, "Inventory of Key Monuments", p. 72; Dani, *MAB*, pp. 107-8; Husain and Bari, "The Sultanate Mosques", pp. 83-87.

Khania Dighi Mosque, Gaur

Location: Police station, Shibganj; district, Nawabganj. The mosque is near the border with India, just southeast of the Kotwali Gate on the Indian side. It is also known as the Rajbibi Mosque.

Date: No inscription. On grounds of style, decoration, and similarity with the Chamkatti Mosque in Gaur, on the other side of the border, which is datable to the late fifteenth to early sixteenth century, a period of active architectural activity in Gaur, this mosque is also attributed a similar date.

Condition: The Department of Archaeology and Museums has done extensive reconstruction, rebuilding the three collapsed domes of the verandah and the piers of the eastern facade of the original mosque which were reduced to stumps.

Fig. 75. Gaur, Khania Dighi Mosque, late fifteenth to early sixteenth century, interior mihrab wall

Dimensions: The interior of the prayer chamber is 8.75 m sq.; the interior of the verandah is 8.75 m x 2.76 m; the wall thickness is 2.00 m.

Material: Brick and stone. Inside, the west wall has stone facing up to the level of the arches (fig. 75); engaged stone pilasters in the prayer chamber and the west wall of the verandah, and a string course of stone along the north, east and south walls of the prayer chamber and the west wall of the verandah.

Plan (fig. 76) and elevation: The verandah has three bays, three entrances from the front, and one each on the north and south sides. These side entrances and the flanking entrances in the east are of the same width (1.20 m); the central entrance is slightly wider. Its east and west walls have engaged pilasters, two in each wall. The prayer chamber also has side entrances from the north and south and three entrances corresponding to the front entrances. The interior west wall has three mihrabs, the central one larger than the other two. It too has engaged stone pilasters in each wall.

Outside are six engaged octagonal towers, four on the corners of the building, and two on each side where the verandah joins the prayer chamber. In the west wall is a projection for the central mihrab.

The curvature of the cornice is barely perceptible. The east facade and the domes of the verandah are entirely reconstructed. The three verandah domes are supported by corbelled pendentives; the large dome over the prayer chamber by squinches. The entrances have pointed arches and are set in recessed rectangles.

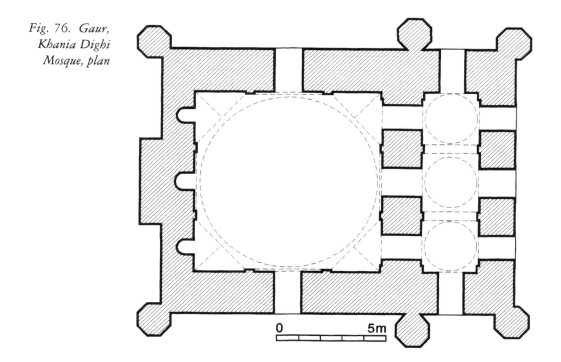

Fig. 76. Gaur, Khania Dighi Mosque, plan

Decoration: There are remnants of original decoration on the upper parts of the west wall, some parts of the north wall, and the base of the northwest corner tower; the cornice had two rows of arcades with small niches carved with vegetal motifs, a band of lozenges, and another of a mesh of four petals. The bases of the corner towers also had arcades of small niches similar to the ones on the cornice, and rows of rosettes. From what remains it is evident that the walls had rows of boldly outlined rectangular panels with arched niches on pillars, lotus buds, and rosettes on spandrels and lush plant motifs in relief inside the arches.

Inside, the mihrab wall is faced with stone up to the level of the arches and retains much of the original decoration (fig. 75). The stone mihrabs have cusped arches with full-blown rosettes carved on the spandrels, the rectangular frames, and the tympana above. They are supported by pillars ornately carved with among other motifs, the hanging bell. The central panel is missing from the central mihrab. An ornate lamp carved with leaves and rosette is the chief decorative motif in the mihrabs. The rectangular frames are intricately carved with vines and topped by *kalashas*. The squinches and the arches between them have elaborate brickwork to emphasize their facades.

The large rosettes wedged between the arches at the base of the dome are carved in terracotta, much like those in the Chamkatti Mosque of Gaur, India. On the spandrels of the arcade, just below these rosettes, are terracotta *kalashas*.

Bibliography: A. S. M. Ahmed, *Choto Sona Mosque*, pp. 125-26; M. A. A. Khan, *Memoirs*, p. 76; Asher, "Inventory of Key Monuments", p. 81; Cunningham, "Report of a Tour", pp. 60-61; Dani, *MAB*, p. 112; S. M. Hasan, *Mosque Architecture*, pp. 117-19; Husain and Bari, "The Sultanate Mosques", pp. 76-82.

Badr Awlia Dargah Jami Mosque, Chittagong

Location: Police station, Chittagong Municipal Area; district, Chittagong (Chawttogram). The mosque is on Badrpati Road in Bokshirhat, one of the oldest areas of Chittagong city, on a hillock opposite the famous *dargah* of Pir Badr, the patron saint of Chittagong, who is popularly associated with the spread of Islam in the region. The whole area is known as Badrpati after the saint.

Date: This mosque has not hitherto been identified as a Sultanate building. It has no inscription, and it is difficult to date, as few original features remain. A tentative late fifteenth-century date is based mainly on the presence of the tomb of Badr Awlia, on the other side of the road, which does seem to be a late fifteenth-century building, although it too has no inscription. Tradition regards them as contemporary, and stylistic grounds support it. The tomb retains most of its original features e.g., curved cornice, pointed arches, and hemispherical dome.

Condition: The building has been renovated and extended on all but the western side. The original mosque has been converted into a "mihrab room", by extending the north,

Fig. 77. Chittagong, Badr Awlia Dargah Jami Mosque, late fifteenth century, prayer chamber

east, and south sides with covered verandahs and additional floors built above. Nothing remains of the old mosque except the original prayer chamber (fig. 77). No original decoration remains, and even the shapes of most of the arches have been altered by reconstruction.

Dimensions: The interior is 7.40 m x 4.14 m; the wall thickness is 1.25 m.

Material: Brick.

Plan (fig. 78) and elevation: The mosque is a rectangular building with three entrances on the east and one each on the north and south. The entrances in the east have been enlarged, and collapsible iron gates inserted. The side entrances are 90 cm wide. In the west wall are three mihrabs: the base of the central one is in the shape of a pointed arch; the other two are rectangular, but the shapes are not the original ones. Two wide arches on the north and south sides of the dome have increased the interior space by 1.65 m on each side.

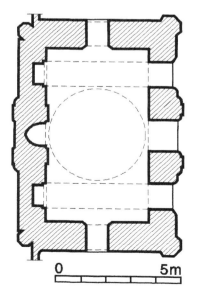

Fig. 78. Chittagong, Badr Awlia Dargah Jami Mosque, plan

Outside, the engaged octagonal corner towers and the mihrab projection in the west remain from the original building.

Pendentives support the large dome. There are two small niches on either side of the north and south entrances. These niches, the north and south entrances, and the mihrabs are set in recessed rectangles. The entrances in the east have lost these recesses to allow the doorways to be enlarged. The two side mihrabs retain their pointed arches but have been converted into closets. The shapes of all the other arches have been changed.

The wide arches are really short barrel vaults spanning the width of the chamber on the north and south sides. The same vault is used in Fath Shah's Mosque in Sonargaon (fig. 70), but it is otherwise an uncommon feature in single-domed mosques. The side mihrabs and the side openings in the east are directly aligned with these arches.

Decoration: No original decoration remains. Plaster and mosaic have changed the appearance of the interior.

Bibliography: Hitherto unpublished.

Shatoir Mosque, Faridpur

Location: Police station, Boalmari; district, Faridpur. The mosque, locally known as Shahi Jami Masjid, is near the marketplace and the railway station in the village of Shatoir. From Faridpur a road goes to Modhukhali, from where it is a half-hour ride by train to Shatoir.

Date: The mosque has no inscription. Only a few original features remain by which to estimate a date. The three other nine-domed mosques (Nine-domed Mosque, Bagerhat; Masjidkur Mosque, Khulna; Kasba Mosque, Barisal) are all in the Khan Jahan style. A later date is assigned to this mosque because, unlike the Khan Jahan style monuments, it combines circular and octagonal corner towers. The only remaining original decoration is on the mihrabs and resembles that of the central mihrab of the Bandar Shahi Mosque (fig. 67), which is dated to 1481. A late fifteenth-century date can therefore also be ascribed to this building.

Condition: This is the largest of the nine-domed mosques. It has been renovated and repaired several times by the villagers, but the inhabitants claim that its appearance has remained unchanged at least over the last fifty years. The corner towers have been made higher, however; the cornice is now straight; and a small verandah with corrugated iron roof in front are clearly new additions.

The ground level has risen considerably—probably by a metre or more—since the mosque was built. All the doorways are half their normal height, just about half of the mihrabs are visible, and the bases and lower parts of the pillar shafts are buried (fig. 79). The villagers said that at one time the river Padma (Pawdda) was so close to the mosque that it was feared it might be washed away. But the river changed course, and the old riverbed is now a large *bil* nearby. Some years ago the south side of the mosque was dug out and two doorways unearthed and turned into windows; the villagers claim that the

Fig. 79. Faridpur, Shatoir Mosque, late fifteenth century, interior

entrances have not been widened. The four corner towers were rebuilt, supposedly as indicated by the old foundations.

Dimensions: The interior is 13.70 m x 13.80 m; the wall thickness is 1.85 m.

Material: Brick; the capitals of both the free-standing and engaged pillars are of stone. The many layers of lime wash make it impossible to tell whether the pillars themselves are stone or brick.

Plan (fig. 80) and elevation: The mosque's square building has three entrances each on the north, east, and south sides. The width of all the entrances is the same (central, 2.02 m; side, 1.86 m). In the west wall, on an axis with the three eastern entrances, are three mihrabs. In the centre of the chamber are four octagonal pillars, and in each wall corresponding to these pillars are engaged octagonal pilasters. In each corner are engaged double-edged pilasters. The interior space is divided into nine equal bays each 4.25 m square.

Outside are four engaged corner towers; the two in front are octagonal and the two at the back are round. If these forms were built on the original foundations, as the local people claim, then this is the only known mosque with this combination. In the west wall is the projection for the central mihrab.

The shallow domes are supported by corbelled pendentives. The interior space is spanned by two intersecting arcades, the pointed arches of which spring from the tops of the free-standing columns in the centre of the chamber and the engaged wall pilasters. The bases of the pillars and pilasters are buried, so it is impossible to say if they are square or round. Although the shapes of the arches are much altered from plastering, there are indications that they were originally all pointed arches. The interior of the mosque is well lit.

Shatoir Mosque, Faridpur

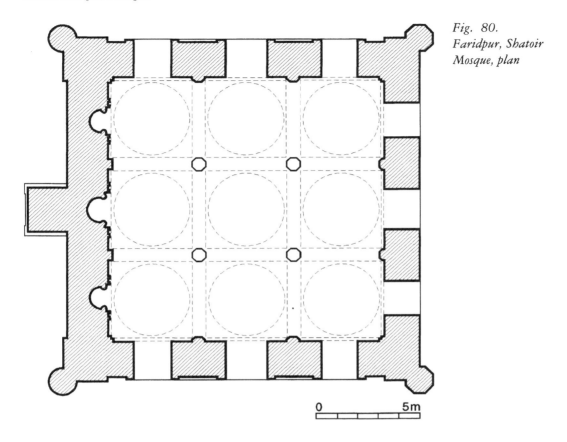

Fig. 80.
Faridpur, Shatoir
Mosque, plan

Decoration: Traces of original decoration remain only in the mihrabs, which had engrailed arches and are set in rectangular frames. The central and northern mihrabs have carved rosettes in their spandrels. The pillars of the central mihrab are elaborately decorated with festoons and a hanging-bell motif. The niche of the mihrab has an arcade of cusped niches with hanging motifs. Over the mihrab arch are bands of miniature cusped niches; their decoration has become indistinct. They are topped by rows of beads and lozenges. The rectangular frame has an interlocking geometric design with rosettes and floral motifs, elaborate versions of the terracotta designs of the Khan Jahan style mosques at Bagerhat. The mihrab niches resemble the central mihrab of the Bandar Shahi Mosque, Narayanganj, of 1481 (fig. 67).

Bibliography: Hitherto unpublished.

KHAN JAHAN STYLE

Shaitgumbad (Shaitgombuj) Mosque, Bagerhat

Location: Police station, Bagerhat; district, Bagerhat. This is the largest mosque in Bangladesh, located about 5 km west of the town of Bagerhat in the village of Shundorghona, on the eastern bank of Ghoradighi, a large pond said to have been excavated by Khan Jahan. It still supplies drinking water to the town of Bagerhat.

Date: The mosque has no inscription. Its mid-fifteenth-century dating is based on its similarity with other buildings in the Khan Jahan style.

Condition: The Department of Archaeology and Museums has restored the building. At the end of the nineteenth century, it was described as being in precarious condition: the corner towers had already fallen down; almost all the domes close to the walls were severely damaged; and the entire roof was covered with thick vegetation. Two *faqir*s kept the interior clean in return for alms from visitors.

Dimensions: The interior is 42.77 m x 24.59 m; the wall thickness is 2.30 m.

Material: Brick, except for the pillars in the prayer chamber, the central mihrab, and the imposts on the walls at the springing of the arches, which are of stone.

Plan and elevation (figs. 33-34): Shaitgumbad literally means "sixty domes" (Beng., *shait*, sixty; Per., *gumbad*, dome). In fact, the mosque has seventy domes and seven *chau-chala* vaults, raising the possibility that the number *shait* (sixty) could refer to the sixty pillars inside the mosque that hold up the domes or to the *chala*s (Beng., *shat*, seven). Since the colloquial word for pillar is *khamba*, another possibility is that *shait khamba* (sixty pillars) was corrupted into Shaitgumbad (sixty domes).

The building is rectangular with eleven aisles and seven bays. The central aisle is the largest and constitutes seven independent rectangular bays measuring 5 m x 3.90 m. The rest of bays are 3.90 m sq. Of the eleven entrances on the east side, the central one is the largest (2.90 m wide). On the north and south sides there are seven entrances each. All the aisles terminate in a mihrab in the west wall, except the one immediately north of the central mihrab, which has an entrance doorway.

Inside the prayer chamber are sixty stone pillars in six rows of ten each (fig. 81). They are about 3.10 m high, ending at the springing of the arches. All but six of the pillars are very slender. Five out of these six have brick casing, while a massive pillar in the northern wing is entirely of stone. Of the engaged brick pilasters in the walls, six are on the north, six on the south, and ten each on the east and west. They have stone imposts at the springing of the arches.

Recesses articulate the south, west, and north exterior walls and there is a projection for the central mihrab. The four corners have massive engaged circular towers. The two

Shaitgumbad (Shaitgombuj) Mosque, Bagerhat

Fig. 81. Bagerhat, Shaitgumbad Mosque, mid-fifteenth century, interior

front towers contain spiral staircases that lead to the chambers above, and the entrance is through a doorway inside the mosque at the base of the tower.

The most unusual architectural feature of this building is its wide central aisle, which connects the largest entrance in the east to the largest mihrab in the west wall, and divides the interior of the mosque into north and south wings. Each rectangular bay in this aisle is roofed independently by a *chau-chala* (fig. 82) which rests directly on the arches springing from the stone pillars below. Small hemispherical domes borne on corbelled pendentives roof the side wings containing seventy square bays. The stone pillars, which vary in thickness, consist of two or three pieces joined together by dowels. They have square, stepped bases and capitals, and octagonal shafts. It appears that at one time all of them were encased in brick because several still have traces of brickwork around their bases. The brick pillars imitated the design of the stone core. The only massive pillar of stone is square and tapers towards the top. All the arches are pointed. The entrances on the north and south sides, with the exception of the central ones, have frontal arches on the exterior. It is said that at one time there were brick platforms at both ends of the aisle immediately north of the central one. No such platforms exist today.

The cornice of the building is curved and comes to a point over the central arched doorway on the east side (fig. 83). This triangular pediment shape, which is aligned to the ridges of the central vaulting of *chau-chalas*, is probably derived from the gable ends of *chala* huts. The corner towers are domed with small cupolas, which copy the corner towers of the Khirki Mosque in Delhi. The two eastern towers have four cardinally set windows; those at the back have two. This is the only example from this period of ascendable towers being attached to a mosque, from which the call to prayer could be given. Circular corner towers are a distinguishing feature of the Khan Jahan style. There was probably an enclosure wall around the building, as a monumental gateway to the mosque area still exists in the east.

Fig. 82. Bagerhat, Shaitgumbad Mosque, chau-chala vaulted roof in central aisle

Decoration: With the exception of the central mihrab, the ornamentation is in terracotta and concentrated on the mihrabs, entrance arches, interiors of the *chau-chalas* of the central aisle, and the moulding of the corner towers. In the interior, parts of the surface still show traces of thin lime plaster.

The stark massive appearance of the exterior, with its minimal terracotta decoration, is in characteristic Khan Jahan style. The cornice moulding featuring a row of lozenges runs around the circular towers. The recessed rectangles, in which all the entrance arches are set, have bands of moulding on top. The central entrance arch on the east has full-blown lotuses in the spandrels and rows of terracotta decoration on top. At the apex of the arch is a lozenge-shaped terracotta plaque. On either side of this entrance are terracotta clusters of rosettes similar to those above the mihrabs in the Masjidkur Mosque in Khulna.

Inside, the spandrels and upper parts of the entrance arches are decorated with rosettes, festoons, interlocking geometric patterns enclosing floral motifs, and vegetal scrolls. The interiors of the *chau-chalas* have thin raised bands of brick that imitate the rafters and purlins of bamboo hut roofs. Some sections still retain the terracotta rosettes that were placed at the intersections of these bands.

The west wall has ten semicircular mihrabs, some of which have engrailed arches. With the exception of the central one, all are of brick with terracotta decoration. They have hanging rectangular motifs descending from the bases of the half-domes. The niches are divided into horizontal panels, some of which still retain a little vegetal decoration. The geometric patterns intertwined with flowers are as lively as the vegetal motifs. The tops of the mihrab rectangles have an arcade of miniature engrailed niches with geometric and plant designs. Each mihrab ensemble is crowned by a row of crested merlons with plants inside. Among the trees depicted, the date and coconut palms are easily discernible. Similar motifs are also found in the Nine-domed Mosque, Bagherhat and the Masjidkur Mosque, Khulna.

Fig. 83. Bagerhat, Shaitgumbad Mosque, pediment over central entrance on the east

The central mihrab is stone with decorations carved in low relief, much of which has worn off. The spandrels of the engrailed arch are decorated with flowering plants and rosettes. A rectangular plaque on a chain descends from the row of rosettes at the base of the mihrab half-dome. The plaque has a trilobed niche with a rosette in the centre. The carvings on the mihrab frame have worn off, but a square tablet of black stone that has a large rosette in the centre encircled by seven smaller ones tops the whole composition.

Bibliography: A. S. M. Ahmed, *Choto Sona Mosque*, pp. 105-6; Asher, "Inventory of Key Monuments", pp. 41-42; Bari, "Khalifatabad and its Monuments", pp. 115-41; Babu Gourdass Bysack, "The Antiquities of Bagerhat", *Journal of the Asiatic Society of Bengal* 2 (1867): 132-33; Dani, *MAB*, pp. 144-47; S. M. Hasan, *Mosque Architecture*, pp. 152-55; W. W. Hunter, *A Statistical Account of Bengal*, (rpt. Delhi, 1973), vol. 2, p. 229; Haque et al, *Pundranagar to Sherebanglanagar*, pp. 50-51; F. A. Khan, "Conservation of Ancient Monuments in East Pakistan: Satgumbad Mosque", *Pakistan Archaeology* 5, (1968): 248-49; Lohuizen de Leeuw, "Monuments at Bagerhat", pp. 165-78; *List of Ancient Monuments*, p. 141; L. S. S. O'Malley, *Bengal District Gazetteers* (Khulna, 1908), pp. 168-69; D. B. Spooner, *ARASI* (1917-18), 1: 9; J. A. Westland, *A Report on the District of Jessore*, rev. ed. (Calcutta, 1871), p. 12.

Mosque adjoining Khan Jahan's Tomb, Bagerhat

Location: Police station, Bagerhat; district, Bagerhat, in the village of Dighir Par. The mosque is west of the mausoleum of Khan Jahan, but within the same enclosure. There was a gateway between the two but it has been blocked and walled up. It is locally known as the mosque of Khan Jahan. There is a very large tank outside the enclosure wall where a number of tame crocodiles are kept. The pilgrims who visit the tomb of Khan Jahan feed them, and acceptance of their offerings by the reptiles is regarded as an auspicious sign.

Fig. 84. Bagerhat, mosque adjoining Khan Jahan's tomb, mid-fifteenth century, south view

Date: There is no inscription. Because of similarity in size and style to the tomb of Khan Jahan next door, which is dated by inscription to 1459, a mid-fifteenth-century date is feasible for this building as well. This mosque and adjoining tomb are the two structures that define the style attributed to Khan Jahan.

Condition: The locals have repaired the mosque and extended it in front by building a verandah between the east facade of the mosque and the gateway to the tomb (fig. 84).

Dimensions: The interior is 7.90 m sq.; the wall thickness is 2.20 m.

Materials: Brick; stone brackets at the springing of the squinch arches.

Plan (fig. 85) and elevation: The mosque is a square building with three entrances on the east side and one each on the north and south. The central entrance in the east is the largest; it is 1.85 m wide; the two on either side are 1.05 m. The north and south entrances are 1.45 m wide. The mihrab projects in the exterior; it is opposite the central entrance on the east. There are two other niches in the west wall, one on either side of the mihrab; two more are on the north and south walls; one on either side of the entrances. On the outside, the four corners have engaged circular towers. The cornice is curved, and the hemispherical dome is supported on squinches whose arches spring from stone brackets projecting out of the walls. The arches of the doorways, the mihrab, and the smaller wall niches are set in recessed panels. The mihrab is semicircular with a half-dome (fig. 86). The circular towers and the exterior in general have very little decoration, which is characteristic of the Khan Jahan style.

Decoration: The exterior retains some original decoration. The two cornice mouldings, which run all around the building, feature lozenge bands. The corner towers are embellished with five more mouldings with rows of lozenges and triangles and a

Mosque adjoining Khan Jahan's Tomb, Bagerhat

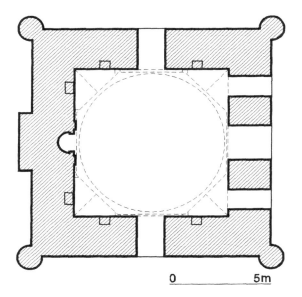

Fig. 85. Bagerhat, mosque adjoining Khan Jahan's tomb, plan

combination of lozenges and rosettes in the lowest moulding. The dome is topped by a *kalasha* finial.

There is no original decoration left in the interior. The walls and the mihrab are covered with modern ceramic tiles up to the level of the springing of the squinch arches. Above that, there is lime wash. The original shapes of the arches have been preserved, and the mihrab has an elegant trefoil-cusped pointed arch.

Bibliography: A. S. M. Ahmed, *Choto Sona Mosque*, p. 113; Bari, "Khalifatabad and its Monuments", pp. 177-79; S. M. Hasan, *MMB*, p. 156; Karim, *Corpus of Inscriptions*, pp. 137-39; Lohuizen de Leeuw, "Monuments at Bagerhat", pp. 165-78; Siddiq, *Islamic Inscriptions of Bengal*, pp. 65-67; D. B. Spooner, *ARASI* (1917-18), 1: 9.

Fig. 86. Bagerhat, mosque adjoining Khan Jahan's tomb, renovated interior

Ranbijoypur Mosque, Bagerhat

Location: Police station, Bagerhat; district, Bagerhat, in the village of Ranbijoypur, a short distance from the Bagerhat-Shaitgumbad road, close to where it branches off toward Khan Jahan's Tomb.

Date: There is no inscription, but similarities with buildings of the Khan Jahan style suggest a mid-fifteenth-century date.

Condition: The Department of Archaeology and Museums protects this imposing structure. Due to the advanced stage of decay of the monument extensive repairs have been made to halt its ruin.

Dimensions: The interior is 10.80 m sq.; the wall thickness is 2.80 m.

Material: Brick.

Plan and elevation (figs. 87-88): The mosque is a large, square building with uninterrupted space in the interior; it has three entrances each on the north, east and south sides. The openings onto the front (eastern) are the largest: the central entrance is 2.00 m wide and the ones flanking it, 1.50 m. Two-centred, pointed front and rear arches flank the central recessed part. The entrances on the north and south sides are small (the centre one is 1.80 m wide and the flanking ones are 1.30 m wide) and simple; one continuous archway runs through the thickness of the wall.

Corresponding to the three front entrances are three mihrabs on the west, of which the largest is the central one (width and depth 1.90 m). These measurements exactly match the dimensions of the mihrabs of Bibi Begni's Mosque nearby. There are two engaged brick pilasters in each wall. Outside are engaged circular towers in the corner; the mihrab projection on the west is recessed on the sides.

This is the largest single-domed mosque in Bangladesh, and almost reaches the proportions of a nine-domed mosque. It has the impact of great massiveness. The huge hemispherical dome rests on squinches with wide front arches (fig. 89), which spring from the tops of engaged brick pilasters in the walls. There is a niche in the southwest section of the south wall. The cornice is gently curved.

Decoration: Very little of the original decoration remains on the exterior. When the Department of Archaeology took over the building, in spite of the dilapidated state, its dome was intact. After repairs it was smoothly plastered. Originally the dome had an exterior decoration of rows of small projecting bricks at regular intervals (fig. 90), a motif very unusual in Bengal architecture, but reminiscent of the decoration on the dome of the Samanid Tomb in Bukhara (for illustration, see Derek Hill and Oleg Grabar, *Islamic Architecture and its Decoration* (Chicago, 1964), pl. 2). They may have provided footholds for the masons who constructed the dome.

Ranbijoypur Mosque, Bagerhat

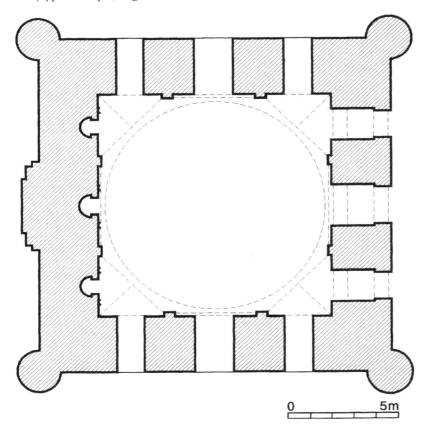

Fig. 87.
Bagerhat,
Ranbijoypur
Mosque, mid-
fifteenth century,
plan

Fig. 88.
Bagerhat,
Ranbijoypur
Mosque

Fig. 89. Bagerhat, Ranbijoypur Mosque, mihrab wall

In the interior, the engaged brick pilasters are octagonal with square bases. The mihrabs are semicircular with half-domes and pointed cusped arches. They are set in rectangular frames and have hanging motifs in their niches. The central rectangle is crowned by merlons. The spandrels of most of the arches are now plain, but the mihrab on the south still has some of its original decoration. Rows of lozenges, small flowers, or combinations of both divide it into horizontal panels. In between are ornamental bands. The first one from the top is a floral scroll with the blossoms shown alternately

Fig. 90. Bagerhat, Ranbijoypur Mosque, before conservation

in frontal and side views; the second is a scroll formed by two intertwined vines with rosettes at intervals; and the third is a conventional trilobed arcade with plant and flower motifs. The central and north mihrabs, now much worn, seem to have had similar decoration. The surfaces of the rectangular hanging plaques in the central and southern mihrabs have been worn smooth, but the one inside the northern mihrab bears a miniature mihrab motif with spandrels decorated with rosettes and a flowering plant in the centre of the arch.

Bibliography: A. S. M. Ahmed, Choto Sona Mosque, p. 114; N. Ahmed, "An Uncommon Group of pre-Mughal Monuments in Bangladesh", The South Asian Archaeology (1981): 309-13; Bari, "Khalifatabad and its Monuments", pp. 179-84; F. A. Khan, "Conservation of Ancient Monuments in East Pakistan", Pakistan Archaeology 5 (1968): 241-42; S. M. Hasan, *MMB*, p. 158; Lohuizen de Leeuw, "Monuments at Bagerhat", pp. 165-78; Haque et al, Pundranagar to Sherebanglanagar, p. 54, D. B. Spooner, *ARASI* (1917-18), 1: 9.

Bibi Begni's Mosque, Bagerhat

Location: Police station, Bagerhat; district, Bagerhat, in the village of Chunakhola, about 200 m west of a huge tank known as Ghoradighi. The building is attributed to Bibi Begni, locally believed to have been Khan Jahan's wife. The name Chunakhola means "lime field"; the lime used in mortar needed for construction was produced here from seashells.

Date: There is no inscription, but the mosque is very similar to the Ranbijoypur Mosque and other buildings in the Khan Jahan style and thus can be ascribed to the mid-fifteenth century.

Condition: Protected by the Department of Archaeology and Museums, which has done extensive repair work.

Dimensions: The interior is 10 m sq.; the wall thickness is 3.10 m.

Material: Brick.

Plan and elevation (figs. 91-92): The mosque is a large square building with three entrances in the east, and one each on the north and south sides: the central one in the east and the north and south entrances are the same size (1.70 m wide); the two other eastern entrances are smaller (1.30 m wide). In the west wall opposite the eastern entrances are three semicircular mihrabs of which the central one is the largest. It has a depth and width of 1.20 m; the corresponding measurement of the side mihrabs is 90 cm.

On the outside are engaged circular towers at the four corners. The mihrab projection of the wall is not very prominent but is accented by two engaged, circular turrets that

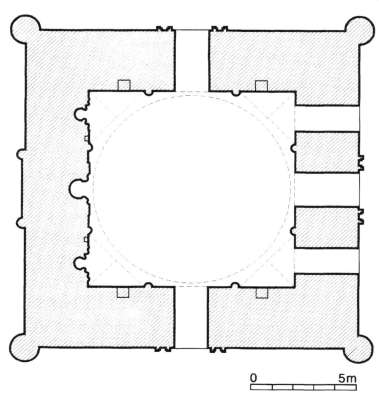

Fig. 91. Bagerhat, Bibi Begni's Mosque, mid-fifteenth century, plan

reach up to the middle of the projection. The central entrance on the east and the entrances on the north and south sides are set in projected rectangular frames.

The cornice is gently curved. The huge hemispherical dome rests on squinches with wide front arches, springing from the tops of the semicircular, engaged brick pilasters.

Fig. 92. Bagerhat, Bibi Begni's Mosque

The corbelled pendentives wedged between the front arches of the squinches are much deeper than those seen in other mosques of the time. The north and south walls have niches, one on each side of the entrances, and there are two small niches on either side of the central mihrab.

Decoration: Very little exterior decoration remains. The cornice moulding, which is continuous around the corner towers, has three rows of lozenges at the base, and the spaces in between are filled with a mesh of four petals and a runner of continuous diamond shapes. The mesh of four petals appears on many of the Khan Jahan style monuments and is similar to brickwork patterns in Persian architecture, e.g., on the southwest main portal of the Masjid-i Jami at Isfahan (twelfth century) and the shrine of Bayazid at Bistam (1120). Between the base and the cornice the corner towers have six more rows of mouldings with lozenges, triangles, and tooth patterns.

Inside the building all the mihrab arches are engrailed and have hanging motifs. The decoration is best preserved in the central mihrab. The rectangular mihrab frame is wider than usual and is decorated in horizontal bands. Each section has arcades of trilobed niches with vegetal motifs inside, the top arcade being crowned by merlons filled with vegetal designs. The mihrab spandrels have rosettes and the interiors of the niches are divided into five horizontal panels filled with variations of the four-petalled mesh motif.

Bibliography: A. S. M. Ahmed, *Choto Sona Mosque*, pp. 116-17; Bari, "Khalifatabad and its Monuments", pp. 184-89; Lohuizen de Leeuw, "Monuments at Bagerhat", pp. 165-78; F. A. Khan, "Conservation of Ancient Monuments in East Pakistan", *Pakistan Archaeology* 5 (1968): 241-42.

Shingra Mosque, Bagerhat

Location: Police station, Bagerhat; district, Bagerhat, in the village of Shundorghona, about 200 m south of the Shaitgumbad Mosque.

Date: There is no inscription. On grounds of stylistic similarities with Khan Jahan style buildings, the mosque is ascribed to the mid-fifteenth century.

Condition: Under the protection of the Department of Archaeology and Museums, which has restored it extensively.

Dimensions: The interior is 7.80 m sq.; the wall thickness is 2.13 m.

Material: Brick.

Plan and elevation (figs. 93-94): The mosque is a square building with three entrances in the east, and one each in the north and south. The width of the eastern central entrance is 1.82 m and of the flanking ones 94 cm. The north and south entrances are 1.50 m wide. The single mihrab in the west wall is on axis with the central entrance in the east.

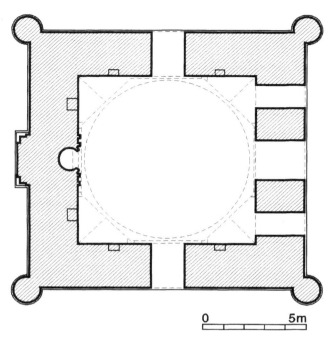

Fig. 93. Bagerhat, Shingra Mosque, mid-fifteenth century, plan

The four corners have engaged circular towers; there is a mihrab projection on the west side. The cornice is gently curved. The hemispherical dome was originally supported on squinches with shallow pointed arches that sprang from stone brackets embedded in the walls, but these have either fallen or been removed, and the squinch arches now spring from brick imposts. There are no engaged pilasters in the interior. Typical corbelled pendentives are wedged between the arches. There are engrailed

Fig. 94. Bagerhat, Shingra Mosque, before conservation

arched niches on either side of the mihrab and in the north and south walls on either side of the entrances.

Decoration: The pointed arched doorways are set in rectangular recesses with rosettes in the spandrels. The cornice has two bands of ornamental moulding; the engaged corner towers have five bands with a lozenge pattern. In the interior, the decoration in the semi-circular mihrab is in four horizontal panels. A rectangular motif whose details are now effaced hangs on a chain from its centre. In the horizontal bands, the first panel from the top has an arcade of miniature mihrabs, and the second row has a mesh of four-petalled flowers. Raised rows of beads and lozenges separate these two bands.

Empty spaces on the spandrels of the mihrab arch indicate that there were rosettes in the original decorative scheme. The niche is within a rectangular frame filled with a four-petalled mesh, and crowned by a frieze of blind merlons. The niche on the north side of the mihrab retains some original decoration. Just above the trefoil-cusped arch is a curving lotus vine similar to those seen in the Masjidkur Mosque in Khulna.

Bibliography: A. S. M. Ahmed, *Choto Sona Mosque*, p. 115; Bari, "Khalifatabad and its Monuments", pp. 193-95; S. M. Hasan, *MMB*, p. 163; Lohuizen de Leeuw, "Monuments at Bagerhat", pp. 165-78.

Nine-domed Mosque, Bagerhat

Location: Police station, Bagerhat; district, Bagerhat, in Dighir Par village on an artificial mound on the western bank of a large tank known as Thakurdighi. It is less than 5 km to the west of the tomb of Khan Jahan.

Date: There is no inscription, but stylistic similarities to Khan Jahan style mosques suggest a date in the mid-fifteenth century.

Condition: The building is under the protection of the Department of Archaeology and Museums. The mosque has been repaired and restored, and is still in use.

Dimensions: The interior is 12.00 m sq.; the wall thickness is 2.25 m.

Material: Brick; four pillars in the centre of the square chamber are of stone. There are stone imposts in the corners of the walls and over the tops of the engaged brick pilasters from where the arches spring.

Plan and elevation (figs. 25-26): The building is square with three entrances each on the east, south and north sides; the central entrances are larger than the flanking ones. The central entrance in the east is the largest (2.00 m wide); the flanking entrances are the same size as the central ones in the north and south (1.30 m).

In the west wall, opposite the three entrances in the east, are three semicircular mihrabs, the central one larger than the other two and projected outside. In the centre of the chamber are four stone pillars, and on each wall corresponding to the pillars, are two engaged brick pilasters. In the corners are engaged, slender, double pilasters. The interior is divided into nine equal bays, each 3.50 m square and covered by a dome.

Four intersecting arcades, the pointed arches of which spring from the capitals of the stone columns in the centre and the engaged brick pilasters of the walls, span the interior space. The pillars, which are in three sections, are all well finished and of the same design. Their capitals are square, and their shafts have square chamfered bases, octagonal middle sections, and square, stepped tops. The hemispherical domes are supported on corbelled pendentives.

There are small lamp niches, two in the west wall on either side of the central mihrab, and two each in the western sections of the north and south walls.

Outside, recesses articulate the walls. There are four circular, engaged corner towers; the cornice is curved.

Decoration: Both the exterior and interior decorations have some unusual features. On the outside the three arched entrances in the east and the central openings in the north and south are set in rectangular recesses with simple mouldings above the arches. The side entrances in the north and south, however, are set in recesses that are narrow and rise vertically almost up to the level of the lower cornice band (fig. 26). They have pointed engrailed tops. Between each side opening and the central entrance on that side are blind recesses of the same type, but with three rows of mouldings at the bottom. This type of tall, narrow, recessed panel is rare in Bengali architecture of the time—the only other examples are in the mosque at Nabagram and the mosque at Shatgachhia—but common in Persian architecture from between the twelfth and the fourteenth century (e.g., the Haruniyya Tomb in Tus, thirteenth to fourteenth century, and the Ribat-i Sharaf caravanserai between Nishapur and Merv, mid-twelfth century, and an earlier example, the Masjid-i Jami, Isfahan, 1088).

The cornice has two rows of mouldings that continue around the corner towers. They enclose an arcade of miniature mihrab motifs. The rectangular frame of the east central entrance has a border mesh of four-petalled flowers. This motif is widely used in the Khan Jahan monuments and has earlier prototypes in Iran.

Inside, the decoration above the entrance archways is more elaborate than usual in mosques of the period. It consists of rows of small rosettes, petals, festoons, a vine with half-palmettes, and a border of small petals. They appear in different scales and are sometimes combined with a lotus motif in the decorative programme of the mihrabs. There is also an interlocking eight-pointed star with a rosette in the centre that has petals arranged in a clockwise swirl as in a pinwheel. It is a simplified version of the geometric mesh with rosettes that is seen in the rectangular outer frame of the central mihrab.

The mihrabs are divided into horizontal panels and profusely decorated (fig. 95). Their programmes include a geometric mesh with rosettes, small rosettes in a chequered

Fig. 95. Bagerhat, Nine-domed Mosque, mid-fifteenth century, mihrab

arrangement, rows of small rosettes and petals, rosettes in a grid, full-blown lotuses, a palmette and rosette vine, and the lotus vine.

The central mihrab has a very naturalistic lotus plant on the spandrel. The top of its rectangular panel has crenellated merlons with fruit and flower-bearing plants, e.g., date and lotus, as in the Masjidkur Mosque, Khulna. The mihrab arches are trefoil-cusped and have hanging motifs down the centre.

Bibliography: A. S. M. Ahmed, *Choto Sona Mosque*, pp. 134-35; Bari, "Khalifatabad and its Monuments", p. 326; Department of Archaeology and Museums, *Protected Monuments and Mounds in Bangladesh* (Dacca, 1975), p. 18; K. N. Dikshit, "Conservation: Eastern Circle, Bengal: Masjidkur", ARASI (1923-24): 32; S. M. Hasan, *MMB*, p. 157; John D. Hoag, *Islamic Architecture* (New York, 1977), pl. 246; Anthony Hutt and Leonard Harrow, *Islamic Architecture in Iran* (London, 1977), vol.1, pls. 94-96; Jalil, *Shundorboner Itihash* (Dacca, 1969), vol. 2, pp. 158-59; F. A. Khan, "Exploration in Pakistan: East Pakistan, Khulna, Nine-Domed Mosque at Bagerhat", *Pakistan Archaeology* 5 (1968): 21-22; Habiba Khatun, "Bagerhater Noy Gumbaj Moshjid", *Bangladesh Itihash Porishod Patrika* (Dacca: Baisakh-Chaitra, 1382 B.S.), pp. 104-13; Haque et al, *Pundranagar to Sherebanglanagar*, pp. 52-53, 160.

Masjidkur (Moshjidkur) Mosque, Khulna

Location: Police station, Koyra; district, Khulna, in the village of Masjidkur, which literally means "excavation of a mosque" on the eastern bank of the river Kabadak (Kapotakshya). It derives its name from the fact that the mosque was discovered by cultivators in the Sundarban (Shundorbon) forest while they were clearing it. The mosque is difficult to reach because of bad road connections.

Date: There is no inscription. On the basis of similarities with mosques of the Khan Jahan style, this mosque is dated to the mid-fifteenth century.

Condition: The mosque is under the protection of the Department of Archaeology and Museums. One of the best preserved of the ancient monuments of Bengal, it is still used as a mosque. At the end of the nineteenth century, it was listed as being in good condition and has been kept in good repair ever since.

Dimensions: The interior is 12.10 m x 12.03 m; the wall thickness is 2.20 m.

Material: Brick; four pillars in the center of the square chamber are of stone.

Plan and elevation (figs. 96-97): A square building with three entrances each on the north, east and south sides. The width of the entrances in the east (central, 1.61 m, flanking, 1.35 m) are the same as those on the south and north sides. In the west wall opposite the three entrances on the east are three semicircular mihrabs, the central one larger than the other two. In the centre of the chamber are four stone pillars, and on each wall, corresponding to the pillars, are four engaged brick pilasters. The interior space is divided into nine equal bays, each one 3.50 m square and covered by a dome.

Outside are four engaged circular towers (diameter 1.55 m) in the corners and a mihrab projection in the centre of the west wall. The cornice is curved. The hemispherical domes are supported on corbelled pendentives.

Masjidkur (Moshjidkur) Mosque, Khulna

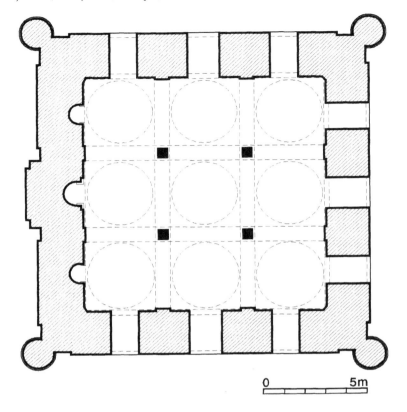

Fig. 96. Khulna, Masjidkur Mosque, mid-fifteenth century, plan

Two intersecting arcades, the pointed arches of which spring from the tops of the stone columns in the centre of the chamber and the engaged brick pilasters in the walls, span the interior space. Each stone pillar is in three sections and has stone capitals. However, the sections are not identical, and the stone is not of uniform quality.

Fig. 97. Khulna, Masjidkur Mosque

Fig. 98. Khulna, Masjidkur Mosque, north mihrab

Decoration: The entrance doorways are all set in rectangular recesses with horizontal bands of terracotta ornamentation above the archways. The decoration on the east side is more elaborate. Over the doorway recess of the central entrance is a rectangular panel with a border depicting a curving vine with half palmettes and rosettes. Inside this frame is a miniature mihrab which is remarkable for its completeness. Similar motifs are also found in the Dakhil Darwaza at Gaur in Malda district of West Bengal. It consists of a semicircular niche and half-dome, with bands of horizontal decoration, pillars and cusped arch with vegetal motifs on the spandrels. Most of the terracotta panels have fallen out, but slightly to the north of this mihrab motif are two panels with exquisite depictions of flowering trees.

The decorative band just underneath the cornice on this side is also unusual. The main motif here is a rosette that appears in various forms and arrangements in sections, as clusters around a larger rosette, in rectangular arrangements in rows, or just as one large single medallion. The band made up of a mesh of four petals is continued all around the building, including the circular engaged corner towers. The bands over the doorways show variations of the intertwined vine with blossoms and the curving vine with rosettes and palmettes. Mouldings divide the corner towers into three sections. The sides of the mihrab projection are recessed and also have three bands of moulding.

In the interior, the mihrabs have horizontal, sunken panels but the motifs are unrecognizable, except for one small section in the north mihrab. Beads and lozenges separate the horizontal sections. The top of the rectangular frame of the north mihrab is decorated with various arrangements of rosettes and flowering trees in panels (fig. 98). On the top centre of the rectangular frame is a miniature mihrab motif much flatter than the one over the east central entrance. It has a flower on an upright stem in its centre. The same motif is repeated over the south mihrab.

In the central mihrab the ornamentation consists of four-petalled flowers in chequed, diamond, or rectangular arrangements, singly or in clusters, and rosettes. Much of the vegetal decoration appears tubular and pasty. The top section of the pillar in the southeastern corner has a hanging chain-and-bell motif.

Bibliography: A. S. M. Ahmed, *Choto Sona Mosque*, pp. 133-34; *ARASI* (1923-24): 32; Bari, "Khalifatabad and its Monuments", pp. 158-64; Dani, *MAB*, pp. 147-48, pl. XX, no. 38; S. M. Hasan, *MMB*, pp. 168-69; Hidayet Hosain, "A Note on the Ruins of Masjidkur and Amadi", *Islamic Culture* 14, no. 4 (October 1949): 454-56; W. W. Hunter, *Statistical Account of Bengal* (Dehli, 1973), vol. 2, pp. 226; *List of Ancient Monuments*, p. 145; C. S. S. O'Malley, *Bengal District Gazeteers (Khulna)* (Calcutta, 1908), p. 183; J. Westland, *A Report on the District of Jessore: Its Antiquities, Its History, Its Commerce*, rev. ed. (Calcutta, 1874), p. 16.

Kasba (Kawshba) Mosque, Barisal

Location: Police station, Gaurnadi (Gournadi); district, Barisal (Borishal), 3.5 km north of Gaurnadi police station, just off the Barisal-Faridpur highway.

Date: No inscription has been found; ascribed to the mid-fifteenth century on the basis of stylistic similarities with other monuments in the Khan Jahan style.

Condition: The Department of Archaeology and Museums has extensively reconstructed the building. The exterior of the west wall is badly damaged. The large pond in front of the mosque has almost dried up.

Dimensions: The interior is 11.60 m x 11.75 m; the wall thickness is 2.17 m.

Material: Brick; four pillars in the centre of the square prayer chamber are of stone.

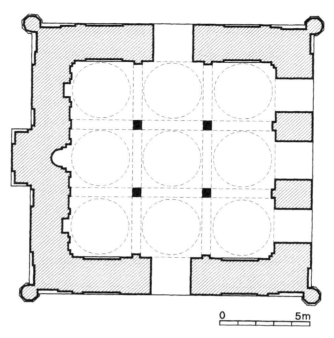

Fig. 99. Barisal, Kasba Mosque, mid-fifteenth century, plan

Plan and elevation (figs. 99-100): A square building with three entrances on the east and one each on the north and the south. The entrances on the north and south and the central entrance on the east are 2.28 m wide; the flanking ones on the east are 2.05 m. On either side of the northern and southern entrances where there are normally flanking doorways are shallow blind arched recesses instead; they are 10 cm deep on the inside, 15 cm deep on the outside.

There are three mihrabs. The four stone pillars in the centre divide the prayer chamber into nine bays each 3.55 m square and covered by a dome. Corresponding to the stone pillars are two engaged brick pilasters in each wall and double ones at the corners.

Fig. 100. Barisal, Kasba Mosque, southwest view

Outside are four circular corner towers with octagonal bases, and a projection for the central mihrab. Shallow recesses articulate the exterior wall surface.

The curve of the cornice is so gentle as to be almost imperceptible. All entrance arches as well as the arches in the recesses flanking the north and south entrances are pointed. They are set in rectangular recesses with gently curved tops. Pointed arches springing from the free-standing pillars and the engaged pilasters span the interior space by forming intersecting arcades. The pillars with square bases and capitals and octagonal shafts are assembled out of two or three pieces of grey stone. The two eastern pillars are bigger (43 cm sq. and 46 cm sq. bases) than the western ones (35 cm sq. and 33 cm sq. bases).

The domes are supported on pendentives. The mihrabs are set in projecting rectangular frames. The central mihrab has a semicircular base; the side mihrabs are rectangular and shallow.

Decoration: The mosque has minimal decoration. On the exterior, the corner towers and the tops of the rectangular doorway recesses have mouldings. Among them diamond-shaped rows of lozenges are prominent. The east central entrance has an arcade of trilobed niches underneath the moulding. The entrance arches have rosettes on their spandrels and a lozenge at the apex of the arches. There is a large rectangular space over the central doorway in the east. This may have held an inscription or perhaps a decorative motif similar to the one seen in the Masjidkur Mosque.

Inside, the only decoration is a row of blind merlons over the rectangular frames of the mihrabs.

Bibliography: A. S. M. Ahmed, *Choto Sona Mosque*, pp. 132-33; Bari, "Khalifatabad and its Monuments", pp. 164-70; Beveridge, *District of Bakarganj*, p. 40; Dani, *MAB*, p. 148; S. M. Hasan, *MMB*, p. 20; J. C. Jack, *Bengal District Gazeteers (Bakerganj)* (Calcutta, 1918), p. 148; *List of Ancient Monuments*, p. 226; Saraswati, "Indo-Muslim Architecture", p. 36.

Shatgachhia Mosque, Barobazar

Location: Police station, Kaliganj; district, Jhenaidah, in the village of Shatgachhia, about 6.5 km west of Barobazar on the Jessore-Khulna road. There is a large pond to its north.

Date: There is no inscription. It is dated to the mid-fifteenth century, on the basis of its similarities to dated monuments in the Khan Jahan style.

Condition: The building was in ruins in 1981-82. The family claiming to own the land on which the mosque stands says that they migrated from India in 1964 and bought the land, which was then forested, from its Hindu owner. In 1978, part of this huge mosque was excavated from underneath a brick mound. It was fully excavated by the Department of Archaeology in 1990 and reconstructed to the height of about 2 m. The mihrab wall is now exposed so that the top halves of the mihrabs in the southwestern side are

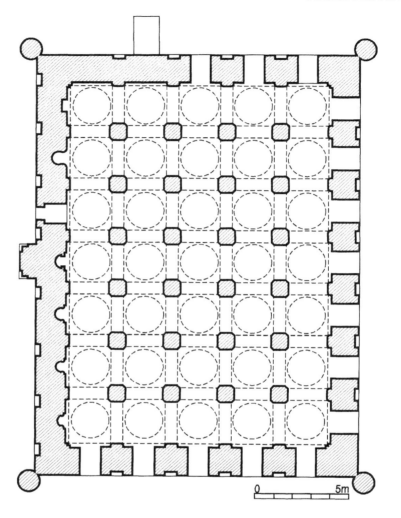

Fig. 101. Barobazar, Satgachhia Mosque, mid-fifteenth century, plan

Fig. 102. Barobazar, Satgachhia Mosque

visible. The present floor level is much higher than the original one. A temporary mosque with clay-tiled roof has been constructed on the northwest side.

Dimensions: The interior is 20.10 m x 14.15 m; the wall thickness is 1.60 m.

Material: Brick.

Plan and elevation (figs. 101-2): Twenty-four massive brick piers (1 m square with 16 cm corner facets) used to divide the rectangular space of the mosque into five bays and seven aisles to be covered by thirty-five domes. The present piers are all reconstructed, but their bases indicate that they were square with chamfered edges. The walls had engaged brick pilasters. There are six mihrabs opposite the seven entrances in the eastern side, there being a door instead of a mihrab at the end of the bay just north of the central mihrab. This door is presently blocked up. The northwest corner mihrab is different from the rest of the semicircular mihrabs, because it is flat and smaller in size, indicating that there may have been a platform in that area which served as a maqsura.

Vertical recesses articulate the exterior wall as in the Nine-domed Mosque in Bagerhat, and indicate the position of the engaged pilasters inside. The mosque originally had engaged, circular, corner towers—the stump of one being still visible in the northwest corner, but its base is buried. Its dimensions seem small for towers attached to a mosque of this size. If the towers were tapered, as in the Shaitgumbad Mosque, their bases would have been slightly larger than the dimensions shown. The central mihrab has an exterior projection.

Decoration: Some terracotta decoration remains on the exposed mihrabs, which have cusped pointed arches. The second mihrab from the north has full-blown lotus blossoms on stems on the spandrels. The central mihrab has rectangular panels with miniature cusped mihrabs and hanging motifs. The southernmost mihrab has two horizontal panels with arcades of colonnettes and cusped arches with motifs inside. It also has a unique hanging rectangular plaque design at the end of a chain of flowers. Details of much of the ornamentation are effaced. Thin lime plaster is visible on some surfaces.

Bibliography: Alamgir, "Archaeological Remains at Barabazar", pp. 269-74; Bari, "Khalifatabad and its Monuments", pp. 148-51; Habiba Khatun and Khoundakar Alamgir, "Satgachhiya Moshjid", *Itihas* 1-3 (1398 B.S., 1992 A.D.): 128-42 (in Bengali).

Galakata Mosque, Barobazar

Location: Police station, Kaliganj; district, Jhenaidah, in the village of Barobazar, on the north side of the Barobazar-Tahirpur road. The previous ruined state of the mosque was probably responsible for its name (*galakata*: lit., beheaded).

Date: There is no inscription, but on the basis of similarities to dated monuments of the Khan Jahan style it is dated to the mid-fifteenth century.

Condition: Was in a ruined state; in some sections the walls had survived upto the height of the mihrabs, and there were no domes. The Department of Archaeology and Museums excavated it in 1992-93 and completely rebuilt it with six domes and in the Khan Jahan style.

Dimensions: The interior is 5.98 m x 9.25 m; the wall thickness is 1.34 m.

Material: Brick; stone pillars.

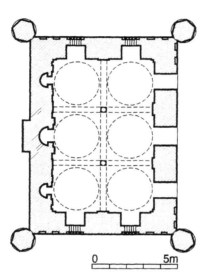

Fig. 103. Barobazar, Galakata Mosque, mid-fifteenth century, plan

Plan and elevation (figs. 103-4): A rectangular building with engaged hexagonal corner towers on circular bases, which have been awkwardly reconstructed. There is a central mihrab projection in the west. Two stone columns divide the interior into two bays and three aisles; the resulting six square bays are domed. There are three entrances in the east, of which the central one is the largest (1.13 m wide; those on either side 97 cm wide). Opposite these are three semi-circular mihrabs in the west

Fig. 104. Barobazar, Galakata Mosque, southeast view

*Fig. 105.
Barobazar,
Galakata Mosque,
central mihrab
before conservation*

wall. The two entrances each on the north and south sides (1.12 m wide) are blocked with brick *jalis* (perforated screens). The exterior surface shows vertical recesses as in the Shatgachhia Mosque nearby and the Nine-domed Mosque in Bagerhat.

Decoration: The stone columns have bases that graduate from square with carved merlons, to octagonal with decorative triangles. The main shaft is dodecagonal with carved chain and bell motifs. All the mihrabs have rectangular frames crowned with merlons. The central frame has some original terracotta lotus scroll decoration and the mihrab niche is decorated with a hanging motif (fig. 105). The side mihrabs have mesh frames, and their interior niches have rows of four-leafed bands alternating with plain ones. A thin lime plaster on the mihrabs indicates that originally the surface was not bare.

Bibliography: Alamgir, "Archaeological Remains at Barabazar", pp. 274-75.

Sailkupa (Shailkupa) Mosque, Jhenaidah

Location: Police station, Sailkupa; district, Jhenaidah, about 16 km north of Jhenaidah town, in a quarter called Dargapara or Masjidpara. Adjoining the mosque are two tombs, one of which is popularly believed to be that of Mawlana Muhammad Arab, a spiritual guide of Sultan Nasir al-Din Nusrat Shah, son of Husayn Shah. To the north is a large pond with an east-west orientation.

Date: There is no inscription. On the basis of similarities with Khan Jahan style mosques of south Bengal it may be dated to the mid-fifteenth century.

Condition: The building has been completely renovated by the local residents, and the corner towers built higher, beyond the cornice (fig. 106). The central entrance in the east is modern, and the remaining six doorways have been converted to windows. The mihrabs have been plastered and much altered in shape. The interior is plastered and whitewashed.

On the outside, remains of old brick can be seen only in the lower half of the west wall on either side of the mihrab projection. Otherwise, the brickwork is completely new. A caretaker (*mutawalli*) appointed by the waqf estate looks after the mosque—at least that was the case in 1982.

Dimensions: The interior is 10.15 m x 6.17 m; the wall thickness is 1.68 m.

Material: Brick; stone pillars.

Plan (fig. 107) and elevation: This rectangular building has three aisles and two bays covered by six domes, three entrances in the east, of which the central one is the largest (1.24 m wide; those on either side and on the north and south sides are 98 cm wide). There are two entrances (90 cm wide) on each of the north and south sides. These are not in the centre of the bays, as they normally are, but almost in the centre of the north and south walls.

In the west wall are three semicircular mihrabs opposite the three front entrances. There are two engaged brick pilasters each in the east and west walls and one each in the north and south walls. In the prayer chamber are two free-standing octagonal pillars of stone which have square bases with chamfered corners and bulging square capitals.

Fig. 106. Jhenaidah, Sailkupa Mosque, mid-fifteenth century, southeast view

On the outside are four engaged circular corner towers. Apart from the mihrab projection in the west wall, the exterior wall surface is plain. The domes are very low and not visible above the cornice. They are borne on corbelled pendentives. Inside, the pointed arches spring from the tops of the engaged brick pilasters and the capitals of the free-standing pillars.

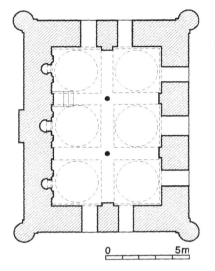

Fig. 107. Jhenaidah, Sailkupa Mosque, plan

Decoration: All three mihrabs retain part of what was probably a hanging chain and bell pattern. The hanging motifs at the end were probably buried as the level of the ground rose. The lower left side of the central mihrab and the top frieze of the southern one have arcades of small niches and colonettes with discs inside. The motifs are much defaced from the many layers of plaster and lime.

Bibliography: A. S. M. Ahmed, *Choto Sona Mosque*, pp. 98-99; Dani, *MAB*, pp. 150-51; S. M. Hasan, *MMB*, p. 145; M. A. Wali, "On the Antiquities and Traditions of the Jami Masjid and the Rauza of Hazrat Muhammad Arab at Sailkupa, Sub-division of the Jhenidah, District of Jessore", *Journal of the Asiatic Society of Bengal* 1 (1901): 15-28.

Masjidbari (Moshjidbari) Mosque, Patuakhali

Location: Police station, Mirzaganj; district, Patuakhali. The village in which the mosque is located has taken its name, Masjidbari, which literally means "mosque house". The only way to reach the village from Patuakhali town is by river. In 1860 when parts of the Sundarban (Shundorbon) area were being reclaimed, the mosque was found in dense jungle. The land was cleared and cultivated in the same year, and when Beveridge visited it in 1874 it was in good order. There are graves on the south side of the mosque.

Date: Dated by inscription to 87 ... (the last digit could not be read). If the date is extended to 870-79, upto the end of Barbak Shah's reign, then it corresponds to 1465-74. The inscription tablet is in the collection of the Indian Museum, Calcutta.

Condition: The Department of Archaeology and Museums, which has carried out extensive restoration and repair work, protects the building.

Dimensions: The interior of the prayer chamber is 6.55 m square; the interior of the verandah is 2.45 m x 6.55 m; the wall thickness 2.00 m.

Material: Brick.

Plan and elevation (figs. 24 and 108): Three entrances on the east and one each on the north and south sides open onto the verandah. Of these, the central entrance in the east is the widest, measuring 1.29 m in width; the others are 1.04 m. The square prayer chamber is provided with three entrances on every side but the west, the central one on the east is the largest (1.40 m wide). The central entrances on the north and south sides are slightly smaller (1.34 m wide); the flanking entrances on every side are the smallest (1.00 m). Corresponding to the three entrances in the east are three semicircular mihrab niches in the west wall. There are engaged brick pilasters, two in each wall in the interior of the prayer chamber.

Outside is a projection for the central mihrab in the west. There are six engaged octagonal towers, four at the corners of the building and two where the verandah joins the prayer chamber. The cornice of the prayer chamber has a curve so gentle that it is almost imperceptible. The roof of the verandah is also curved following the forms of a *chau-chala* (fig. 109). All the entrances have pointed arches and are set in recessed rectangles. Front and rear arches with vaulted spaces in between frame the verandah entrances. Inside, the shallow hemispherical dome is supported on squinches with wide front arches springing from the tops of the engaged brick pilasters.

The bare massive quality of the building is characteristic of the Khan Jahan style, but the octagonal corner towers and the addition of a verandah represent an innovation in that style.

Decoration: The exterior has no decoration except the mouldings at the base of the corner towers. Inside, the *chau-chala* vault of the verandah has ribs prominently marked out with brickwork (fig. 109) in imitation of the bamboo frame of *chau-chalas* over huts.

Fig. 108. Patuakhali, Masjidbari Mosque, 1465-74, southeast view

Fig. 109. Patuakhali, Masjidbari Mosque, interior of verandah chauchala vault

The doorways have mouldings at the top of the rectangular recesses and rows of four-petalled flowers seen so often in Bagerhat. All the mihrabs are framed in rectangular projections and have heavily restored cusped arches (fig. 110). The central mihrab has been totally redone. Those on either side of it have an interlocking mesh border in the rectangular frames similar to those on the cornice band of the Chunakhola Mosque and on the mihrab frame of Zinda Pir's Mosque in Bagerhat. High above the mihrabs and doorways in the interior of the prayer chamber are full-blown rosettes similar to the ones seen in the Shaitgumbad Mosque in Bagerhat, adding to the several stylistic links with the Bagerhat monuments.

Inscription: The inscription is in Arabic. The parental name of the builder and the last part of the date could not be read properly. This inscription is evidence that Muslim rule, perhaps for the first time was extended up to the coastal belt of Barisal during the reign

Fig. 110. Patuakhali, Masjidbari Mosque, interior southwest

of Sultan Rukn al-Din Barbak Shah. The text reads: "The Prophet, peace and blessings of Allah be upon him has said, 'He who builds a mosque, Allah builds (for him) seventy palaces in Paradise' [Hadith]. This mosque was built in the reign of the great Sultan Rukn al-Dunya wal-Din Abil Muzaffar Barbak Shah, son of Mahmud Shah the Sultan; it was built by the great Khan Ajyal Khan, son of Munjh ... Malaku Mazhar al-Din ... Dated in the months of 87 ... ? [1465-74?]."

Bibliography: A. S. M. Ahmed, *Choto Sona Mosque*, pp. 123-24. S. Ahmed, *IB*, 4:81-83; Asher, "Inventory of Key Monuments", p. 86; Beveridge, *District of Bakarganj,* pp. 39-40; Dani, *MAB*, pp. 148-50; C. Dutt, *Catalogue of Arabic and Persian Inscriptions in the Indian Museum, Calcutta* (Calcutta, 1967), p. 14; Eaton, *The Rise of Islam,* p. 324; S. M. Hasan, *MMB,* p. 196; J. C. Jack, *Bengal District Gazeteers, (Bakerganj)* (Calcutta, 1918), pp. 151-52; Karim, *Corpus of Inscriptions,* pp. 171-73; S. C. Mitra, *Jawshorore Khulnar Itihash*, 2 vols. (Calcutta, 1963), vol. 1 pp. 370-71.

Chunakhola Mosque, Bagerhat

Location: Police station, Bagerhat; district, Bagerhat. Located in the middle of rice fields in the village of Chunakhola about 72 km northwest of the Shaitgumbad Mosque.

Date: There is no inscription. Based on the decoration on the east side it is judged to date from the late fifteenth century and probably marks a transition from the pure Khan Jahan style to monuments of a later date such as the Zinda Pir's Mosque, also in Bagerhat.

Condition: Restored and protected by the Department of Archaeology and Museums.

Dimensions: Interior, 7.70 m square; wall thickness, 2.24 m.

Material: Brick.

Plan and elevation (figs 111-12): The mosque is a square building with three entrances on the east and one each on the north and south sides. The central entrance in the east is 1.33 m wide and the ones flanking it are 87 cm. The north and south entrances are 1.51 m wide. There are four circular engaged towers in the corners.

There are three mihrabs in the west wall. The central one is the largest and is also projected on the exterior. Squinches with half-domes and wide frontal arches support a hemispherical dome. Their arches spring directly from the walls and not from engaged pilasters or brackets as is the norm. Arches over the rectangular frame of the central mihrab or over the north and south entrances, to match the front arches of the squinches are conspicuously absent here (fig. 113). The mihrabs are semicircular with half-domes and cusped arches. There are two small trefoil arched niches in the north and south walls. The cornice is gently curved.

Decoration: On the exterior, the central entrance in the east and those on the north and south are enclosed by wide rectangular borders filled with a mesh pattern (fig. 114).

Chunakhola Mosque, Bagerhat

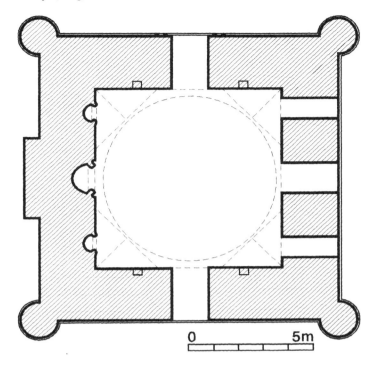

Fig. 111. Bagerhat, Chunakhola Mosque, late fifteenth century, plan

These frames, as well as the one around the central mihrab, are crowned with merlons enclosing lively plant motifs. A couple of merlons on the east central entrance have miniature mihrabs with hanging motifs. A bold *kalasha* motif marks the centre of the row.

Only on the east facade are four rectangular panels with borders of a foliated scroll topped by merlons enclosing plant motifs. This type of exterior decoration is not found

Fig. 112. Bagerhat, Chunakhola Mosque

Fig. 113. Bagerhat, Chunakhola Mosque, interior mihrab wall

Fig. 114. Bagerhat, Chunakhola Mosque, terracotta pattern within rectangular frame of eastern entrance

in any of the mosques in the Khan Jahan style. The cornice has three rows of mouldings; a decorative band below the lowest moulding consists of sections of different mesh designs. The cornice mouldings continue around the corner towers. There are also four rows of mouldings around the base and three more with lozenge and tooth patterns at regular intervals around the shaft.

Bibliography: A. S. M. Ahmed, *Choto Sona Mosque*, pp. 117-18; Bari, "Khalifatabad and its Monuments", pp. 189-92; S. M. Hasan, *MMB*, p. 164; Saif Ul Haque et al, *Pundranagar to Sherebanglanagar* (Dhaka, 1997), pp. 55, 162.

LATE SULTANATE PERIOD

Chhota Sona (Chhoto Shona) Mosque, Gaur

Location: Police station, Shibganj; district, Nawabganj. This area was part of ancient Gaur, but is now in the Nawabganj district of Bangladesh. The rest of the ancient city is just across the border in the Indian district of Malda in West Bengal. The mosque is located in the centre of an open court that is approached by a monumental gateway in the east. Also in the east, at a little distance from the mosque, are two tombs.

Date: According to the inscription it was built by Wali Muhammad, a courtier, during the reign of Sultan Ala al-Din Husayn Shah (r. 899-925/1493-1519). The inscription plaque is fixed over the central entrance in the east. The lower left-hand corner which had the date is broken, so it cannot be dated more precisely.

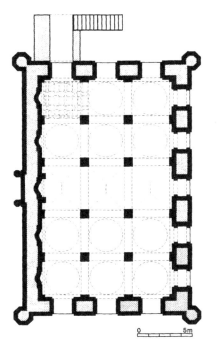

Fig. 115. Gaur, Chhota Sona Mosque, 1493-1519, plan

Condition: Restored and protected by the Department of Archaeology and Museums. Creighton, and later Cunningham, noticed the gilding in the ornamentation that had given the building its name (Chhota Sona Masjid means "small golden mosque"), but nothing of the gilding remains.

During an earthquake in 1897, three of the hemispherical domes, three of the *chauchalas* of the central aisle, and much of the west wall collapsed. A brick pillar has replaced one of stone that supported the platform in the northwestern bay. The gateway has also been restored. The stone facing of the central mihrab is missing.

Dimensions: Interior, 21.46 m x 12.19 m; wall thickness, 1.83 m.

Material: Brick and stone. Brick walls are completely faced with stone on the outside. Inside, the walls are faced with stone up to the arches. All pillars and pilasters and the platform on the northwest corner bay are also of stone.

Plan and elevation (figs. 115-16): The building is rectangular. Two rows of four pillars each running in the north-south direction divide the prayer chamber into twelve squares and three rectangular bays. Each square bay is 3.50 m square and is roofed by a hemispherical dome. The three rectangular bays are in the middle running in an east-west direction, each measuring 3.50 m x 4.49 m and covered by a *chau-chala* vault. There are five entrances on the east, three on the south, and four on the north sides. One of the northern entrances provides access to the raised platform in the northwest, and is located directly above a smaller entrance at the ground floor level. The usual hierarchical scheme of widths is absent here: all the ground floor entrances are 1.75 m wide.

At the northwest corner, additional prayer space has been created by adding a mezzanine level in the form of a raised platform that occupies the corner of the square bay. The platform is of stone and is supported on a frame of stone beams and two additional pillars (fig. 117).

Along the west wall, opposite the eastern entrances, are five semicircular mihrabs. An additional mihrab is at the platform level directly above the one on the ground floor. Corresponding to the main pillars are two engaged pilasters each in the east and west walls and in the four corners.

Outside are four engaged octagonal corner towers. A flight of steps on the northwest leads up to the entrance at the platform level. A long tunnel vault underneath the staircase

Fig. 116. Gaur, Chhota Sona Mosque, northeast view

platform links the outside with the small doorway below the platform in the interior. The central mihrab is reflected on the outside by a shallow projection with turrets on either side. The cornice is gently curved and has stone gutters to drain off rainwater.

Fig. 117. Gaur, Chhota Sona Mosque, platform in interior northwest

The domes are supported on corbelled pendentives, the arches of which spring from the tops of the pillars and engaged pilasters. No pendentives are required in the central aisle because the *chauchalas* have rectangular bases that rest directly on the four columns. The eight free-standing stone pillars and the engaged pilasters are similar in design. They have crenellated square bases and capitals, and square-sided shafts. Of the two pillars supporting the stone platform in the northwest, one is of stone, with a square base, wide capital, and octagonal shaft (fig. 117); the other is brick and seems to be modern. Cunningham reports that the upper platform was partitioned off by screens of trelliswork, but there are no screens now. This is the second non-imperial mosque with a platform, suggesting that the nobility also liked to separate themselves from the masses. The doorways in the east are cusped both inside and out.

Decoration: On the outside there is abundant stone carving in low relief. A prominent horizontal moulding divides the exterior wall surface into two sections with niches decorating the upper one (fig. 118). In the east, all the doorways except the central one have wide rectangular frames with curving vines and rosettes. The frame of the central

Fig. 118. Gaur, Chhota Sona Mosque, exterior west wall

doorway is carved with ornamental cusped niches with hanging motifs. Niche, rosette, and *kalasha* motifs are used repeatedly. Ornamental niches in rectangular panels are found between the doorways, on the west wall, and on the corner towers. Mouldings are used to emphasize outlines and mark off sections.

Inside, the mihrabs are similarly decorated. The central mihrab is bare, and it is believed that the stone structure is now in the Royal Scottish Museum in Edinburgh (S. M. Hasan, *Mosque Architecture*, pp. 199-200). There is also some terracotta decoration. The *chau-chalas* are similar to those seen in the Shaitgumbad Mosque, but here the terracotta rosettes are not only in the intersections of the rafters and purlins, but also in the spaces between them. A pendant motif imitating jewellery hangs from the ends of curved flower- and leaf-bearing stems and descends from the bases of the *chau-chalas*.

Inscription: The inscription is written in Arabic. The text reads:

> "In the name of Allah, the Merciful and the Compassionate. The Almighty Allah says, 'The mosques of Allah shall be visited and maintained by such as believe in Allah and the Last Day, establish regular prayers, and practice regular charity, and fear none except Allah. It is they who are expected to be on true guidance' {Quran 9:18}. And the Prophet, may peace and blessings of Allah be upon him, has said, 'He who builds a mosque for Allah, Allah will build a similar house in Paradise' {Hadith}. The building of this Jami mosque [took place] during the reign of the Sultan of Sultans, the Sayyid of Saiyids, the fountain of auspiciousness, who has mercy on Muslim men and women, who exalts the words of truth and good deeds, who is aided by the assistance of the Supreme Judge, the warrior in the path of the Merciful, Khalifah of Allah by proof and testimony, defender of Islam and the Muslims, Sultan Ala al-Dunya wal-Din Abul Muzaffar Husain Shah, the Sultan al-Husaini, may Allah perpetuate his kingdom and sovereignty. This Jami mosque was built from pure and sincere motives, and trusting in Allah, by Wali Muhammad, son of Ali, who bears the title Majlis al-Majalis Majlis-Mansur [the title of a noble, lit. court of courts, court of the victor], may the Almighty Allah help him in this world and the next. Its auspicious date is the 14th day of the month of the blessed Rajab, may Allah increase its value and dignity ... " {year has broken off}.

Bibliography: A. S. M. Ahmed, *Choto Sona Mosque*, pp. 26-80. S. Ahmed, *IB*, 4: 199-202; Asher, "Inventory of Key Monuments", p. 69; Beveridge, "Notes on the Khurshid-i Jahan Numa", pp. 224-25; M. M. Chakravarti, "Pre-Mughal Mosques of Bengal", pp. 29-30; Cunningham, "Report of a Tour", pp. 73-76; Dani, *MAB*, pp. 136-40; Eaton, *The Rise of Islam*, p. 325; S. M. Hasan, *Mosque Architecture*, pp. 160-65; A. B. M. Husain, ed., *Gawr-Lakhnawti* (Dhaka: Asiatic Society of Bangladesh, 1997), pp. 88-98; Karim, *Corpus of Inscriptions*, pp. 311-14; M. A. A. Khan, *Memoirs*, pp. 79-83; J. H. Ravenshaw, *Gaur: Its Ruins and Inscriptions* (London, 1878), pp. 38-39; Haque et al, *Pundranagar to Sherebanglanagar*, pp. 48, 49, and 157; Saraswati, "Indo-Muslim Architecture", p. 27; Siddiq, *Islamic Inscriptions of Bengal*, pp. 189-90.

Shankarpasha Mosque, Habiganj

Location: Police station and district, Habiganj, about a mile from Shahzibazar (Shahjibajar) railway station. The village of Shankarpasha is better known by the name of its *pargana* (an administrative unit), Uchail. The mosque is popularly known as the Gayebi Masjid (mosque of the unseen, i.e. created without any human intervention). The myth associated with all Gayebi mosques is that they suddenly appeared one day.

Date: The inscription is not legible, but the name Sultan Husayn Shah (r. 899-925/ 1493-1519) can be discerned.

Condition: The mosque has been renovated and painted by the villagers. Shallow barrel vaults resting on steel beams that are supported on two steel columns have replaced the domed roof. There is a shallow vault over the verandah. The parapet is modern; the corner towers extend above it. The northwest corner tower bulges out in the middle.

Dimensions: The interior of the prayer chamber is 6.55 m x 6.62 m; the interior of the verandah is 2.45 m x 6.55 m; the wall thickness is 1.40 m.

Material: Brick; stone imposts on the engaged brick pilasters formerly at the springing of the squinch arches which had carried the dome.

Plan and elevation (figs. 119-20) : The rectangular building consists of a square prayer chamber with a verandah in the east. The verandah has three entrances in the east, and one each in the north and south. Of these the central eastern entrance is 1.00 m wide; the flanking ones are 77 cm wide. The north and south verandah entrances are only 66 cm wide.

The square prayer chamber is provided with three accesses on each of the north, east and south sides, of which the ones in the east have the same dimensions as those on the east side of the verandah. The central entrances on the north and south sides are 97 cm wide and the flanking ones are 66 cm. On axis with the eastern entrances are three mihrabs in the west wall.

Originally, a large probably hemispherical dome which, in the interior, would be carried on squinches covered the prayer chamber. The tops of the engaged brick pilasters in the interior of the prayer chamber have stone imposts from which the squinch arches would have sprung. The pilasters, with square bases and octagonal shafts are now continued up to the roof. Similar engaged pilasters divide the verandah into three square bays, which are domed.

Outside are six engaged octagonal corner towers, four in the corners of the building, and two where the verandah joins the prayer chamber. The centre of the west wall is prominently projected on the outside (fig. 40). The cornice has been straightened in modern times.

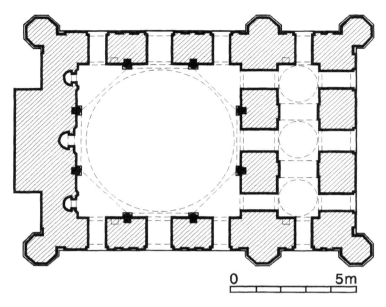

Fig. 119. Habiganj, Shankarpasha Mosque, 1493-1519, plan

Decoration: The exterior of the mosque is profusely decorated. Although gaudily painted—and disfigured in the process—most of the original decorations have been preserved. The entrance arches have cusped indentations and are set in rectangular recesses that are emphasized by wide, raised rectangular frames. Between the entrances are tall narrow recessed panels with an arch and hanging ornament motif. This distinctive articulation breaks up the continuity of the wall surface. A row of recessed panels above the entrances gives the impression of a two-storeyed building. The tall and narrow proportions of the mihrabs in the interior and of the panels in the exterior emphasize verticality. A stone slab inserted over the central doorway bears an inscription, which is now almost illegible.

Among the decorative motifs, the rectangular panel enclosing a cusped arch with hanging ornament is the most predominant. Although derived from the Gaur monuments such as the Chhota Sona Mosque, the execution is different. The panels are more elongated and the conventional bell and chain has been turned into jewellery-like design filling two-thirds of the panels. The panels are featured on each facet of the octagonal corner towers that have moulded bases. On the outside, the central mihrab projection (fig. 40) has a spectacular composition of a large central panel surrounded by smaller ones. There are two large panels on the flanking receding wall planes on either side of the mihrab projection. The rectangular recesses above the entrance arches also have terracotta decoration.

In the verandah, the bottoms of the engaged pilasters have sunken rectangular panels with cusped arches filled with terracotta reliefs of fruit-bearing trees, e.g., mango, jackfruit and pomegranate. Their crests have five-lobed leaves, and the spandrels have flowering plants.

Fig. 120. Habiganj, Shankarpasha Mosque, southeast view

In the prayer chamber, the mihrabs are conspicuous for their narrow, elongated shapes and garish paint. Their pillars have hanging-bell motifs, and the spandrels of the arches have highly ornamental vegetal forms in terracotta. Inside the mihrabs are arcades of niches which have been changed from their earlier forms, as seen in the Bandar Shahi Mosque in Narayanganj, to a completely ornamental design.

Inscription: In Arabic. The text has not been published; part of it was read by M. Abdul Qadir, an epigrapher formerly with the Department of Archaeology and Museums. He confirms what K. N. Dikshit had reported earlier: "The stone inscription fixed in the centre of the front wall, however refers itself to the reign of Alauddin Husain Shah, probably the greatest of the Sultans of Bengal (1493-1518 A.D.) and its construction may, therefore, be assigned to the beginning of the sixteenth century" (*ARASI*, 1928-29: 43). Only the name of Husayn Shah, the ruling sultan, could be deciphered.

Bibliography: A. S. M. Ahmed, *Choto Sona Mosque*, pp. 131-32; Dani, *MAB*, pp. 157-58: K. N. Dikshit, "Bengal and Assam: Shankarpasha", *ARASI* (1928-29): 42-44; Eaton, *The Rise of Islam*, p. 325; S. M. Hasan, *MMB*, pp. 249-50.

Aroshnagar Mosque, Khulna

Location: Police station, Dumuria; district, Khulna. Foundations dug from the banks of the pond in front of the mosque suggest that there was once a gateway from the pond to the mosque.

Date: Dated by inscription to 907 (1501-2). The inscription is now in the Varendra Research Museum, Rajshahi.

Condition: The villagers discovered this mosque in a mound; they rebuilt it entirely and crudely but did not enlarge it. The roof is a *do-chala* of clay tiles over a bamboo frame.

Dimensions: The interior is 5.18 m x 5.30 m; the wall thickness is 1.33 m.

Material: Brick.

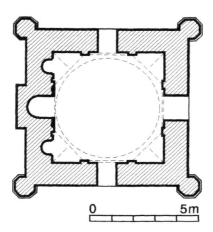

Fig. 121. Khulna, Aroshnagar Mosque, 1501-2, reconstructed plan

Plan and elevation (figs. 121-22): The mosque is a square building with three doorways, one each on the north, east, and south sides, but the north and south entrances have been converted to windows. There are three mihrabs in the west wall; the central one is projected on the outside. The stumps of four octagonal corner towers are still partially preserved. A single dome carried on squinches originally covered the building. The walls show traces of the engaged brick pilasters from the tops of which the squinch arches had sprung. No trace of the squinches remains, however, due to the crude renovation work. Two brick pillars have been erected in the middle of the prayer chamber to support the new roof.

Fig. 122. Khulna, Aroshnagar Mosque

Decoration: All that remains of the original terracotta decoration are four rectangular tiles, fixed arbitrarily on the front of the mihrab bases, two on either side of the central mihrab and one each in front of the north and south mihrabs. Scrolls with lotus or pine-cone motifs are depicted on them in a style reminiscent of the terracotta decoration in the Shabekdanga building in Bagerhat, which is datable to the early sixteenth century.

Inscription: The inscription is in Arabic. It reads:

> "The Prophet, the peace and blessings of Allah be upon him, said: 'For whoever builds a mosque on the earth, Allah will build seventy palaces in Paradise' [Hadith]. The sultan of the period and the age [*sultan al-ahd wa al-zaman*] Ala al-Dunya wa al-Din Abu al-Muzzaffar Husain Shah al-Sultan, the noblest one on the earth and the sea, may Allah perpetuate his kingdom and sovereignty; in the year nine hundred and seven [1501-2]."

Bibliography: Bari, "Khalifatabad and its Monuments", pp. 204-5; Siddiq, *Islamic Inscriptions of Bengal*, pp. 144-45.

Baba Saleh's Mosque, Narayanganj

Location: Police station, Bandar; district, Narayanganj. The mosque adjoins the tomb of Baba Saleh and is within 1 km of the Bandar Shahi Mosque, which the inscription attributes to the same patron.

Date: Dated by inscription to 911(?)/1505. Part of the date has been chipped off the inscription tablet. Blochmann supplied the missing words that yield this date. The inscription tablet is now in the Bangladesh National Museum, Dhaka. Another inscription from a tomb in Bandar records the death of Baba Saleh in 912/1506-7.

Condition: Completely renovated and enlarged.

Dimensions: The original mosque was 3.60 m sq.; the wall thickness was 1.20 m.

Material: Brick.

Plan (fig. 123) and elevation: The original square chamber of the mosque has been retained as the central unit. To this, northern and southern domed wings have been added after removing the lower parts of the walls. The upper parts were retained as wide shallow arches and indicate the original thickness of the walls (1.20 m). The largest extension is on the eastern side, where a verandah with a roof of corrugated iron sheeting has been added. The mihrab is a semicircular niche with a half-dome. The west wall has a mihrab projection. The minbar, which is in front of a shallow niche, is to the north of the mihrab. The shallow niche behind it probably indicates the position of the original north mihrab.

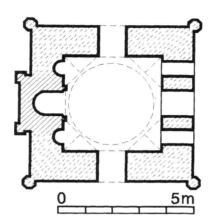

Fig. 123. Narayanganj, Baba Saleh's Mosque, 1505, reconstructed plan

The front entrances have been altered to accommodate doors of a uniform size. The three entrances on the east, the entrances on the north and south, and the three mihrabs follow the conventional arrangement. The enlarged building has engaged octagonal corner towers, which were probably modelled after the corner towers in the original mosque, and thus are indicated in the conjectural plan of the original structure.

Remnants of the squinches on which the dome rested are still visible at the base of the dome. They have been imitated in the northern and southern extensions.

Decoration: No original decoration remains. The building is now plastered, lime washed, and painted.

Inscription: The inscription is in Arabic. The text reads:

> "Allah the Most Propitious and the Most High has said, 'And the places of worship are for Allah {alone}: so invoke not anyone along with Allah' [Quran 72:18]. This blessed mosque was built during the time of the Sultan Ala al-Dunya-wal-Din Abul Muzaffar Husain Shah the Sultan, may Allah perpetuate his kingdom; by the exalted and liberal Malik, the servant of the Prophet, the pilgrim to Makka {Mecca} and Madina {Medina}, the visitor to the two footprints (of the Prophet), Haji Baba Saleh dated 900 … { words are missing} from the Hijra of the Prophet."

Bibliography: A. S. M. Ahmed, *Choto Sona Mosque*, p. 119; S. Ahmed, *IB*, 4: 170-71; Blochmann, *Contributions*, p. 78; P. Hasan, "Eight Sultanate Mosques", p. 185; Karim, *Corpus of Inscriptions*, pp. 273-74 and 275-76; Siddiq, *Islamic Inscriptions of Bengal*, pp. 158-59.

Goaldi Mosque, Sonargaon

Location: Police station, Sonargaon; district, Narayanganj. In the village of Goaldi, near Panam, within the area that belonged to the ancient capital of Sonargaon.

Date: Dated by inscription to 15 Shaban 925 (12 August 1519). The current location of the inscription tablet is not known.

Condition: Completely restored by the Department of Archaeology and Museums. Before restoration, the dome, and major portions of the north, east and south walls had fallen; only the mihrab wall to the west remained.

Dimensions: The interior is 4.93 m x 4.97 m; the wall thickness is 2.29 m.

Material: Brick; the central mihrab is of dark basalt; pillars at the doorway are made of sandstone.

Plan and elevation (figs. 18-19) : The mosque is a square building with three entrances on the east, and one each on the north and south. The central entrance on the east and the side entrances are 1.68 m wide. The two doorways on either side of the main entrance are each 1.20 m wide. Recesses of the same width appear as blind doorways on either side of the side entrances. Outside, these recesses are shallow (16 cm), but inside the building they are 87 cm deep. Corresponding to the three arched entrances in the east are three mihrabs in the west wall of the mosque, the central one being higher, wider, and deeper than those on either side. There are no pillars inside the square hall, but two stone pilasters are embedded in each wall.

The four corners have circular towers. The central mihrab projection on the western wall is 2.44 m wide. Recesses 1.52 m wide (slightly less on the western wall) and 10 cm to 15 cm deep break up the wall surface.

A hemispherical dome covers the building. The transition from the square of the mosque interior to the circular base of the dome is made by squinches with heavy front arches. Wedged between the arches and the base of the dome are shallow, triangular corbelled pendentives. Each wall has two engaged stone pilasters with square bases and arches springing from their tops. The cornice is very gently curved.

Decoration: Mouldings reminiscent of temple plinths run in three bands around the lower end of the corner towers and into the recesses on either side. Similar bands appear in the corners of the mihrab projections on the exterior surface of the western wall. Bands of vines run between the mouldings, and the whole is topped by a row of decorated merlons. The top of the curved cornice and the engaged corner towers have two mouldings running all around the building. Just below the second one is an ornamental band of miniature pilasters forming a continuous arcade below the cornice and across the towers. Each miniature niche in this arcade has a vegetal motif inside. There are similar

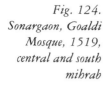
Fig. 124. Sonargaon, Goaldi Mosque, 1519, central and south mihrab

decorative bands on top of the rectangular recesses of the archways of the north, east, and south sides.

The pilasters between the entrances and blind doorways in the north and south have decorative rectangular panels. They frame an ornamental miniature mihrab niche with a hanging motif, and are crowned with a row of merlons. The exterior of the mihrab wall is bare except for the decorative band along the cornice and the sections of moulding at the bottom.

The central mihrab (fig. 124) is made of black basalt. There is a rectangular stone frame (lintel and posts) carved with a flowering vine and crowned by a row of merlons with vegetal motifs inside. The mihrab arch is a piece of carved stone resting on a pair of stone pillars. It is trefoil cusped, and a wide border of vine defines the arch. The spandrels feature two full-blown lotuses on stems, reminiscent of similar blossoms held by the Hindu god Surya in stone images of the eighth to twelfth centuries (for illustration, see N. K. Bhattasali, *Iconography of Buddhist and Brahmanical Sculptures in the Dacca Museum* (Dacca, 1929), pl. LVIII). The semicircular niche, also of stone, is carved with motifs of ornamental lamps hanging in arches. The side mihrabs, made entirely of brick decorated with terracotta tiles, has a crowning row of merlons over a rectangular frame, and a vegetal scroll bordering the mihrab arch. A full-blown lotus motif occupies a very prominent position in each tympanum of the mihrab wall.

Inscription: The inscription is in Arabic, except for the number 15 and the word for month (*mah*) which are in Persian. The text reads:

> "The Almighty Allah says, 'And the places of worship are for Allah [alone]: so invoke not anyone along with Allah' [Quran 72:18]. Allah is the best knower of the right [things]. The Prophet, may peace and blessings of Allah be upon him, says, 'He who builds a mosque in this world, Allah will build

for him seventy palaces in Paradise' [Hadith]. This mosque was built during the reign of the Sultan of Sultans, Sultan Husain Shah, son of Ashraf al-Husaini, may his kingdom and authority be perpetuated. This mosque was built by Mulla Hizbar Akbar Khan, on the 15th of the month of Shaban, in the year 925 [12 August 1519]."

Bibliography: A. S. M. Ahmed, *Choto Sona Mosque*, p. 120; S. Ahmed, *IB*, 4: 198-99; Asher, "Inventory of Key Monuments", p. 133; Blochmann, *Contributions*, pp. 90-91; Chakravarti, "Pre-Mughal Mosques of Bengal", p. 26; Dani, *MAB*, p. 236; P. Hasan, "Eight Sultanate Mosques", p. 186, and "Muslim Architecture", pp. 75-77; S. M. Hasan, *MMB*, p. 125; Karim, *Corpus of Inscriptions*, p. 311; *List of Ancient Monuments*, pp. 205-6; Saraswati, "Indo-Muslim Architecture", p. 22; Siddiq, *Islamic Inscriptions of Bengal*, pp. 186-87; Wise, "Notes on Sonargaon", p. 88.

Ten-domed Mosque, Bagerhat

Location: Police station and district, Bagerhat. Earlier sources located the mosque in the village of Krishnanagar, but local people claim that Krishnanagar is north of the mosque and that the building is properly in Ranbijoypur, on the Shaitgumbad-Bagerhat town road.

Date: It has no inscription and the features that characterize the Khan Jahan style are absent. It cannot be dated precisely as it has been reconstructed and very few of the original features are left, but it seems to belong to a period later than the Khan Jahan buildings. An early sixteenth-century date is likely as local tradition attributes the building to the reign of Husayn Shah.

Condition: Many of the original features are lost due to alterations and repairs made by the villagers. The outside is plastered. The two northern entrances and the southernmost eastern entrance have been blocked.

Dimensions: The interior is 7.40 m x 19.25 m; the wall thickness is 1.67 m.

Material: Brick.

Plan (fig. 125) and elevation: Rectangular building with five aisles and two bays covered by ten domes. There are five entrances in the east and two each on the north and south sides. The central entrance is 1.58 m wide, slightly wider than the flanking ones, which, along with the northern and southern entrances, are 1.48 m wide.

The west wall has five semicircular mihrabs opposite the five front entrances. The first and second mihrabs from the south and the second mihrab from the north are almost all of the same size (71 cm wide), and the central mihrab is only slightly larger (75 cm wide). The mihrab on the extreme north is much smaller (54 cm wide) and placed higher on the wall (fig. 126). The smallness of the northern mihrab can only be explained if the floor on that part is assumed to have had a raised platform. This is a possibility because, wherever

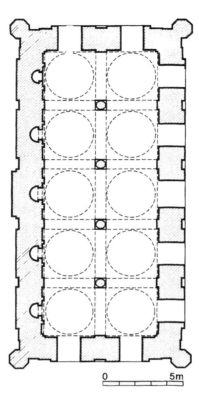

Fig. 125. Bagerhat, Ten-domed Mosque, early sixteenth century, plan

such platforms exist, they are always in the northwest corner, as, e.g., in the Adina Mosque in Pandua (1375), the Darasbari Mosque (late fifteenth century) and the Chhota Sona Mosque (1493-1519) in Gaur.

Along the centre of the rectangular chamber are four extremely short, but massive brick pillars. They are 65 cm in diameter, each face measuring about 17 cm, and stand on square bases which are now almost buried underneath the floor. There are engaged brick pilasters on the walls, one each on the north and south sides, and four each on the east and west. In the corners are pairs of slender engaged pilasters.

The domes are very low and rest on corbelled pendentives and pointed arches which spring from the tops of free-standing pillars and engaged pilasters in the walls.

Fig. 126. Bagerhat, Ten-domed Mosque, interior northwest corner

Decoration: The mihrabs are set in rectangular recesses which have a band of diamond-shaped lozenges on top. The shapes of the mihrab arches are much altered and gaudily painted, but the niches still bear traces of a hanging rectangular motif. On the exterior, the original parts have mouldings with a central band of lozenges.

Bibliography: Bari, "Khalifatabad and its Monuments", pp. 146-48; S. C. Mitra, *Jawshohore Khulnar Itihash* (Calcutta, 1963), vol. 1, pp. 376-77.

Bagha Mosque, Rajshahi

Location: Police station and district, Rajshahi, about 56 km southeast of Rajshahi town. The mosque is on the banks of a very large pond in a walled enclosure with a monumental gateway on the southeast (fig. 127). Near the mosque are the ruins of a village that is popularly believed to belong to the descendants of the well-known saint Mawlana Shah Muazzam Danishmand, commonly known as Shah Dawlah. According to tradition they received the land from an emperor of Gaur.

Date: Dated by inscription to 930 (1523-24). The stone inscription tablet with the date is fixed above the central doorway in the east. It is one of the two mosques in Bangladesh built under royal patronage, the other being the Darasbari Mosque in Gaur.

Condition: The building was reconstructed and renovated by the Department of Archaeology and Museums, Government of Bangladesh. The mosque was severely damaged in an earthquake in 1897 when the eastern wall together with the ten domes fell.

Dimensions: The interior measures 21.60 m x 8.30 m; the wall thickness is 2.30 m.

Fig. 127. Rajshahi, Bagha Mosque, southeast view

Materials: Brick; except for the plinth, a string course at the level of the springing of the arches that runs all around the building both inside and outside, and the pillars and pilasters in the prayer chamber which are of stone.

Plan (fig. 128) and elevation: The approach gateway has a vaulted space in the centre which is roofed by a structure in three segments, two semicircular sections on either side, bridged by a barrel vault in the middle, and four octagonal engaged corner towers capped by cupolas. The niches on either side are high enough for a standing person; they were probably used by guards.

The building is rectangular. Outside, the walls have very shallow recesses. The centre of the west wall has a projection for the mihrab and an engaged octagonal tower in each corner. The cornice of the mosque is gently curved. The ten low domes are carried on corbelled pendentives. The corner towers have cupolas with faceted vertical sections and a flat disc finial.

Inside, a row of four pillars runs north-south, forming ten squares, each covered by a dome. There are five entrances in the east; the central one is slightly larger (1.90 m wide) than the others. The two entrances each on the north and south sides have brick screens. There are three semicircular mihrabs in the west wall, the central one and two to its south according to normal practice. But in the bay immediately north of the central one there is no mihrab, and the end bay in the northwest corner has a small mihrab not at floor level but above the string course in the wall. The side opening in the north wall at this corner has two arches, one above the other, the apex of the lower one is below the string course; the one above springs from it. This unusual feature leads to the conclusion that there must have been a raised royal platform on this side, as in the Darasbari, Chhota Sona, and Kusumba Mosques. The platform was probably between these two arches at the same level as the stone string course. However, there is no special entrance from the exterior or other indication of any access to a platform. Access could have been gained through the northern entrance in the east and then by a flight of stairs to the platform, as in the Kusumba Mosque. No trace of either platform or stairs remains. It is also possible that the platform was never built, the idea being discarded at some point during construction.

Corresponding to the four free-standing stone pillars in the centre of the prayer chamber are engaged stone pilasters, four each in the east and west walls, one each in the north and south walls, and slender half-pilasters in the corners. All the pillars and engaged pilasters are identical in design and dimension. They have square bases and crenellated capitals, shafts that are square at the ends, and octagonal mouldings in the middle.

Decoration: The terracotta decoration is both profuse and rendered in a style that becomes a touchstone for dating several other mosques. On the exterior, the string course topped with a band of moulding divides the wall into an upper and lower zone. Each zone has rows of rectangular panels with cusped arches and hanging motifs. These have lost the vegetal quality of earlier terracotta motifs to become designs imitating jewellery: the

Bagha Mosque, Rajshahi

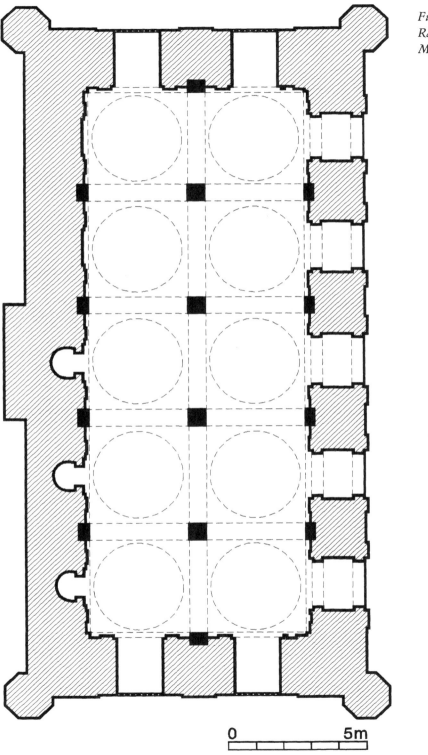

Fig. 128.
Rajshahi, Bagha
Mosque, plan

Fig. 129. Rajshahi, Bagha Mosque, mihrab

Fig. 130. Rajshahi, Bagha Mosque, terracotta panel with mango tree motif

rectangular motifs that descend down the arches no longer have bells or lanterns, but pendants with abstract designs. Chains have disappeared to be replaced by beads and pearls sometimes adorned with a bunch of grapes. The same decoration is carried around the corner towers. The entrances are set in recessed rectangles with rosettes in the spandrels and crescents at their apexes.

Inside, both sides of the entrance arches have pennants that are stylized to an upright half of a five-lobed leaf. The apexes of the arches have finials composed of a crescent over a five-lobed leaf. The cusp-arch mihrabs, divided into rows of rectangular panels with ornamental niches, are profusely decorated (fig. 129). The pillars have festoons and hanging bells with tasselled ends. Their outer rectangular frames have panels with niches holding roses and pomegranate and mango trees (fig. 130). The bases of the domes are decorated with bands of five-lobed leaves.

Inscription: The inscription is in Arabic. The text reads:

> "The Prophet, may peace and blessings of Allah be upon him, has said, 'He who builds a mosque for Allah, Allah will build for him a house in Paradise' [Hadith]. This Jami mosque was built by the Sultan, son of the Sultan, Nasir al-Dunya wal-Din Abul Muzaffar Nusrat Shah, the Sultan, son of Husain Shah, the Sultan, al-Husaini, may Allah perpetuate his kingdom and sovereignty, in the year 930 [1523-24]."

Bibliography: A. S. M. Ahmed, *Choto Sona Mosque*, pp. 96-97; S. Ahmed, *IB*, 4: 212-14; Asher, "Inventory of Key Monuments", p. 44; Chakravarti, "Pre-Mughal Mosques", p. 30; Dani, *Bibliography*, p. 68; *idem*, *MAB*, pp. 159-60; S. M. Hasan, *Mosque Architecture*, pp. 136-37; Karim, *Corpus of Inscriptions*, pp. 333-35; *idem*, *Social History*, pp. 140-41; M. H. Khan, *Terracotta Ornamentation in Muslim Architecture of Bengal* (Dhaka, 1988), pp. 180-82; Saraswati, "Indo-Muslim Architecture", p. 28; Siddiq, *Islamic Inscriptions of Bengal*, pp. 201-2; Wali, "On Some Archaeological Remains in the District of Rajshahi", *Journal of the Asiatic Society of Bengal* 73, no.1 (1904): 108-13.

Majlis (Mojlish) Awlia's Mosque, Faridpur

Location: Police station, Bhanga; district, Faridpur. The mosque is located in the village of Pathrail and known after the Pir Majlis Abd Allah Khan, better known as Majlis Awlia Saheb, whose tomb is in front of the mosque. A large pond, also in front of the mosque, oriented in the north-south direction, is mostly dried up.

Date: No inscription. Stylistic similarities with the Bagha Mosque make it datable to the early sixteenth century. Over the central doorway on the east is a stone slab that was broken in two pieces, but was later cemented together. Faint traces of writing are visible on one half. Two pieces of stone (perhaps door jambs) with traces of writing are lying in front of a mihrab inside the mosque.

Condition: Protected by the Department of Archaeology and Museums. The building was in ruins with no roof when visited by the author, but has recently been reconstructed with all the domes. There are still some traces of thin lime plaster on the exterior. There has been some settling, exposing the wall foundations for about 25 cm below floor level.

Dimensions: The interior is 8.60 m x 21.55 m; the wall thickness is 2.05 m.

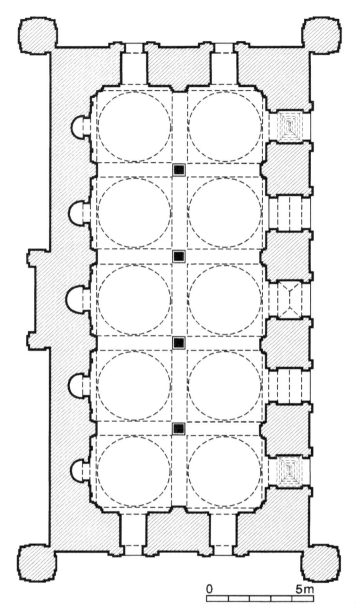

Fig. 131. Faridpur, Majlis Awlia's Mosque, early sixteenth century, plan

Material: Brick. Fragments of the original stone pillars, which used to be inside the prayer chamber, are now lying outside the mosque. In the interior they have been replaced by brick pillars. There are also stone imposts on top of the engaged columns in the walls from which the arches in the interior of the prayer chamber once sprang.

Plan (fig. 131) and elevation: The mosque is a rectangular building with five aisles and two bays. There are five entrances in the east, the central one being the largest (1.73 m wide), diminishing in size towards the corners: the ones flanking the central entrance are

1.61 m wide; the ones nearest the two corners are 1.38 m wide. There are two entrances each on the north and south sides; they are 1.25 m wide. In the west wall are five semicircular mihrabs; like the eastern entrances, they diminish in size towards the corners. There are engaged brick pilasters, four each on the east and west walls, and one each on the north and south walls. In each corner is a pair of unusually elaborate engaged half-pilasters.

On the exterior, recesses and projections articulate the surface of the wall. The corner towers are attached to the building by very small sections. They are square with vertical projections on all sides as in temple architecture (*ratha*). Similar towers are seen in the Parbajpur Mosque in Satkhira district.

The exterior west wall has an unusual mihrab projection, which is framed by engaged square towers with vertical projections in the centre. The ten hemispherical domes that have now fallen once covered the interior, supported on corbelled pendentives. The cornice has a pronounced curve. The stone pillars that were once in the interior of the prayer chamber and are now lying outside have square bases and capitals and octagonal shafts. The sections were held together by short dowels which are now exposed. The interior arches sprang from these pillars and the stone imposts above the engaged brick pilasters in the walls. The pilasters are well developed and are paired in the corners. They have square bases with vertical central projections and octagonal shafts with mouldings and decoration.

The entrance arches are set in rectangular projections. The eastern entrances have unusual two-centred pointed front and rear arches with a variety of vaults in between. The central vault is a *chau-chala*, the ones flanking it are *do-chala*, and the ones nearest the corners are corbelled (fig. 132). The entrances are very high, and originally must have been fitted with doors as the hinge stones are still intact. The stone threshold of the central entrance has a hole in the centre, probably for drainage. The side entrances have only

Fig. 132. Faridpur, Majlis Awlia's Mosque, corbelled entrance vault

Fig. 133. Faridpur, Majlis Awlia's Mosque, exterior mihrab projection

exterior arches, so that their width is narrower on the outside. The level of the floor was higher on the mihrab side, as one can see more of the exposed foundation on the east.

Decoration: Traces of thin lime plaster on the facade indicate that the exteriors of Sultanate mosques were lime washed and painted, and did not always have the bare brick-coloured exterior that they have now. The east facade also bears traces of the profuse ornamentation it once had, but most of the terracotta plaques have fallen. Just underneath the cornice moulding is a row of hanging flowers, combining the usual lotus with a tiered cup-shaped flower and a feathery blossom.

Between the entrances, the wall surface is divided into two rows of rectangular panels. The horizontal division is achieved by rows of full-blown rosettes, a recurrent motif executed in high relief. Each rectangular panel has a curving vine-and-tendril border which frames a cusped niche, the spandrels of which are filled with tendrils and two large rosettes. There is a *kalasha* at the apex of the niche from which tendrils and leaves descend with a rectangular motif at the end. The vegetal decoration has a fluttering, ribbon-like quality.

Majlis (Mojlish) Awlia's Mosque, Faridpur

Fig. 134. Faridpur, Majlis Awlia's Mosque, south mihrab

The entrance arches have rectangular frames with *kalashas* on the crown. They are filled with geometric designs, except for the central one which has a vine motif that originates in a small niche at the bottom.

On the north and south sides, the entrance arches also have *kalasha* crowns. All but a few examples of the five-lobed leaf (also seen in the Parbajpur and Gorar Mosques of Jessore) with a crest have disappeared. This motif is also seen in the square corner towers that have recessed surfaces like the *ratha* mouldings on temple plinths.

Three rows of horizontal mouldings with a leaf border starts from the southeast corner of the east wall, goes around the corner towers and three sides of the mosque up to the northeast corner of the east wall. Engaged pilasters with vertical projections resembling those in the Shubhorara Mosque in Jessore frame the mihrab projection in the exterior west wall (fig. 133). The engaged pilasters are very elaborate with mouldings and bands of leaf and wreath designs. There is a chain-and-bell motif in the centre of the shallow projection. As most of the plaques have fallen, it is impossible to tell whether the motif had started from the apex of a niche.

All the mihrabs appear to have been similarly ornamented (fig. 134). Their rectangular frames match those of the corresponding ones around the entrance arches, and their pillars have *amalakas* (fluted fruit motif common in temple architecture) just below the capitals. The niches are divided into horizontal panels of smaller niches with *kalasha* and fern motifs, upright and hanging lotus buds, and rosettes. Some of the niches and the outermost whorl of rosette petals are serrated. Chains with an end motif descend down the middle of the mihrab niches. The motif is visible only in the southern mihrab, which is the best preserved of the five. Taking the place of the rectangular motif which usually terminates a hanging chain, there is what seems to be a bundle of reeds tied in the middle, which is of the same width as the chain. A similar motif turns up in the Shabekdanga building in Bagerhat, which is now being used as a mosque, but was not originally built for that purpose.

Bibliography: A. S. M. Ahmed, *Choto Sona Mosque*, pp. 97-98; Dani, *MAB*, pp. 158-59; F. A. Khan, "Exploration in Pakistan", *Pakistan Archaeology* 5 (1968): 23-24; M. H. Khan, *Terracotta Ornamentation in Muslim Architecture of Bengal* (Dhaka, 1988), pp. 191-94.

Gorar Mosque, Barobazar

Location: Police station, Kaliganj; district, Jhenaidah, about 80 m from the marketplace of Barobazar. There is a large north-south oriented pond in front of the mosque. The name literally means "first mosque" or "oldest mosque".

Date: There is no inscription. Because of stylistic similarities with the Bagha Mosque of 1523, and Majlis Awlia's Mosque at Faridpur, it can be dated to the early sixteenth century.

Condition: The building was in ruins; the dome and verandah had collapsed, the two side entrances in the east were blocked, and the floor had settled about 15 cm, because the brickwork below the stone bases of the engaged pilasters was exposed. The Department of Archaeology and Museums has completely rebuilt it.

Dimensions: Interior, 6.15 m square; wall thickness, 1.67 m; verandah, 1.81 m x 6.97 m.

Material: Brick, except for four engaged stone pilasters in the interior, two in the west wall, and one each in the north and south.

Plan (fig. 135) and elevation: The square prayer chamber has three entrances in the east, the central one being the largest, and one each in the north and south. The central doorway in the east is 1.24 m wide, those flanking it are 81 cm. The north and south openings of the prayer chamber are 1.32 m wide. The verandah in front also has three front entrances and one each on the north and south according to convention. The six engaged towers, four at the corners and two where the verandah is attached to the prayer chamber, are octagonal.

Corresponding to the three entrances in the east are three semicircular mihrabs in the west wall; the central one is the largest. In the western half of the prayer chamber there

Gorar Mosque, Barobazar

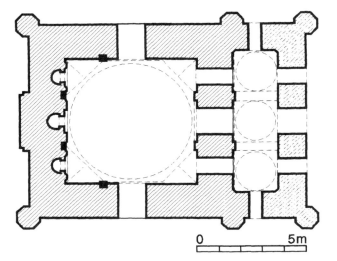

Fig. 135. Barobazar, Gorar Mosque, early sixteenth century, plan

are four engaged pilasters of stone, two in the west wall and one each in the north and south walls. They have square bases with merlons, octagonal shafts and crested capitals. The corresponding brick pilasters in the eastern half imitate the stone ones. Both in plan and decoration the mosque is similar to the Parbajpur Mosque.

Squinches with wide front arches carry the hemispherical dome of the prayer chamber. There are shallow, corbelled pendentives between the arches and the base of the dome. The pointed arches have nearly rounded tops.

Decoration: Some original terracotta decoration—horizontal bands of four-petalled flowers very common in Bagerhat monuments, and an upright leaf motif like that in the Parbajpur Mosque—is still visible on the south side (fig. 136). There are horizontal moulded bands that run all around the exterior facade. Inside, the semicircular mihrabs with half-domes, cusped pointed arches, and rosettes in their spandrels are set in

Fig. 136. Barobazar, Gorar Mosque, part of exterior south wall

ornamented rectangular panels crowned with merlons. From the cusped border of the central mihrab, stemmed leaf motifs reach out to the spandrels as in the Parbajpur Mosque. Its frame has a lively lotus vine with a wide meandering stem. The interior of the niche is divided into rectangular panels with the traditional rectangular hanging motif on a chain. A row of merlons surrounds the base of the dome, and the arches supporting the dome are topped by a band of four-petalled flowers.

On the exterior west and north sides and parts of the original wall base there are residues of thin lime plaster.

Bibliography: Sohrabuddin Ahmed, "Antiquities of Barabazar", pp. 71-80; Alamgir, "Archaeological Remains at Barabazar", pp. 265-68; Bari, "Khalifatabad and its Monuments", pp. 201-4.

Manohar Dighi Mosque, Barobazar

Location: Police station, Kaliganj; district, Jhenaidah. There is a pond on the north side.

Date: Extremely difficult to date because of the ruined condition. A broad early sixteenth-century date is ascribed because most of the monuments in Barabazar belong stylistically either to the Khan Jahan group of the mid-fifteenth century, or to the early sixteenth century. The octagonal corner towers preclude attribution to the Khan Jahan style.

Condition: Excavated in 1993-94 it is in an utterly ruined state (fig. 138).

Dimensions: 22.88 m x 16.17 m; wall thickness. 1.54 m.

Material: Brick.

Plan and elevation (figs. 137-38): There are stumps of twenty-two free-standing square brick pillars in the interior, and the bases of walls on the east and west sides. From the arrangement of the pillars it seems that the mosque had five bays and seven aisles and was roofed over by thirty-five domes. The remaining octagonal towers on circular bases in the northwest and southeast corners indicate that there were similar towers in the other two corners as well. Remains of extra construction in the four northwestern bays suggest that there may have been a platform on that side, as was common in many of the larger mosques. These platforms usually functioned as maqsuras to ensure security of the rulers. The ruins also indicate that there was a room attached to the mosque in the exterior northwest corner with an entrance on the west side. The function of the room is to be ascertained.

Decoration: The pillar bases have merloned patterns.

Bibliography: Alamgir, "Archaeological Remains at Barabazar", pp. 277-80.

Manohar Dighi Mosque, Barobazar

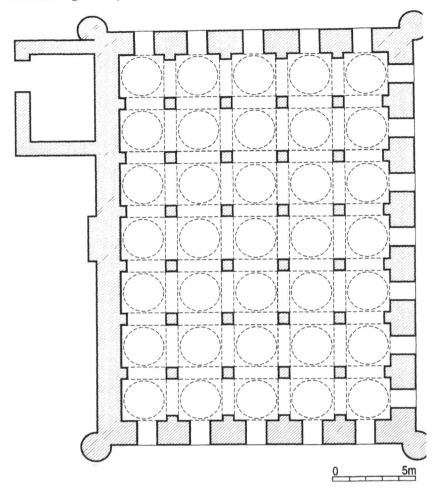

Fig. 137.
Barobazar,
Manohor Dighi
Mosque, early
sixteenth century,
plan

Fig. 138.
Barobazar,
Manohar Dighi
Mosque, ruins

Pirpukur Mosque, Barobazar

Location: Police station, Kaliganj; district, Jhenaidah; in the village of Belat Daulatpur. There is a pond on the eastern side of the mosque. Several graves were unearthed during excavation.

Date: It is difficult to date such a ruined structure, but taking into account other contemporary monuments in the area, an early sixteenth-century date is ascribed.

Condition: Was in an utterly ruined condition when excavated in 1993-94. The Department of Archaeology and Museums has reconstructed the building up to a height of 1.50 m on the west side and the top of the arches on the other three sides (fig. 140). Eight brick pillars in the interior have also been reconstructed with square bases and shafts with chamfered corners. There is no roof.

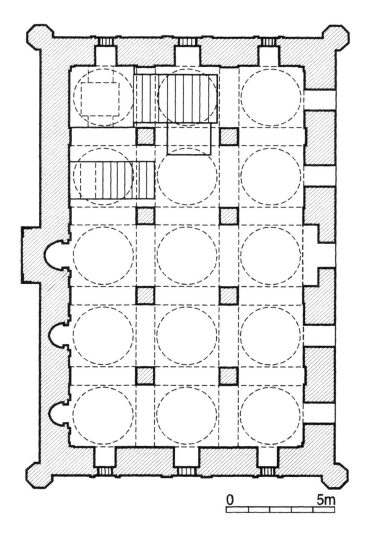

Fig. 139. Barobazar, Pirpukur Mosque, early sixteenth century, plan

Fig. 140. Barobazar, Pirpukur Mosque, ruins

Dimensions: 10.80 m x 18.35 m; wall thickness, 1.41 m.

Material: Brick.

Plan and elevation (figs. 139-40): On the basis of the eight free-standing pillars and engaged pilasters in the walls it is possible to say that this rectangular mosque had three bays, five aisles and fifteen domes. There are octagonal corner towers and a mihrab projection in the west. Each bay has an entrance in the east, but there are corresponding mihrabs only at the end of the central and two southern bays. On the northwestern side there are no mihrabs, but two flights of stairs indicate that there was a maqsura platform in the northwestern corner and a minbar in the bay next to the central one. The three windows on the north and south sides are closed with brick grills (*jalis*), original pieces of which were found in the north side.

Decoration: The bases of the pillars have merlon decoration. The corner towers and the recessed edges of the exterior mihrab projection have bead and lozenge mouldings.

Bibliography: Alamgir, "Archaeological Remains at Barabazar", pp. 280-83.

Nabagram Mosque, Sirajganj

Location: Police station, Taras (Tarash); district, Sirajganj, in the village of Nabagram, popularly known as Naoga. To its north is the tomb of Hazrat Haji Shah Sharif Jinnani, locally venerated as the grandfather of Khwaja Moinuddin Chishti of Ajmer. A large madrasa is attached to the mosque.

Date: Dated by inscription to 4 Rajab 932 (16 April 1526). The inscription was found lying loose inside the mosque. It is now in the collection of the Varendra Research Museum, Rajshahi.

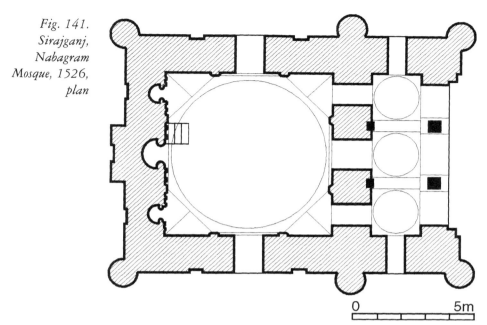

Fig. 141. Sirajganj, Nabagram Mosque, 1526, plan

Condition: The villagers have renovated the mosque, and almost none of the original decoration has survived. A large new verandah supported by concrete beams was added to the front in 1962 and the grave of the saint is in an enclosure in the northeast side of the verandah. The original dome had collapsed and the caretaker (*khadem*) reported that it was reconstructed ca. 1950. The cupolas on the engaged towers are probably new.

Dimensions: The interior of the prayer chamber is 7.25 m sq.; the interior of the verandah is 7.25 m x 2.05 m; the wall thickness is 1.70 m.

Material: Brick, except for the stone verandah pillars, pilasters, and imposts at the springing of the arches in the interior of the prayer chamber.

Plan (fig. 141) and elevation: The verandah has three bays and three wide entrances on the east side, and single narrow entrances on the north and south sides. Of the front (east) entrances, the largest one in the centre is 2.40 m wide; the northern and southern entrances are only 75 cm wide. There are two free-standing stone pillars at the verandah entrance and two engaged stone pilasters in the opposite wall.

The square prayer chamber has three entrances from the verandah side and one each from the north and south sides. Of these, the largest is the central one in the east (1.50 m wide). The flanking ones are 90 cm; the side entrances are 1.30 m. There are three semicircular mihrabs in the west wall, and two engaged brick pilasters set in each wall.

On the outside, recesses articulate the walls; the projection for the central mihrab is in the west wall. There are six engaged circular (Dani describes them as octagonal) towers, four at the corners of the building and two where the verandah is joined to the prayer chamber. The stone pillars at the entrance of the verandah are an unusual feature and are

Fig. 142. Sirajganj, Nabagram Mosque, verandah facade

remarkable for their shortness and their thick proportions (fig. 142). They have square bases and capitals and octagonal shafts with mouldings in the centre. Over their capitals are huge slabs of stone, much bigger than the base; and wide arches spring from them.

The cornice of the prayer chamber is gently curved. A very shallow dome covers each verandah bay. There is no drum to the dome of the prayer chamber, and it is carried on squinches with wide front arches and corbelled pendentives wedged between the arches. The arches spring from the stone imposts on top of the engaged brick pilasters. This part of the interior retains most of its original character. On the exterior, recesses similar to the ones seen in the Nine-domed Mosque at Bagerhat rise vertically and have pointed tops just below the cornice moulding.

Decoration: Almost all the original decoration is lost. The corner towers have mouldings at the base and cornice, and the shaft is divided into three sections by two rows of moulding. Dani described them as fluted, but they are now plain, plastered and lime washed. The bases of the narrow vertical recesses are also moulded. There were rectangular terracotta panels on the exterior of the verandah facade, one of which still remains in situ (fig. 142). It has a miniature mihrab consisting of a trefoil-cusped niche in a decorated frame, with a rectangular motif suspended from a rope, and rosettes on the spandrels of the niche arch. There are two more terracotta panels on the north wall. Their rectangular frames are crowned with merlons filled with plant motifs, and the cusped arches have flowering lotus plants on the spandrels and bells hanging from their apexes. Lotus vines fill the background.

The mihrabs are set in rectangular frames crowned by a row of merlons with plant motifs. The frame of the central mihrab has a band of interlocking vines, and its niche is divided into rectangular panels with arched niches and hanging motifs inside. The pillars and spandrels of the mihrab arches are new; the front of the central one is awkwardly rendered.

Inscription: Written in Arabic. The text reads:

> "The Prophet may the peace and blessings of Allah be upon him, has said, 'He who builds a mosque in the world, the Almighty Allah will build seventy palaces in Paradise' [Hadith]. This mosque was built during the reign of the Sultan, son of the Sultan Nasir-al-Dunya wal-Din Abul Muzaffar Nusrat Shah, the Sultan, son of Husain Shah, the Sultan, may Allah perpetuate his kingdom and sovereignty, and elevate his affairs and dignity. The builder of this great mosque is Ajyal Mina, *Jangdar*, son of Munawwar Ana [or Manurana], *Mir Bahr* [admiral of the fleet]. [It was built] during the time of Khan Muazzam Mubarak Khan *Nazir* [an officer of the Revenue Department], may Allah keep them both in peace in both the worlds. Dated 4 Rajab, may its position be dignified, in the year 932 [16 April 1526]; [engraved by] Bahlol."

Bibliography: S. Ahmed, *IB*, 4: 218-20; Dani, *MAB*, p. 160; Karim, *Corpus of Inscriptions*, pp. 340-44; Siddiq, *Islamic Inscriptions of Bengal*, pp. 203-4.

Jorbangla Mosque, Barobazar

Location: Police station, Kaliganj; district, Jhenaidah, in the village of Barobazar on the left side of the Barabazar-Tahirpur road. The name (*jorbangla*, twin huts or two huts attached to each other) may be derived from twin huts that are said to have once existed on its east side. Situated on the western side of a platform which has a gateway on the northeast leading to a large pond. A recently built road runs between this gateway and the *ghat* (steps going down to the water) of the pond.

Date: Dated to 1532-38 on the basis of a few fragmented pieces of a terracotta inscription discovered from the site. These record the building of a mosque during the reign of Ghiyath al-Din Mahmud Shah (r. 939-44/1532-38), son of Ala al-Din Husayn Shah.

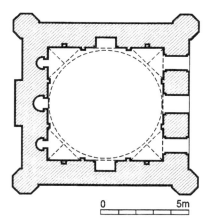

Fig. 143. Barobazar, Jorbangla Mosque, early sixteenth century, plan

Condition: Excavated in 1992-93 by the Department of Archaeology and Museums, and almost entirely reconstructed from a ruined state. Only the bases of the octagonal corner towers and interior walls up to the height of the mihrab arches of the original had survived.

Jorbangla Mosque, Barobazar

Fig. 144. Barobazar, Jorbangla Mosque, northeast view of reconstructed mosque

Dimensions: The interior is 6.44 m x 6.36 m; wall thickness, 1.44 m. Platform, 19.35 m x 17.03 m; height, 55 cm.

Material: Brick.

Plan and elevation (figs. 143-44): Square single-domed mosque with octagonal corner towers. The three entrances on the east (central, 1.07 m wide; side entrances, 86 cm) correspond to three semicircular mihrabs in the west wall. The central mihrab is larger and is projected in the exterior. Recesses and offsets articulate the exterior wall. The interior north and south walls have deep recesses flanked by small niches on either side. There are two engaged pilasters in each wall.

Decoration: The mihrabs are flanked by engaged pilasters, and have rectangular frames whose mesh patterns resemble the Bagerhat mosques. The central mihrab has a flamboyant five-lobed arch. Its stylized bell and chain of flowers resembles those seen in the Bagha Mosque of 1523-24. It has a lotus-bud finial. The side mihrabs have no hanging motifs.

The engaged pilasters have octagonal shafts on square bases and pot capitals. In the exterior there are bold horizontal mouldings on the corner towers.

Inscription: As some of the terracotta fragments are missing the text is partially lost. The text here is exactly as published by Muhammad Abdul Qadir:

> "The Prophet, may Peace and Blessings of Allah be upon him, said, 'Whoever builds a mosque, Allah will build for him a palace in the Heaven' [Hadith]. The Mosque has been constructed during the reign of Ghiyathud Din Abul Muzaffar Mahmud Shah Sultan, son of Husain Shah Sultan. May Allah make his Kingdom and Authority lasting. Its builder is the Dignified and Revered General malik Mihkhan ... the humble Kamhina, the Wazir of the city [Shahr] Muhammadabad in the year 9."

Bibliography: Alamgir, "Archaeological Remains at Barabazar", pp. 276-77; Eaton, *The Rise of Islam*, p. 325; Muhammad Abdul Qadir, "Eight unpublished Sultanate Inscriptions of Bengal", *Journal of Bengal Art* 4 (1999): 250-51.

Noongola Mosque, Barobazar

Location: Police station, Kaliganj; district, Jhenaidah; in the village of Mithapukur. The name of the mosque indicates that the area was at some point a depot for salt collection. There is a pond in the east and two graves on the south side of the mosque.

Fig. 145. Barobazar, Noongola Mosque, early sixteenth century, reconstructed east facade

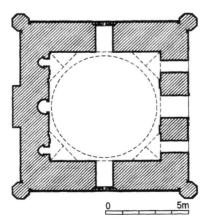

Fig. 146. Barobazar, Noongola Mosque, plan

Date: On the basis of other mosques in the area, an early sixteenth-century date is ascribed.

Condition: The building was in an utterly ruined state, the Department of Archaeology and Museums excavated it in 1993-94 and has reconstructed it up to the level of the springing of the arches (fig. 145). Only the lower parts of the walls had survived; parts of the mihrab wall and the lower half of the northern mihrab are original.

Dimensions: The interior is 6.78 m x 6.69 m; the wall thickness is 1.70 m.

Material: Brick.

Plan (fig. 146) and elevation: The dome and the upper parts of the walls had fallen. The octagonal corner towers are on circular bases. Corresponding to the three entrances in front there are three semicircular mihrabs in the west wall inside, the central one being the largest. Each wall has two engaged brick pilasters. The two entrances in the north and south are closed with brick screens; they have niches on either side.

Decoration: Vertical offsets and recesses articulate the exterior wall; the recesses have horizontal mouldings. The brick pilasters inside have merlon bases. The mihrabs are within rectangular frames with a mesh pattern; the northern mihrab has traces of a bell and chain motif in the interior. There are traces of lime plaster in the exterior southwest corner.

Bibliography: Alamgir, "Archaeological Remains at Barabazar", p. 283.

Pathagar Mosque, Barobazar

Location: Police station, Kaliganj; district, Jhenaidah. There is a pond in the east.

Date: On the basis of the exterior articulation of the walls and corner towers, an early sixteenth-century date is ascribed.

Condition: Was in a ruined state with only the lower parts of the walls and corner towers, and no dome. There are some original remains in the interior west wall up to a height of 1.05 m. The Department of Archaeology and Museums excavated it in 1995 and rebuilt it up to a height of 1.70 m.

Dimensions: The interior is 4.03 m x 4.00 m; wall thickness, 1.44 m.

Material: Brick.

Plan (fig. 147) and elevation: It is a small square building with octagonal corner towers on circular bases. There is only one entrance in front (1.26 m wide), and two others in the north and south sides (1.11 m wide)

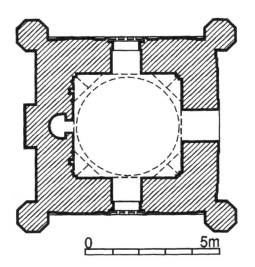

Fig. 147. Barobazar, Pathagar Mosque, early sixteenth century, plan

Fig. 148. Barobazar, Pathagar Mosque, interior mihrab wall

which are closed with brick screens. Of the three mihrabs inside, only the central one is semicircular and is projected outside, but the two side ones have rectangular bases and are very shallow (fig. 148).

Decoration: The entrance arches are framed with a rectangular mesh border, and the exterior wall has offsets and recesses with horizontal mouldings at the bases. The northwest corner tower has mouldings of rows of four-petalled flowers and lozenges. The interior of the central mihrab has traces of a rectangular panel design with arcades, and the side mihrabs, which have remnants of lime plaster on the surface, are decorated with chain and bell motifs inside.

Bibliography: Alamgir, "Archaeological Remains at Barabazar", pp. 283-86.

Shukur Mallik Mosque, Barobazar

Location: Police station, Kaliganj; district, Jhenaidah; in the village of Hasilbagh.

Date: No inscription. Attributed stylistically to the early sixteenth century.

Condition: Was in a ruined state; excavated in 1995 by the Department of Archaeology and Museums and rebuilt up to the level of the springing of the arches. There is no dome but a tin roof has been erected to protect the interior. The mihrab wall in the interior had survived up to the level of the central mihrab arch (fig. 149), but there were only the lower parts of the other walls and octagonal towers.

Shukur Mallik Mosque, Barobazar

Fig. 149. Barobazar, Shukur Mallik Mosque, early sixteenth century, interior mihrab wall

Dimensions: The interior is 3.76 m sq.; the wall thickness is 1.11 m.

Material: Brick.

Plan (fig. 150) and elevation: This was a very small square mosque with engaged octagonal towers and a central mihrab projection in the exterior. Like the Pathagar Mosque there is only one entrance in front (1.09 m wide) and one each on the north and south sides (83 cm wide), and also three mihrabs of which only the central one is semicircular. The two side mihrabs are flat against the wall with no niche.

Decoration: All the mihrabs have hanging motifs in the middle composed of rectangular plaques at the end of a long chain. The side mihrabs are cusped and the southern one, which retains more original features has flamboyant motifs in the interstices as in the Jorbangla Mosque. In the Gorar and Parbajpur Mosques these motifs are more clearly defined as stemmed leaves. The five-lobed leaf motif at its apex is also similar to those of the Gorar and Parbajpur Mosques. There are large terracotta motifs in the spandrels.

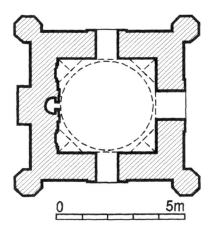

Fig. 150. Barobazar, Shukur Mallik Mosque, plan

Bibliography: Alamgir, "Archaeological Remains at Barobazar", p. 286.

Parbajpur Mosque, Satkhira

Location: Police station, Kaliganj; district, Satkhira, in a thickly vegetated area. There is a large tank on the north side of the mosque.

Date: No inscription was found, but there is an empty rectangular space above the central doorway on the east, which indicates that there was an inscription tablet there. Based on similarities with the Gorar Mosque in Barobazar and Majlis Awlia's Mosque in Faridpur, it is assigned to the early sixteenth century.

Condition: The interior and the exterior east side of the mosque have been plastered, lime washed and painted. There is no roof over the verandah. One Shaykh Abdul Moudud, who now owns the land on which the mosque stands, is the caretaker (*mutawalli*). There is a new staircase on the southeast corner of the verandah, from the top of which the muezzin gives the call for prayer. The low enclosure wall in front is probably a later addition.

Dimensions: The interior of the prayer chamber is 6.45 m x 6.50 m; the wall thickness is 1.86 m.

Material: Brick.

Plan (fig. 151) and elevation: From the east are three entrances into the prayer chamber; the central entrance is much larger (1.39 m wide) than the flanking ones (76 cm wide). There are two other entrances into this chamber, one each from the north and south sides (1.15 m wide). Opposite the front entrances are three semicircular mihrabs in the west—the central one is much larger than the other two—and two engaged brick pilasters in each wall.

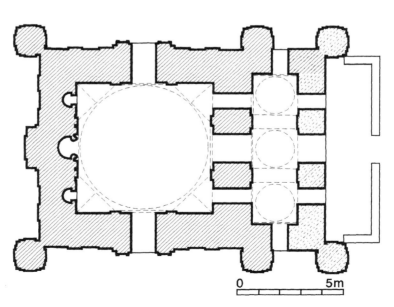

Fig. 151. Satkhira, Parbajpur Mosque, early sixteenth century, plan

Parbajpur Mosque, Satkhira

The north and south entrances to the verandah are still extant, but since the front of the verandah has disappeared, the three entrances shown in the plan on the east side of the verandah are conjectural. Engaged pilasters on the east wall of the prayer chamber, which are still intact up to the springing of the arches, indicate that the verandah was covered with three domes. There are six square, engaged corner towers, whose projections are similar to those in Majlis Awlia's Mosque. The exterior wall also has many recesses, and on the west side is the projection for the central mihrab.

A hemispherical dome with a finial covers the square prayer chamber. Due to roof repairs, details of the original cornice are not clear, but a gentle curve can be seen on all sides except the east.

The dome is borne on squinches with front arches, which spring from the tops of engaged brick pilasters similar in design to the stone pilasters of the Gorar Mosque. The zones of transition, the engaged double brick pilasters in the corners of the verandah and the exterior east wall of these two mosques are similar.

Decoration: The building is profusely decorated with vegetal designs. On the exterior, some of the original decoration is retained in the south, west and north sides; the west wall is the best preserved (fig. 152). It is decorated with bands of four-petalled flowers, upright five-lobed leaves (as in the Gorar Mosque, fig. 136), palmettes and arcades of small pilasters and cusped arches with vegetal motifs inside.

The centre of the mihrab projection has a rectangular framed panel. It has lost its central motif, but it was probably a miniature reproduction of a mihrab. The square corner towers have recesses and mouldings that recall the *ratha* (wall projections of north Indian temples) mouldings on temple plinths and are similar to those of Majlis Awlia's Mosque in Faridpur.

Inside, much of the detail is lost because of later applications of plaster and paint. A decorative band of four-petalled flowers as in the Gorar Mosque (fig. 136) tops the

Fig. 152. Satkhira, Parbajpur Mosque, exterior west wall

arches of the transition zone. The mihrabs are well preserved and set in rectangular recessed frames topped by merlons with vegetal and floral motifs inside. The central mihrab is much larger than the two side ones. Its rectangular frame has a vine design with rosettes at intervals; sections have palmette motifs. The mihrab itself has a pointed, cusped arch with full-blown lotuses on the spandrels. The niche is covered by a half-dome with a row of upright trefoil leaves at its base. The rest is divided into panels, each having a lively vegetal motif. Descending from the apex is a chain with a hanging rectangular vegetal motif at its end. As in the Gorar Mosque, the cusped border of the mihrab arch has stemmed leaves that spread over the spandrel. This resembles the "flamboyant" motifs of some of the other Barobazar mosques, e.g., Shukur Mallik.

Bibliography: S. M. Hasan, *MMB*, p. 84; S. C. Mitra, *Jawshohore Khulnar Itihash* (Calcutta, 1963), vol. 2, p. 86.

Rezai Khan's Mosque, Bagerhat

Location: Police station and district, Bagerhat, on the roadside between the villages of Shundorghona and Ranbijoypur. On the other side of the road is the mosque and tomb of Zinda Pir. Its builder is believed to be Rezai Khan, a contemporary of Khan Jahan, but the mosque is unlike most of the monuments of Bagerhat, which are in the distinctive Khan Jahan style.

Date: There is no inscription. An early sixteenth-century date is ascribed to it on the grounds that it is close in style to the Bagha Mosque (1523-24).

Condition: Protected by the Department of Archaeology and Museums. The building is in ruins. All the domes have fallen. Only one side of the east wall with an entrance remains. The lower part of the south wall, the west wall up to the mihrab level (fig. 153),

Fig. 153. Bagerhat, Rezai Khan's Mosque, early sixteenth century, ruined interior

the north wall with only the lower part of the northwest entrance, the complete northeastern entrance, and the northeast corner tower still exist. Engaged pilasters on the west, north and on the remaining parts of the east wall remain. The bases of the stone pillars are in situ but other sections are scattered around in the prayer chamber. A small mosque with a corrugated iron roof occupies a small area inside.

Dimensions: The interior is 12.10 m x 8.05 m, the wall thickness is 1.73 m.

Materials: Brick except for two stone pillars lying on the ground in the centre of the prayer chamber.

Plan (fig. 154) and elevation: A rectangular building with three aisles and two bays once covered by six domes. There are three entrances on the east side, of which the central one is 1.95 m wide; the two on either side are 1.80 m wide. There are two openings each in the north and south walls; the ones on the eastern end are almost the same size as the corner entrances in the east facade. The openings on the western end measure 1.60 m across. Corresponding to the three entrances on the east side are three mihrabs in the west wall with semicircular niches. The interior walls have engaged brick pilasters, two each in the east and west walls, and one each in the north and south. In the corners are thin engaged pilasters revealing angular surfaces.

The arches in the interior sprang from the tops of the engaged brick pilasters and the twelve-sided, free-standing stone pillars. The domes rested on the arches and corbelled pendentives, the oversailing courses of which are visible in the northeastern corner.

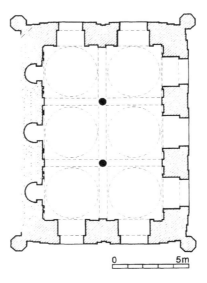

Fig. 154. Bagerhat, Rezai Khan's Mosque, plan

Outside are four engaged octagonal towers and the wall is articulated by recesses. The openings on the western end of the north and south walls were screened and are smaller in size than the other doorway openings. There are some perforated bricks in situ in the southwest. The wall foundation of the window in the north side indicates that it was also screened.

The Department of Archaeology claims that there was a courtyard in front of the mosque enclosed by a brick wall with a monumental gateway in the east, but no trace of either exists above ground.

Decoration: Only a small amount of decoration is left; it is on the exterior of what remains of the east and north walls and on the mihrabs. Traces of rectangular panels are still visible on the east facade; within each is a cusped arch motif with rosettes and leaves in the spandrels, and a chain descending from its apex. Vertical recesses that are broken in the lower portions by horizontal bands with a cresting of five-lobed leaves articulate the northern wall. The five-lobed leaf is also featured in the decoration of the central mihrab, where a row of small leaves is set over larger ones. The same five-lobed leaf motif is featured prominently in the decorative program of the Gorar Mosque in Barobazar, the Parbajpur Mosque in Satkhira and Majlis Awlia's Mosque in Faridpur, all of which are assigned to the sixteenth century. The shafts of the pillars of the central mihrab have small bells hanging from chains. In the north mihrab a delicate flower motif is still preserved on the rectangular plaque also hanging from a chain. The panels and the vertical recesses of the exterior facade are also similar to those on the facade of the Qadam Rasul building in Gaur, Malda (1530). The bases of the pillars in the northern mihrab have projected merlons with three-lobed leaf finials.

Bibliography: Bari, "Khalifatabad and its Monuments", pp. 142-45; A. F. M. A. Jalil, *Shundorboner Itihash* (Dacca, 1969), vol. 2, p. 144.

Hammad's Mosque, Chittagong

Location: Police station, Sitakunda; district, Chittagong. The mosque is on the east side of the Dhaka-Chittagong road in the village of Masjida about 1 km from the Masjida High School and about 20 km from Chittagong city. One Hammad, about whom nothing is known, presumably built the mosque and dug a large pond with a north-south orientation. Karim identifies Hammad with Hamid Khan, an officer of Sultan Ala al-Din Husayn Shah, who is mentioned by the medieval Bengali poet Bahram Khan in his poetical work, *Laili Majnu*.

Date: Dated by inscription to the reign of Ghiyath al-Din Mahmud Shah (r. 939-44/ 1532-38), the son of Husayn Shah. The stone inscription slab is just below the curved cornice in front. It is covered with a layer of lime and obliterated to the extent of near illegibility.

Condition: The mosque is in a walled enclosure. The building was renovated, a verandah added in front and the original *do-chala* gateway demolished. Both interior and exterior have been plastered and lime washed. Much of the decoration in the interior seems to have been painted over. The lotus finials on the large central dome and the cupolas may date from Mughal times. The side entrances have been converted to windows and renovation has transformed the arch of the southern entrance and the central entrance in the east to four-centred forms.

Dimensions: The interior is 4.30 m sq.; the wall thickness is 1.55 m.

Hammad's Mosque, Chittagong

Material: Brick; the central and northern mihrabs are of stone. There are stone brackets at the springing of the front and rear arches of the entrance and stone gutters on the roof for drainage.

Plan and elevation (figs. 155-56): The mosque is a square building with three entrances in the east, and one each on the north and south sides. The central entrance is the largest (1.05 m wide). The flanking entrances are 60 cm wide. The altered side entrances now measure 85 cm in the interior. There are three mihrabs in the west wall of which the central one, the largest, is semicircular. The side ones, which are much smaller, have rectangular bases.

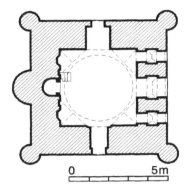

Fig. 155. Chittagong, Hammad's Mosque, 1532-38, plan

Outside, the four corners have engaged circular towers. There is a small semicircular projection for the central mihrab in the west (diameter at base, 3.27 m), and the building is inside a walled enclosure.

The cornice is curved; stone gutters drain water from the curved roof. The entrance arches are low and set in rectangular recesses with mouldings on top. The eastern ones have front and rear arches with *chau-chala* vaults in between. The level of the verandah, which is extended up to the eastern and northern limits of the enclosure wall, is higher than the floor of the prayer chamber, so that one has to step down to enter the chamber. The large dome is supported on squinches. The mihrab projection and the four corner

Fig. 156. Chittagong, Hammad's Mosque, southwest view

towers extend above the parapet and are covered with cupolas. Parts of the original enclosure wall still exist in the west.

Decoration: On the outside, the corner towers and mihrab projection have rows of mouldings. The large central dome (the shape of which also indicates later renovation) and the cupolas have water-pot finials. Inside, the mihrabs are set in rectangular frames. The central and north mihrabs are of stone, but heavy painting obscures most of the carving. The southern mihrab is bare. Both the central and northern mihrabs have trefoil-cusped niches with hanging rectangular motifs on chains. On the rectangular frame of the northern mihrab, in spite of its many layers of paint, a pattern of interlocking geometric shapes with rosettes can still be seen. On the central mihrab the relief carving of the niche also shows through the paint. Its rectangular frame has Quranic verses inscribed on it. The base of the dome has an arcade of miniature niches as seen in Faqir's Mosque in Chittagong.

Inscription: The inscription, in Arabic, originally contained two lines of writing, but most of the writing is now effaced. What could be read of the text is the following:

"... al-Dunya wal Din Abul Muzaffar Mahmud the Sultan son of a Sultan ..."

There are three Mahmuds in the Sultanate history of Bengal, but this one must be Ghiyath al-Din Mahmud Shah (r. 1532-38), who had the title of Abul Muzaffar.

Bibliography: A. S. M. Ahmed, *Choto Sona Mosque*, pp. 118, 122; Eaton, *The Rise of Islam*, p. 325; Karim, "Two Unnoticed Sultanate Mosques", pp. 321-31, esp. 328-30; *idem, Corpus of Inscriptions*, pp. 379-82; Bahram Khan, *Laili Majnu*, ed. Ahmed Sharif (Dacca, 1966), pp. 10-11; *List of Ancient Monuments*, p. 228; Siddiq, *Islamic Inscriptions of Bengal*, p. 223.

Osmanpur Gayebi Mosque, Sylhet (Silet)

Location: Police station, Balaganj; district, Sylhet, in village of Osmanpur, also known as Lamapara (quarter of Buddhist priests), 27 km from Sylhet town and about 3 km off the Dhaka-Sylhet road. The name Lamapara indicates that there may have been a settlement of Buddhist monks there.

Date: There is no inscription. The mosque is not mentioned in any account and is not known to be a Sultanate building. It is impossible to date it precisely, but an early to mid-sixteenth-century date is given because it still shares some of the features of small Sultanate mosques, several of which were built at that time.

Condition: The building has been thoroughly renovated. A verandah has been added in front and both the interior and exterior plastered, lime washed and painted with brightly coloured designs. The side entrances have been turned into windows, and corner towers are capped with cupolas and finials. Recognizable vestiges of the original construction remain to indicate that the original building dates from the Sultanate period.

Osmanpur Gayebi Mosque, Sylhet (Silet)

Dimensions: The interior is 5.80 m sq.; the wall thickness is 1.69 m.

Material: Brick.

Plan (fig. 157) and elevation: The building is square. Of the three eastern entrances the central one is 1.04 m wide and the two flanking ones only 62 cm wide. The north and the south entrances are 93 cm wide. The interior is plain because of the plaster and whitewash. There is only one mihrab in the west with the mihrab projection outside, and no engaged pilasters. The four engaged corner towers are octagonal with circular base, but the octagon is slightly rotated so that none of its sides are parallel to the sides of the building, a feature not seen in any other Sultanate building.

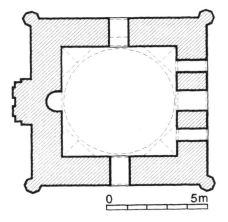

Fig. 157. Sylhet, Osmanpur Gayebi Mosque, early to mid-sixteenth century, plan

The mosque has a squat appearance; the structure is dominated by the large dome, whose irregular shape indicates that it has been reconstructed. The square building with single dome, the low entrances with pointed arches set in recessed rectangles, the absence of a drum and a dome carried on squinches all suggest a Sultanate building. The small pendentives between the squinch arches that carry the dome seem to have been corbelled, but now have painted designs, some of which imitate brickwork (fig. 158). The mihrab is semicircular, but it has been reconstructed very crudely. The interior is well lit.

Fig. 158. Sylhet, Osmanpur Gayebi Mosque, interior east

Decoration: No original decoration remains. The corbelled pendentives in the zone of transition between the squinch arches and the dome have been replaced with painted triangular panels, some of which have designs imitating the brickwork of the originals.

Bibliography: P. Hasan, "The Gayebi Mosque in Osmanpur, Sylhet", *Chetana: Architecture and the Arts* 2 (Feb. 1987): 44-45.

Sura (Shura) Mosque, Dinajpur

Location: Police station, Ghoraghat; district, Dinajpur; the mosque is about 11 km west of the Ghoraghat police outpost. It is on a raised platform and approached by a flight of steps and a monumental gateway.

Date: There is no inscription. The resemblance to the decorative styles of the Bagha and Kusumba Mosques (1523-24 and 1558) suggests a mid-sixteenth-century date.

Condition: Restored by the Department of Archaeology and Museums which protects the building.

Dimensions: The interior of the prayer chamber is 4.87 m sq. The interior of the verandah is 4.87 m x 1.70 m; the wall thickness is 1.29 m.

Material: Brick, with stone used in the central mihrab and the engaged pilasters inside; and over the six engaged towers, the thresholds, entrances and a string course at the level of the springing of the arches on the outside. Contrary to what Dani has written, the exterior walls are not faced with stone (*MAB*, p. 161).

Plan and elevation (figs. 159-60): The verandah has three entrances in the east, all of nearly the same size (1 m wide), and one each on the north and south sides that are slightly smaller. The square prayer chamber has three accesses from the east, corresponding to the front entrances in the verandah (the central one is 80 cm wide and the flanking ones 70 cm) and one each on the north and south sides. These two side entrances are the widest (1.05 m) in the mosque. On the west side of the prayer chamber are three semicircular mihrabs, of which the central one is the largest. Each wall of the prayer chamber as well as the east and west walls of the verandah have two engaged brick pilasters. The verandah also has a pair of half-pilasters in the corners. On the exterior are six engaged octagonal towers, four at the corners of the building and two where the verandah is joined to the prayer chamber. There is a projection for the central mihrab in the west wall.

The mosque is on a raised platform with a monumental gateway. The cornice is very gently curved. The exterior surface of the wall is articulated by shallow offsets and recesses and the stone string course mid-way up the wall appears as a moulding. Structurally, the string course serves as a tie for masonry construction, and in weak soil can minimize the effect of localized settling of the superstructure above the stone course.

Sura (Shura) Mosque, Dinajpur

In the verandah, the lateral arches springing from the tops of the stone pilasters divide the space into three bays, each covered by a dome on corbelled pendentives. These domes are spaced so close together that their bases touch. The verandah entrances have front and rear arches with pointed barrel vaults in between. All the entrance arches are pointed and set in rectangular recesses. In the interior of the prayer chamber, the dome is high, but there is no drum and its base rests on the wide front arches of squinches.

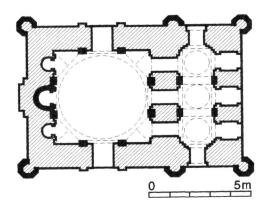

Fig. 159. Dinajpur, Sura Mosque, mid-sixteenth century, plan

Decoration: The stone string course and prominent moulding divides the exterior surface of the wall into an upper and lower zone. Each half has a row of rectangular panels with an ornamental border, and the interior is filled with a cusped niche with a flamboyant motif that has the decorative quality of jewellery. The delicate terracotta relief is similar to the panels in the Bagha Mosque (1523-24). The stone encasing of the engaged octagonal corner towers has rows of mouldings and indentations similar to those of the Kusumba Mosque (1558).

The engaged stone pilasters inside have square bases and capitals and octagonal shafts with decorative mouldings at intervals. The three mihrabs have cusped arches and are set in ornamented rectangular frames with *kalasha* motifs on the centre top. The central mihrab is of stone with a terracotta rosette with a pendant suspended above its rectangular frame (fig. 161). Its arch is supported on pillars with square bases with a central

Fig. 160. Dinajpur, Sura Mosque, northeast view

Fig. 161. Dinajpur, Sura Mosque, central mihrab

projection and rows of mouldings. This projection rising vertically up to a short height and ending in a *kalasha* finial bears crude resemblance to a temple profile. The octagonal shafts of the pillars have hanging-bell motifs. The spandrel of the mihrab arch is filled with curving tendrils that have lost their vegetal quality and are reduced to dots. They are related to the mihrab carvings of the Kusumba Mosque. The niche has a central zone of rectangular panels with cusped arches and hanging motifs. The same motif appears in the rectangular frame and seems to imitate not mihrabs, but jewellery. The side mihrabs are filled with terracotta decoration, whose lines and curves give a nervous quality to the design.

Bibliography: A. S. M. Ahmed, *Choto Sona Mosque*, p. 130; Asher, "Inventory of Key Monuments", p. 134; Dani, *MAB*, p. 161; S. M. Hasan, *MMB*, pp. 138-39; M. H. Khan, *Terracotta Ornamentation in Muslim Architecture of Bengal* (Dhaka, 1988), pp. 185-86; M. R. Tarafdar, *Husain Shahi Bengal, 1494-1538 A.D. A Socio-Political Study*, 2nd rev. ed. (Dhaka, 1999), p. 325.

Kusumba (Kushumba) Mosque, Naogaon (Naoga)

Location: Police station, Manda; district, Naogaon. Manda is on the west bank of the Atrai River, and the village of Kusumba is about 6.5 km to its south.

Date: The inscription tablet that dates the building to 966 (1558-59) is fixed over the central entrance in the east. It was built during the period of Afghan rule under one of the last Sur rulers Ghiyath al-Din Bahadur Shah by Sulayman who was probably a high-ranking official.

Condition: Restored and protected by the Department of Archaeology and Museums. Three of the domes collapsed during the earthquake of 1897 but were later rebuilt.

Dimensions: The interior is 12.34 m x 8.07 m; the wall thickness is 1.82 m.

Material: Brick and stone. The entire exterior wall is faced with stone. Inside, the staircase and the walls up to the arches of the pendentives have stone facing. The pillars, platform, floor and perforated side screens are also of stone.

Plan and elevation (figs. 162-63): The mosque is a rectangular building with three aisles and two bays covered by six domes. There are three entrances in the east, all of the same size (1.25 m wide), and screened openings, two each on the north and south sides. On the west wall, opposite the central and southeastern entrances are two semicircular mihrabs on the floor level. The mihrab in the northwestern bay is not on the same level as the other two, but is above a raised platform ascended by a staircase. The presence of such platforms in non-imperial mosques such as this one and the Chhota Sona Mosque indicates that not only royalty, but nobility and high-ranking officials were separated from the general public during prayers. There are pillars in the centre of the prayer chamber and engaged pilasters, two each in the east and west walls, and one each in the north and south walls. The corners

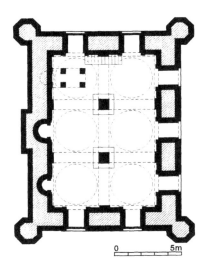

Fig. 162. Naogaon, Kusumba Mosque, 1558-59, plan

of the chamber have half-pilasters. Outside are four engaged octagonal corner towers and a projection for the central mihrab in the west.

The building is inside a walled enclosure with a monumental gateway that has standing spaces for guards. Undoubtedly, the sponsor was a wealthy person of high position. Although built during Sur rule, it is not influenced at all by the earlier Sur architecture of north India. Instead, it is well grounded in the Bengal style.

The cornice of the mosque is gently curved and the corner towers stop at the parapet. In the northwest corner there are two arches, one above the other.

Inside, the hemispherical domes are carried on corbelled brick pendentives. The arches spring from the tops of the two pillars in the centre of the chamber and engaged stone pilasters in the walls. The pillars are on square stone platforms and have crenellated square bases and capitals. Their shafts have square ends and an octagonal middle section with mouldings. The engaged pilasters are similar in shape.

The platform in the northeastern bay is reached by a flight of stairs on the east (fig. 164). It is supported by four short stone pillars, the engaged pilasters in the west wall, the stairs and the walls of the prayer chamber.

Decoration: The decoration is carved stone; mouldings are the most prominent decorative feature on the exterior, especially on the east and west sides. They divide the walls into upper and lower sections, run all along the curved cornice, around the corner towers, in a straight line below the cornice and along the upper and lower borders of rectangular panels on the east, south and north walls, in a way similar to the mouldings in the exterior of Qutb Shah's Mosque in Kishoreganj. The indentation in the moulding of the corner towers, especially the base, is similar to the mouldings on the turrets of the Sura Mosque. The coarse stone facing of the east facade is carved in shallow relief. The spandrels of the central entrance arch are filled with small *kalashas* and rosettes. The north and south sides have screened windows and more elaborate carving.

Inside, all the mihrabs are very elaborately carved (fig. 46). They have cusped arches crowned with *kalasha* motifs, supported on intricately worked stone pillars. The pillar bases have projections and tasselled decorations hanging down from chains. *Kalashas,*

Fig. 163. Naogaon, Kusumba Mosque

Fig. 164. Naogaon, Kusumba Mosque, platform in interior northwest

tendrils, and rosettes are reduced to dots as on the stone facing of the central mihrab of the Sura Mosque. Bunches of grapes and vines curve in an almost serpentine manner. Large rosettes are featured at intervals on the mihrab wall. The platform edge is decorated with a row of grapes, and the spandrels and frames of the arches that support it are decorated with rosettes.

Inscription: Written in Arabic (only the phrase *bana kardeh* meaning "built by" is in Persian). The text reads:

> "The Prophet, may the peace and blessings of Allah be upon him, has said, 'He who builds for Allah a mosque, seeking thereby the favour of Allah, Allah will build for him a similar house in Paradise.' During the reign of the exalted and honoured Sultan Ghiath al-Dunya wal-Din Abul Muzaffar Bahadur Shah the Sultan, son of Muhammad Shah Ghazi, may Allah perpetuate his kingdom and sovereignty and elevate his position and dignity and may his army and proof be honoured. Built by Sulaiman, may his justice endure; in the year 966 [1558-59]."

Bibliography: S. Ahmed, *IB*, 4: 242-44; Asher, "Inventory of Key Monuments", p. 85; Chakravarti, "Pre-Mughal Mosques", p. 29; Dani, *MAB*, pp. 163-64; K. N. Dikshit, "Conservation: Eastern Circle, Bengal, Kusumba", *ARASI* (1923-24), p. 33; Karim, *Corpus of Inscriptions*, pp. 393-94; F. A. Khan, "Conservation of Ancient Monuments in East Pakistan: Kusumba Mosque", *Pakistan Archaeology* 5 (1968): 242; Saraswati, "Indo-Muslim Architecture", p. 26; Siddiq, *Islamic Inscriptions of Bengal*, pp. 225-26; M. A. Wali, "On the Archaeological Remains in the District of Rajshahi", *Journal of the Asiatic Society of Bengal* 73, pt. 1(1904): 117.

Shialghuni Mosque, Barisal (Borishal)

Location: Police station, Bakerganj; district, Barisal. The village of Shialghuni is about 11 km from the police station; it can be reached by road or boat.

Date: There is no inscription. The only original decoration is on the mihrab facade (fig. 165). Its similarity to that executed in stone on the mihrab facade of the Kusumba Mosque in Naogaon (fig. 46), dated 1558, allows a mid-sixteenth-century date to be assigned to this mosque.

Condition: The mosque has been completely rebuilt; the walls are now thinner, but their original thickness can be surmised from the ground outside. In the northeast corner is the remnant of an octagonal corner tower. The interior retains the original area and the large rectangular facade for the mihrab that is filled with terracotta decoration. According to the villagers, the large dome that covered the mosque fell in the mid-1950s. In 1969 the walls were plastered, and the mosque was given a concrete roof supported by beams.

Dimensions: The interior is 4.45 m sq.; the wall thickness is 1.37 m.

Material: Brick.

Plan (fig. 166) and elevation: The mosque is a square building with a single entrance in the east and one each on the north and south sides. The original dimensions of the doorways can no longer be ascertained. The side entrances have been turned into small windows. Normally there would have been three entrances on the east, but even the oldest living villager does not remember having seen more than one. However, the single entrance corresponding to the single large mihrab inside is within the standard formula of mosques in Bengal.

Fig. 165. Barisal, Shialghuni Mosque, mid-sixteenth century, mihrab facade

Outside, there are signs of engaged octagonal corner towers and a mihrab projection. Inside, corresponding to the entrance on the east is a semicircular mihrab in the west wall. The large space taken up by the single mihrab frame rules out the possibility of multiple mihrabs. No other original features remain except the octagonal base of the northeast corner tower. No structural features of the original mosque are preserved.

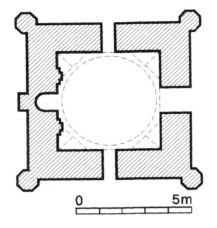

Fig. 166. *Barisal, Shialghuni Mosque, plan*

Decoration: The only remaining decoration in the mihrab area is the terracotta facade for the mihrab (fig. 165), the decoration is similar to that executed in stone in the mihrab of the Kusumba Mosque in Naogaon. The terracotta decoration derived from vegetal sources is not very lively. The plant motifs on the spandrels look dry and brittle and the curving tendrils resemble snail shells. The rosettes have been reduced to a purely schematic design. A similar facade is found in Sadi's Mosque in Egarosindur (1652), where it frames both the mihrab and the central doorway in the east. Such facades are found on the doorways of several late medieval temples in Bengal, e.g., the Shyama-Raya Temple in Bishnupur, West Bengal (1643), and Kantaji's Temple in Dinajpur (1704-22), showing a continuity of style well into the seventeenth and eighteenth centuries. The niche itself has only two bands of horizontal mouldings. The arched niche is set in a very elaborate rectangular projection that has rows of rectangular bands.

Bibliography: Asher, "Inventory of Key Monuments", p. 64; Beveridge, *District of Bakarganj*, p. 40; George Michell, ed., *Brick Temples of Bengal* (Princeton, 1983), figs. 417 and 608.

Qutb Shah's Mosque, Kishoreganj

Location: Police station, Astogram (Awshtogram); district, Kishoreganj. Astogram is in the middle of a marshy (*haor*) area. The mosque is named after Qutb Saheb, a local saint whose tomb is nearby.

Date: There is no inscription. On stylistic grounds the building is dated to the late sixteenth century. This is the earliest mosque in the district, and has the most developed form of the plan seen earlier in Fath Shah's Mosque and the Badr Awlia Jami Mosque (figs. 35 and 78). The terracotta decoration is also in a late style.

Condition: The mosque, protected by the Department of Archaeology and Museums, is well preserved. The exterior has traces of lime plaster; the interior is plastered and lime-washed.

Dimensions: The interior is 5.30 m x 10.90 m; the wall thickness is 1.46 m.

Material: Brick.

Plan and elevation (figs. 37-38): The mosque is a rectangular building with three entrances in front and two each on the north and south sides. The three front entrances are of the same size and have front and rear arches with vaulted spaces in between. The side entrances are smaller on the exterior than in the interior.

The building is on a high plinth, mounted by steps. The plinth moulding skirts the entire building. Other prominent mouldings on the exterior wall surface give the impression of a two-storeyed building. The cornice has a very pronounced curve. Five domes, a large hemispherical one in the centre and bubble-shaped ones in the corners, cover the mosque. Four engaged, octagonal corner towers rise slightly above the cornice, and circular towers frame the mihrab projection in the west.

Inside, corresponding to the three front entrances are three semicircular mihrabs in the west wall; the central one is the largest. On each of the north and south walls are two engaged, short, brick pilasters. The central bay in the interior single-aisled, three-bayed space is the largest, a square 5 m on a side. Wide transverse arches (1.16 m) springing from the tops of the engaged brick pilasters mark off the central bay. The central dome is carried on the pilasters, transverse arches, and deep corbelled pendentives.

Fig. 167. Kishoreganj, Qutb Shah's Mosque, late sixteenth century, makara head in ornamental vine motif at entrance

The north and south bays are again divided into two equal portions by small arches between the east-west transverse arches and the north and south walls. These small areas have corbelled pendentives that carry the four bubble-shaped corner domes of the roof. The Jamatkhana Mosque of Delhi (1310-16) has a similar arrangement of five domes, but there the side wings are separated by walls. These corner domes and two entrances each in the north and south sides give the impression of two side aisles—an innovation, which soon gives way to the rectangular, single-aisled, three-domed

Mughal type of mosque. The exterior elevation of a cluster of domes (a large dome surrounded by smaller ones) recalls the Sur architecture of Bihar, especially Sher Shah's Mosque in Patna (1540), and the multiple clusters of the mid-fourteenth-century Khirki Mosque of Delhi. The arches are pointed. The vaulted spaces between the front and rear arches on the east side have small pointed barrel vaults or *do-chalas*. Inside, just above floor level is a skirting about 2 cm wide.

Decoration: On the east facade, the curve of the cornice and the horizontal moulding that marks the upper limits of the panel decoration produces a prominent gable effect. Rectangular panels filled with blind niches break up the entire exterior wall surface. This enhances the two-storeyed effect and heralds the early Mughal style. The arched niches of the panels have *kalasha* crowns, but their interiors are bare. The same decoration is repeated on all sides. The corner towers have stepped bases and mouldings. All the entrance doorways have large rosettes on their arch spandrels with an outer circle of serrated leaves which recall the mihrab decoration of Majlis Awlia's Mosque in Faridpur. The large and small rosettes on the rectangular frame of the central doorway in the east are similarly treated. In the smaller ones this outer circle looks much like a pinwheel. The style of the terracotta ornamentation is close to that of Sadi's Mosque in Egarasindur (1652), also in Kishoreganj district.

The most extraordinary decoration is on the exterior, inside the rectangular frame of the central entrance. On the right and left sides, at the bases, are fruit-bearing date palms on platforms, with jars on either side of the tree similar to those used for tapping date palms for their syrup. Above these trees are *kalashas* from which lush vines grow. A *makara* (crocodile-like creature in Hindu mythology) head complete with snout, tongue, eyes and ears appears at every bend of the vine (fig. 167). This is the only appearance of this motif in Islamic architectural decoration in Bengal. The vine motif originally in its Hindu/Buddhist context as the auspicious *purna kalasha*, or overflowing pot, was animated in a similar manner. The Muslims reduced the motif to purely vegetal form by substituting leaves and tendrils for the *makaras*. In this mosque the original form makes an unexpected and rare reappearance.

In the interior all entrances and arches have *kalasha* crowns. The central mihrab niche has a rectangular frame with a curved top similar to the one in the Shialghuni Mosque. The interior decoration consists of rows of moulding. The hanging motif on a chain is absent.

Bibliography: Asher, "Inventory of Key Monuments", p. 39; Dani, *MAB*, pp. 164-65; *List of Ancient Monuments*, figs. 105, 112, 114; Anthony Welch and Howard Crane, "The Tughluqs", *Muqarnas* 1 (1983): 138-39.

Zinda Pir's Mosque, Bagerhat

Location: Police station and district, Bagerhat. The mosque is located in the village of Ranbijoypur in a large enclosure that also contains the tomb of Zinda Pir and a number of other graves. The mosque and tomb are in the same architectural style. The name literally means "living saint". Local legend has it that while a saint named Ali was being buried, he rose and asked the mourners to bring his Quran.

Date: There is no inscription. The building differs from the Khan Jahan style monuments of Bagerhat. The massiveness of the bare, heavy walls of the Khan Jahan monuments is replaced by articulation with recesses and mouldings (fig. 168) that characterize a later style best represented by the Qadam Rasul building in Gaur, Malda dated 1531. The octagonal corner towers in this mosque first appeared in the Khan Jahan style in the Masjidbari Mosque, Patuakhali, dated 1465. The high dome is unlike the shallow hemispherical ones seen in Khan Jahan style buildings, but closely resembles the profile of Sadi's Mosque in Egarasindur (1652). Based on this stylistic evidence, this mosque can be dated to the late sixteenth century.

Condition: The mosque is in ruins. Much of the dome has fallen and is overgrown with vegetation. Some repair work was done by local residents, as is evident from the altered shapes of the arches and the cement and brickwork around them.

Dimensions: The interior is 4.92 m x 4.88 m; the wall thickness is 1.28 m.

Material: Brick.

Plan (fig. 169) and elevation: The mosque is a square building with three entrances in the east and one each on the north and south sides. In front, the central entrance is the largest (1.30 m wide); the other two are 1.00 m wide. The entrances in the north and

Fig. 168. Bagerhat, Zinda Pir's Mosque, late sixteenth century, northeast view

south are 1.20 m wide. There is only one semicircular mihrab in the west wall, opposite the central entrance in the east, and two engaged brick pilasters in each wall. Outside are engaged octagonal towers in the four corners; the mihrab is projected on the west side, and the wall is articulated by recesses.

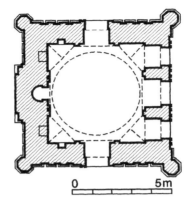

Fig. 169. Bagerhat, Zinda Pir's Mosque, plan

The building was once covered by a hemispherical dome carried on squinches whose arches sprang from the tops of engaged octagonal brick pilasters with square bases. There are cusped niches on either side of the mihrab. The southwest and northwest walls have smaller niches. The entrances are set in rectangular projections and have front arches that make them larger inside than outside. The cornice of the building has disappeared.

Decoration: Shallow recessed pilasters articulate the exterior surface of the walls. They have four horizontal bands of moulding up to a height of almost half the wall surface. The mouldings are similar to those in the Qadam Rasul in Gaur and have prominent lozenge and bead motifs. Deep shadows are cast in the recesses of the wall surface. The rectangular frames of the entrances probably had terracotta decoration, but it has disappeared.

Inside, the engaged brick pilasters are decorated at intervals with ornamental bands. The rectangular frame of the mihrab has a wide border of an interlocking mesh pattern similar to some sections of the cornice decoration of the Chunakhola Mosque. The top of the frame has a row of lozenges crowned by a row of merlons. The mihrab niche is in a very dilapidated state. Its lower half, decorated by a lush curving vine, still has some terracotta decorations. This section has an arcade of three miniature mihrabs complete with ornamental hanging lamps on chains, fully fashioned pillars, and trefoil-cusped arches with flowering plants in their spandrels. The terracotta motifs are conspicuous for their fleshiness; even the curving tendrils seem to have weight, and the ornate lamp is almost like a vegetal motif. The decoration on the square plaques of the mihrab pillars has the same quality.

Bibliography: Asher, "Inventory of Key Monuments", p. 43; Bari, "Khalifatabad and its Monuments," pp. 196-97; L. S. S. O'Malley, *Bengal District Gazeteers (Khulna)* (Calcutta, 1908), p. 167.

Shubhorara Mosque, Jessore (Jawshore)

Location: Police station, Abhaynagar (Awbhoynawgor); district, Jessore. The village of Shubhorara is on the east bank of the old Bhairab River, about 4.5 km from the Abhaynagar police station. The village is reached from Phultola in the Khulna district, from where there is a motorable road to Shikarhat 1.5 km away. The last kilometre to Shubhorara is by boat. The mosque is in a small clearing in an otherwise thickly vegetated area.

Date: There is no inscription. Based on stylistic similarity to Zinda Pir's Mosque in Bagerhat, this mosque is also dated to the late sixteenth century.

Condition: The original roof collapsed and has been replaced by a roof made of corrugated iron sheets on a bamboo frame. The level of the floor seems to have settled about 30 cm, since the square bases of the mihrab pillars are about 30 cm above floor level. Below these bases are layers of brick which seem to be part of the foundation wall. The rectangular brick tiles of the mihrab frames also stop at the same point, and the entrances and mihrabs look unusually elongated, also suggesting a lowering of the floor level.

Dimensions: The interior is 5.05 m sq.; the wall thickness is 1.56 m.

Material: Brick.

Plan (fig. 170) and elevation: A square building with single entrances on the north, east and south sides; the eastern entrance is the widest (1.43 m wide); the side ones are 95 cm wide. The west wall has three mihrabs, of which the central one is the largest and projected on the outside.

The exterior corners have four engaged octagonal towers. Offsets and recesses break up their surfaces just as in the Zinda Pir's Mosque in Bagerhat. The building was originally covered by a single dome carried on squinches. Traces of the squinch arches are visible on either side of the eastern entrance. The walls have no pilasters. The entrance and mihrab arches are pointed. The central mihrab is semicircular and has a half-dome (fig. 171); the side mihrabs have rectangular bases. There are small

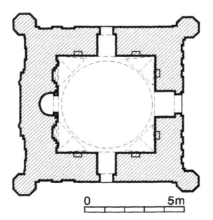

Fig. 170. Jessore, Shubhorara Mosque, late sixteenth century, plan

Shubhorara Mosque, Jessore (Jawshore)

Fig. 171. Jessore, Shubhorara Mosque, interior mihrab wall

niches on either side of the entrances on the east, south and north sides.

Decoration: The mihrabs are set in rectangular recesses but the wall looks bare and unfinished. The rectangles of the side mihrabs are continuous with the central one. The central mihrab has a cusped facade. *Kalasha* motifs are visible on the shafts of the pillars and the top left-hand corner of the mihrab. The side mihrabs have double arches, one recessed about 10 cm from the face of the other.

The corner towers have horizontal mouldings and bands of merlons. The exterior mihrab projection is large, with vertical recesses (fig. 172). The mihrab motif on it occupies the entire length of the wall, but the square plaque at the end of the long descending chain is missing. This exterior projection and its decoration are similar in

Fig. 172. Jessore, Shubhorara Mosque, exterior west wall with mihrab projection

style to Majlis Awlia's Mosque in Faridpur of the early sixteenth century. Other mosques with prominent mihrab motifs in the projection of the central mihrab are the Muazzampur Shahi Jami Mosque, Sonargaon (1432-45), Baba Adam's Mosque, Munshiganj (1483), and Shankarpasha Mosque, Habiganj (1493-1519).

Bibliography: S. C. Mitra, *Jawshohore Khulnar Itihash* (Calcutta, 1963) vol. 1, p. 344.

Appendix 1

Independent Muslim Rulers (Sultans) of Bengal

(Dates after Richard M. Eaton)

Rulers	Principal capital	Dates
Governors of the Delhi Sultanate (some declared independence and became sultans)	Lakhnawti (Gaur) and Devkot	1204–1338
Independent Sultans		
Fakhr al-Din Mubarak Shah	Sonargaon	1338–49
Ikhtiyar al-Din Ghazi Shah	Sonargaon	1349–52
Ala al-Din Ali Shah	Lakhnawti	1341–42
Ilyas Shahi Dynasty (1342–1415)	Firuzabad (Pandua)	
Shams al-Din Ilyas Shah		1342–57
Sikandar Shah		1357–89
Ghiyath al-Din Azam Shah		1389–1410
Saif Hamza Shah		1410–11
Shihab al-Din Bayazid Shah		1411–14
Ala al-Din Firuz Shah		1414
Raja Ganesh Dynasty (1415–33)		
Jalal al-Din Muhammad Shah		1415–32
Shams al-Din Ahmad Shah		1432–33

Restored Ilyas Shahi Dynasty (1433–86) Lakhnawti

Nasir al-Din Mahmud	1433–59
Rukn al-Din Barbak Shah	1459–74
Shams al-Din Yusuf Shah	1474–89
Sikandar	1481
Jalal al-Din Fath Shah	1481–86

Abyssinian Sultans (1486-93) Lakhnawti

Barbak Shah-zadah	1486
Saif al-Din Firuz Shah	1486–90
Shams al-Din Muzaffar Shah	1490–93

Husayn Shahi Dynasty (1493–1538) Lakhnawti

Ala al-Din Husayn Shah	1493–1519
Nasir al-Din Nusrat Shah	1519–32
Ala al-Din Firuz Shah	1532
Ghiyath al-Din Mahmud Shah	1532–38

Sher Shah Sur and Successors (1538–64) Lakhnawti

Sher Shah Sur	1538
(Emperor Humayun)	(1538–39)
Sher Shah Sur	1539–45
Islam Shah	1545–53
Shams al-Din Muhammad Shah	1553–55
Ghiyath al-Din Bahadur Shah	1556–60
Ghiyath al-Din II	1560–63
Ghiyath al-Din III	1563–64

Karrani Dynasty (1564–75) Gaur and Tanda

Taj Khan Karrani	Gaur	1564–65
Sulayman Karrani	Tanda	1565–72
Bayazid Karrani		1572
Daud Karrani		1572–75

Appendix 2

Dated Sultanate Mosques of Bangladesh

Muazzampur Shahi Jami Mosque, Dhaka	1432-33
Binat Bibi's Mosque, Dhaka	1456-57
Gopalganj Mosque, Dinajpur	1460
Masjidbari Mosque, Patuakhali	1465-74
Faqir's Mosque, Chittagong	1474-81
Darasbari Mosque, Nawabganj	1479-80
Bandar Shahi Mosque, Narayanganj	1481
Baba Adam's Mosque, Munshiganj	1483
Fath Shah's Mosque, Narayanganj	1484
Chhota Sona Mosque, Nawabganj	1493-1519
Shankarpasha Mosque, Habiganj	1493-1519
Aroshnagar Mosque, Khulna	1501-2
Baba Saleh's Mosque, Narayanganj	1505-6
Goaldi Mosque, Narayanganj	1519
Bagha Mosque, Rajshahi	1523-24
Nabagram Mosque, Sirajganj	1526
Jorbangla Mosque, Jhenaidah	1532-38
Hammad's Mosque, Chittagong	1532-38
Kusumba Mosque, Naogaon	1558

— Appendix 3 —

Sultanate Mosques by District

Bagerhat
    Shaitgumbad Mosque, police station: Bagerhat
    Mosque adjoining Khan Jahan's Tomb, police station: Bagerhat
    Ranbijoypur Mosque, police station: Bagerhat
    Bibi Begni's Mosque, police station: Bagerhat
    Shingra Mosque, police station: Bagerhat
    Nine-domed Mosque, police station: Bagerhat
    Chunakhola Mosque, police station: Bagerhat
    Ten-domed Mosque, police station: Bagerhat
    Rezai Khan's Mosque, police station: Bagerhat
    Zinda Pir's Mosque, police station: Bagerhat

Barguna
    Bibi Chini's Mosque, police station: Betagi

Barisal
    Kasba Mosque, police station: Gaurnadi
    Shialghuni Mosque, police station: Bakerganj

Bogra
    Mankalir Bhita Mosque, police station: Shibganj

Chittagong
    Faqir's Mosque, police station: Hathazari
    Badr Awlia Dargah Jami Mosque, police station: Chittagong Municipal Area
    Hammad's Mosque, police station: Sitakunda

Dhaka
   Binat Bibi's Mosque, police station: Sutrapur

Dinajpur
   Gopalganj Mosque, police station: Kotwali
   Sura Mosque, police station: Ghoraghat

Faridpur
   Majlis Awlia's Mosque, police station: Bhanga
   Shatoir Mosque, police station: Boalmari

Habiganj
   Shankarpasha Mosque, police station: Habiganj

Jessore
   Shubhorara Mosque, police station: Abhaynagar

Jhenaidah
   Shatgachhia Mosque, police station: Kaliganj
   Sailkupa Mosque, police station: Sailkupa
   Galakata Mosque, police station: Kaliganj
   Gorar Mosque, police station: Kaliganj
   Manohar Dighi Mosque, police station: Kaliganj
   Pirpukur Mosque, police station: Kaliganj
   Jorbangla Mosque, police station: Kaliganj
   Noongola Mosque, police station: Kaliganj
   Pathagar Mosque, police station: Kaliganj
   Shukur Mallik Mosque, police station: Kaliganj

Khulna
   Aroshnagar Mosque, police station: Dumuria
   Masjidkur Mosque, police station: Koyra

Kishoreganj
   Qutb Shah's Mosque, police station: Astogram

Munshiganj
   Baba Adam's Mosque, police station: Munshiganj

Naogaon
   Kusumba Mosque, police station: Manda

Narayanganj
   Bandar Shahi Mosque, police station: Bandar
   Fath Shah's Mosque, police station: Sonargaon
   Yusufganj Mosque, police station: Sonargaon

  Baba Saleh's Mosque, police station: Bandar
  Goaldi Mosque, police station: Sonargaon
  Muazzampur Shahi Jami Mosque, police station: Sonargaon

Nawabganj
  Chhota Sona Mosque, police station: Shibganj
  Darasbari Mosque, police station: Shibganj
  Dhunichak Mosque, police station: Shibganj
  Khania Dighi Mosque, police station: Shibganj

Patuakhali
  Masjidbari Mosque, police station: Mirzaganj

Rajshahi
  Bagha Mosque, police station: Rajshahi

Satkhira
  Parbajpur Mosque, police station: Kaliganj

Sirajganj
  Nabagram Mosque, police station: Taras
  Makhdum Shah's Mosque, police station: Shahzadpur

Sylhet
  Osmanpur Gayebi Mosque, police station: Balaganj

Principal Abbreviations

ARASI	*Annual Report of the Archaeological Survey of India*
A. S. M. Ahmed, *Choto Sona Mosque*	Abu Sayeed Mostaque Ahmed, *The Choto Sona Mosque in Gaur: An Example of Early Islamic Architecture in Bengal* (Dusseldorf, 1997)
N. Ahmed, *Mahasthan*	Nazimudin Ahmed, *Mahasthan* (Dhaka, 1975)
S. Ahmed, *IB*	Shamsud-din Ahmed, *Inscriptions of Bengal*, vol. 4 (Rajshahi, 1960)
Sohrabuddin Ahmed, "Antiquities of Barabazar"	Sohrabuddin Ahmed, "Antiquities of Barabazar", *Journal of the Varendra Research Museum* 4 (1975-76): 71-80
Alamgir, "Archaeological Remains at Barabazar"	Khoundkar Alamgir, "Archaeological Remains at Barabazar, Jhenidah District", *Journal of Bengal Art* 3 (1998): 263-90
Asher, "Inventory of Key Monuments"	Catherine B. Asher, "Inventory of Key Monuments", in *The Islamic Heritage of Bengal*, ed. George Michell (Paris, 1984), pp. 37-140
Banerji, *The Architecture of the Adina Mosque*	Naseem Ahmed Banerji, *The Architecture of the Adina Mosque in Pandua, India: Medieval Tradition and Innovation* (Lewiston, 2002)
Bari, "Khalifatabad and its Monuments"	M. A. Bari, "Khalifatabad and its Monuments", M. Phil. thesis, Rajshahi University, 1980
Beveridge, *District of Bakargunj*	H. Beveridge, *The District of Bakargunj, Its History and Statistics* (London, 1876. Rpt. Barisal, 1970)
Beveridge, "Notes on the Khurshid-i Jahan Numa"	H. Beveridge, "Notes on the Khurshid-i Jahan Numa", *Journal of the Asiatic Society of Bengal* 44, pt.1, no.3 (1895): 194-236.
Blochmann, *Contributions*	H. Blochmann, *Contributions to the Geography and History of Bengal (Muhammadan Period)* (Calcutta, 1968)

Principal Abbreviations

Chakravarti, "Pre-Mughal Mosques"	M. M. Chakravarti, "Pre-Mughal Mosques of Bengal", *Journal of the Asiatic Society of Bengal* 2 (1867): 126-35
Cunningham, "Report of a Tour"	Alexander Cunningham, "Report of a Tour in Bihar and Bengal in 1879-80 from Patna to Sunargaon", *Archaeological Survey of India* Report 15 (1882)
Dani, *MAB*	A. H. Dani, *Muslim Architecture in Bengal* (Dacca, 1961)
Dani, *Bibliography*	A. H. Dani, *Bibliography of the Muslim Inscriptions of Bengal (down to 1538)*, Appendix to *Journal of the Asiatic Society of Pakistan* 2 (Dacca, 1957)
Department of Archaeology	Department of Archaeology and Museums, Government of Bangladesh
Eaton, *The Rise of Islam*	Richard M. Eaton, *The Rise of Islam and the Bengal Frontier 1204-1760* (Berkeley, 1993)
Haque et al, *Pundranagar to Sherebanglanagar*	Haque et al, *Pundranagar to Sherebanglanagar: Architecture in Bangladesh* (Dhaka, 1997)
P. Hasan, "Eight Sultanate Mosques"	Perween Hasan, "Eight Sultanate Mosques in Dhaka District", in *The Islamic Heritage of Bengal*, ed. George Michell (Paris, 1984), pp. 179-92
S. A. Hasan, *Notes*	S. A. Hasan, *Notes on the Antiquities of Dhaka* (Dacca, 1904)
S. M. Hasan, *Mosque Architecture*	Syed Mahmudul Hasan, *Mosque Architecture of Pre-Mughal Bengal* (Dacca, 1979)
S. M. Hasan, *MMB*	Syed Mahmudul Hasan, *Muslim Monuments of Bangladesh* (Dacca, 1980)
Husain and Bari, "The Sultanate Mosques"	A. B. M. Husain and M. A. Bari, "The Sultanate Mosques", in *Gawr-Lakhnawti*, ed. A. B. M. Husain (Dhaka, 1997), pp. 65-98
Karim, *Corpus of Coins*	Abdul Karim, *Corpus of Muslim Coins of Bengal* (Dacca, 1960)
Karim, *Corpus of Inscriptions*	Abdul Karim, *Corpus of the Arabic and Persian Inscriptions of Bengal* (Dhaka, 1992)
Karim, *Social History*	Abdul Karim, *Social History of the Muslims of Bengal (up to A.D. 1538)* 3rd ed. (Dhaka, 2001)
Karim, "Two Unnoticed Sultanate Mosques"	Abdul Karim, "Two Hitherto Unnoticed Sultanate Mosques of Chittagong", *Journal of the Asiatic Society of Pakistan* 12, no. 3 (1967): 321-31
M. A. A. Khan, *Memoirs*	M. Abid Ali Khan, *Memoirs of Gaur and Pandua* (Calcutta, 1931)
List of Ancient Monuments	*List of Ancient Monuments in Bengal. Revised and Corrected up to 31st August 1895* (Calcutta, 1896)
Lohuizen de Leeuw, "Monuments at Bagerhat"	J. E. Lohuizen de Leeuw, "The Early Muslim Monuments of Bagerhat", in *The Islamic Heritage of Bengal*, ed. George Michell (Paris, 1984), pp 165-78

Saraswati, "Indo-Muslim Architecture"	S. K. Saraswati, "Indo-Muslim Architecture in Bengal", *Journal of the Indian Society of Oriental Art* 9 (1941): 12-36
Siddiq, *Islamic Inscriptions of Bengal*	Mohammad Yusuf Siddiq, *Arabic and Persian Texts of the Islamic Inscriptions of Bengal* (Watertown, 1992)
Wali, "On the Antiquities and Traditions"	Maulavi Abdul Wali, "On the Antiquities and Traditions of Shahzadpur", *Journal of the Asiatic Society of Bengal* 1, no. 3 (1904): 262-71
Wise, "Notes on Sonargaon"	J. Wise, "Notes on Sonargaon, Eastern Bengal", *Journal of the Asiatic Society of Bengal* 63 (1874): 88-92

Glossary

A = Arabic
B = Bengali
Bu = Burmese
P = Persian
S = Sanskrit
T = Turkish
U = Urdu

amalaka (S)	round, fluted, cushion-like architectural member resembling fruit of the same name
amir (A)	commander
ariz (A)	paymaster of the forces
azan (A)	the ritual call to prayers
baraka (A)	blessing
Baro Bhuiyan (B)	group of twelve feudal landlords of Bengal who fought for independence against the Mughal army
bhadra (S)	horizontal platform-like division of the superstructure of Bengal temples
bil (B)	marsh or lake. Low-lying depressions where the accumulation of water has converted large areas into swamps and marshes
Bismillah (A)	"In the name of God, the Clement, the Merciful." The beginning of each of the Quranic verses, with the exception of Sura 9
brahman (S)	highest caste among Hindus
chahar taq (P)	pavilion-like structure in which four arches support a dome
chaitya (S)	originally a tumulus, but subsequently any Buddhist temple
chala (B)	hut roof

chau-chala (B)	a hut roof which slopes down in four directions away from the centre of the room. Over a rectangular room the longer slopes form a ridge at the top and the end slopes are triangular in shape. The roofing material is generally reed over a bamboo frame
chhatri (S)	umbrella; small domed pavilion
Chishti (P)	a Sufi order named after Muin al-Din Chishti (1142-1236) of India
dabir-i-khas (P)	private secretary
dargah (P, B)	tomb or shrine of a holy person
dighi (B)	a large, deep pond or tank
do-chala (B)	a hut roof which slopes down in two directions. The ridge at the top formed by the meeting of the two slopes is curved if the roofing material is bamboo and reed
faqir (A)	pious ascetic, beggar
Firdawsi (A)	a Sufi order named after Najib al-Din Firdawsi (d. 1291) and established by Sharaf al-Din Maneri (1263-1381) in Bihar and Bengal
galakata (B)	headless, beheaded
ghat (B)	steps going down to the water
ghazi (A)	Muslim warrior of the Faith
Gosvamin (S)	title of Vaishnava guru
Habshi (P)	Abyssinian
Hadith (A)	traditions dealing with the deeds and utterances of the Prophet Mohammad
haj (A)	annual pilgrimage to Makkah (Mecca)
haji (A)	one who has performed the haj
Hanafi (H)	one of the four schools of law among Sunni Muslims founded by Abu Hanifa (d. 769)
hansa torana (S)	(*hansa* = goose; *torana* = arched gateway) gateway design used in ancient Indian architecture
haor (B)	depressed, water-filled area
hat (B)	market
imam (A)	prayer leader
jagir (P)	revenue assignment granted by king
jali (S)	pierced stone screen
jamdar ghayr mahalli (P)	superintendant of royal robes
jami (A)	mosque where Friday afternoon congregational prayer is held
jandar (P)	sword-bearer; executioner
jangdar (P)	soldier; one who attained prominence by his bravery
jorbangla (B)	two huts attached to each other

Glossary

jhum (B)	shifting and temporary cultivation in jungle or forest clearings on hills
Kaaba (A)	the nearly cubic building in Makka (Mecca), which is the holiest sanctuary in Islam
kalasha (B)	water-pot: vase-like member usually crowning a Shiva temple
khadem (A)	caretaker, servant
khal (B)	canal
khalifa (A)	successor, vice-regent, caliph
khamba (U)	column
khan (P)	title of nobility
khan-i-azam (P, A)	high-ranking officer
khanqa (P)	meeting place of dervishes or Sufis
khaqan (P)	title of Chinese emperors
khutba (A)	sermon made in a jami mosque before Friday afternoon prayer
kirtimukha (S)	a decorative sculptural motif showing the head of a lion-like creature with strings of beads issuing from its mouth
madrasa (A)	theological college
mahal (A)	administrative unit of an estate
majlis al-majalis majlis mansur (A)	a great noble attached to the royal court
makara (S)	mythical crocodile-like creature, the vehicle of the Hindu river-goddess Ganga
malik (A)	lord
malik al-muazzam (A)	exalted lord
maqsura (A)	enclosure within a mosque for the protection of the ruler
masjid (A)	mosque; place of prostration
mihrab (A)	niche indicating the direction of Makka (Mecca) (qibla)
minbar (A)	pulpit in a jami mosque used by the imam for preaching the Friday sermon
mir bahr (A)	admiral of the fleet
muezzin (A)	the man who makes the call to prayer
mulla (A)	title of religious scholar or dignitary
mutawalli (A)	the legally appointed administrator of waqf property
muqarrab al-dawla (A)	adherent to the state, i.e. "great noble"
nagara (S)	northern style of temple characterized by a cruciform plan and high curvilinear tower
naskh (A)	a cursive style of Arabic calligraphy
nazir (A)	superintendent; an officer employed in a judicial court superior to all peons and bailiffs
pargana (P)	an administrative unit

pir (P)	saintly or holy person with a following
puja (S)	devotional rites in a temple or before a deity
Purana (S)	sacred text of Hindus
pyatthat (Bu)	modern Burmese word for the ancient *prasat*, derived from *prasada* (S) meaning palatial building or pavilion with multiple roofs
qibla (A)	direction of prayer, i.e. the Kaaba in Makka (Mecca)
Quran (A)	sacred text of the Muslims believed to be the revelation of Allah made to the Prophet Mohammad
raja (S)	king
ratha (S)	central or subsidiary projections of a wall of a north Indian temple
ratna (S)	single or multiple towers in a temple
sar-i-lashkar (P)	commander of an army
shahada (A)	profession of faith fundamental to Islam
shahr (P)	city, town
shaykh (A)	head of a Sufi order
shikhara (S)	tower of a temple
shiqdar (A)	head of an administrative unit known as *shiq*, which was like a district of today
silahdar (P)	arms bearer
stupa (S)	mound. Originally contained relics of Buddha, later became a symbol of Buddhist faith
stupa-shirsha (S)	topped by stupa
suba (P)	Mughal province
Sufi (A)	mystic
Sura (A)	chapters of the Quran
thana (B)	police station or outpost
tilak (S)	auspicious mark on the forehead
tughra (A)	elaborate calligraphic style used in the seals of Ottoman sultans
Ulugh (T)	powerful, great
Vaishnava (S)	in Hinduism, followers of the god Vishnu
Veda (S)	sacred text of Hindus
waqf (A)	land or property perpetually endowed with a pious institution
wazir (A)	vizier, minister
zamindar (P)	landholder, peasant proprietor
zulla (A)	shaded area in a mosque; hence, sanctuary

Select Bibliography

Abul Fazl Allami. *Ain-i-Akbari*, 3 vols.: vol. 1, trans. H. Blochmann, ed. D. C. Phillott; vols. 2-3, trans. H. S. Jarrett, ed. Jadunath Sarkar. First published Lucknow: Nawal Kishore, 1869, 2nd ed. Calcutta: Asiatic Society, 1927, rpt. Calcutta: Asiatic Society, 1993.

Ahmad, Khwaja Nizam al-Din. *Tabaqat-i-Akbari*, 3 vols., trans. Brajendranath De. First published Calcutta: Asiatic Society, 1927, rpt. Calcutta: Asiatic Society, vol. 1, 1973, vols. 2-3, 1996.

Ahmad, Qeyamuddin. *Corpus of Arabic and Persian Inscriptions of Bihar*. Patna: K. P. Jayaswal Research Institute, 1973.

Ahmed, Abu Sayeed Mostaque. *The Choto Sona Mosque in Gaur: An Example of Early Islamic Architecture in Bengal*. Dusseldorf: Institut für Baugeschichte der Universitat Karlsruhe, 1997.

Ahmed, Nafis. *An Economic Geography of East Pakistan*. London: Oxford University Press, 1968.

Ahmed, Nazimuddin. *Mahasthan*. Dacca: Department of Archaeology and Museums, Government of Bangladesh, 1975.

―― "An Uncommon Group of Pre-Mughal Monuments in Bangladesh". *South Asian Archaeology* (1981): 309-13.

―― *Discover the Monuments of Bangladesh*. Dhaka: University Press Ltd, 1984.

―― *The Buildings of Khan Jahan in and around Bagerhat*. Dhaka: University Press Ltd, 1989.

Ahmed, Rafiuddin. *The Bengal Muslims 1871-1906: A Quest for Identity*. Delhi: Oxford University Press, 1981.

Ahmed, Shamsud-din. *Inscriptions of Bengal*, vol. 4. Rajshahi: Varendra Research Museum, 1960.

Ahmed, Sohrabuddin. "Antiquities of Barabazar". *Journal of the Varendra Research Museum* 4 (1975-76): 71-80.

Alamgir, Khoundkar. "Archaeological Remains at Barabazar, Jhenidah District". *Journal of Bengal Art* 3 (1998): 263-90.

Al-Bukhari. *Sahih al-Bukhari*. 9 vols., trans. Muhammad Muhsin Khan. Ankara: Hilal Yayinlari, 1976.

Ali, Abdullah Yusuf. *The Holy Quran: Text, Translation and Commentary*, 3 vols. Lahore: Sh. Muhammad Ashraf, 1967, reprinted 1988.

Ali, Muhammad Mohar. *History of the Muslims of Bengal*, vols. 1A-B. Riyadh: Department of Culture and Publications, Imam Muhammad Ibn Saud Islamic University, 1985.

Ananda Bhatta. *Vallala Caritam*, ed. H. P. Shastri. Calcutta: Asiatic Society, 1904.

Asher, Catherine B. "Inventory of Key Monuments". *The Islamic Heritage of Bengal*, ed. George Michell. Paris: UNESCO, 1984, pp. 37-140.

―― *The New Cambridge History of India, Architecture of Mughal India,* vol. 1: 4. Cambridge: Cambridge University Press, 1992.

Asher, Frederick M. "Ancient Slate Quarry Revisited: A Source Located". *Journal of Bengal Art* 4 (1999): 263-66.

Askari, S. H. "New Light on Rajah Ganesh and Sultan Ibrahim Sharqi of Jaunpur from Contemporary Correspondence of Two Muslim Saints". *Bengal Past and Present* 57, no. 130 (1948): 32-39.

—— "The Correspondence of Two 14th-Century Sufi Saints of Bihar with the Contemporary Sovereigns of Delhi and Bengal". *Journal of the Bihar Research Society* 42, pt. 2 (1956): 177-95.

Aslanapa, Oktay. *Turkish Art and Architecture*. New York: Praeger, 1971.

Bagchi, Prabodh Chandra. "Political Relations between Bengal and China in the Pathan Period". *Visva-Bharati Annals* 1 (1945): 96-134.

Banerji, Naseem Ahmed. *The Architecture of the Adina Mosque in Pandua, India: Medieval Tradition and Innovation*. Mellen Studies in Architecture, vol. 6. Lewiston: Edwin Mellen Press, 2002.

Bangladesh in Maps. Dacca: University of Dacca, 1981.

Barani, Zia al-Din. *Tarikh-i Firoz Shahi*, ed. Saiyid Ahmad Khan. Calcutta: Asiatic Society of Bengal, 1862. Extracts reproduced in *The History of India as Told by Its Own Historians*, 8 vols., trans. and ed. H. M. Elliot and John Dowson. Allahabad: Kitab Mahal, 1964, vol. 3, pp. 93-268.

Bari, M. A. "Khalifatabad and Its Monuments". M.Phil thesis, Rajshahi University, 1980.

Basak, Radhagovinda. "Tipperah Copper-Plate Grant of Lokanatha: The 44th Year". *Epigraphia Indica* 15 (1919-20): 301-15.

Beveridge, H. "Notes on the Khurshid-i-Jahan Numa". *Journal of the Asiatic Society of Bengal*, 44, pt. 1, no. 3 (1895): 194-236.

—— *The District of Bakarganj, its History and Statistics*. London: Trubner & Co., 1876, rpt. Barisal: Bakerganj District Council, 1970.

Bhattasali, Nalini Kanta. *Iconography of Buddhist and Brahmanical Sculptures in the Dacca Museum*. Dacca: Dacca Museum Committee, 1929.

—— *Coins and Chronology of the Early Independent Sultans of Bengal*. Cambridge: W. Heffer & Sons, 1922, rpt. New Delhi: Indological Book Corporation, 1976.

Birashk, Ahmad. *A Comprehensive Calendar of the Iranian, Muslim Lunar, and Christian Eras for Three Thousand Years (1260 B.H.-2000 A.H./639 B.C.-2621 A.D.)*. Costa Mesa, CA: Mazda Publishers in association with Bibliotheca Persica, 1993.

Blair, Sheila S., and Jonathan Bloom. *The Art and Architecture of Islam 1250-1800*. New Haven, CT, and London: Yale University Press, 1994.

Blochmann, H. "Notes on Places of Historical Interest in the District of Hugli". *Proceedings of the Asiatic Society of Bengal* 4 (April 1870): 109-27.

—— *Contributions to the Geography and History of Bengal (Muhammadan Period)*. *Journal of the Asiatic Society of Bengal* 42, no. 3 (1873); 43, no. 3 (1874); 44, no. 3 (1875), rpt. Calcutta: Asiatic Society, 1968.

Bloom, Jonathan. *Minaret: Symbol of Islam*. Oxford: Oxford University Press, 1989.

Brown, P. *Indian Architecture (Islamic Period)*. 5th ed. Bombay: Taraporevala, 1968.

—— *Indian Architecture (Buddhist and Hindu Periods)*. 7th ed. Bombay: Taraporevala, 1976.

Bysack, Babu Gourdass. "The Antiquities of Bagerhat". *Journal of the Asiatic Society of Bengal* 2 (1867): 126-35.

Chakravarti, M. M. "Bengal Temples and their General Characteristics". *Journal of the Asiatic Society of Bengal* n.s. 5, no. 5 (1909): 141-51.

—— "Pre-Mughal Mosques of Bengal". *Journal of the Asiatic Society of Bengal* n.s. 6, no. 1 (1910): 23-38.

Chowdhury, A. M. *Dynastic History of Bengal*. Dacca: Asiatic Society of Pakistan, 1967.

Coomaraswamy, A. K. *Essays in Early Indian Architecture*, ed. M. W. Meister. New Delhi: Oxford University Press, 1992.

Select Bibliography

Creighton, H. *Ruins of Gaur*. London: Black, Parbury, and Allen, 1817.
Creswell, K. A. C. *Early Muslim Architecture*, vol. 1, pts. 1-2. Oxford: Clarendon Press, 1969.
Cunningham, Alexander. "Report of a Tour in Bihar and Bengal in 1879-80 from Patna to Sunargaon". *Archaeological Survey of India, Report*, vol. 15. Calcutta: Government of India, 1882.
Dani, A. H. *Bibliography of the Muslim Inscriptions of Bengal (Down to 1538)*, Appendix to Journal of the Asiatic Society of Pakistan, vol. 2. Dacca: Asiatic Society of Pakistan, 1957.
—— *Muslim Architecture in Bengal*. Dacca: Asiatic Society of Pakistan, 1961.
Dasgupta, Shashi Bhusan. *Obscure Religious Cults: As Background of Bengali Literature*. Calcutta: University of Calcutta, 1946, 2nd ed. Calcutta: K.L. Mukhopadhyaya, 1962.
Dasgupta, Tamonesh Chandra. *Aspects of Bengali Society from Old Bengali Literature*. Calcutta: University of Calcutta, 1935.
Dayel, K. al-, S. al-Hilwa, and N. Mackenzie. "Preliminary Report on the Third Season of Darb Zubaydah Survey 1978". *Atlal: The Journal of Saudi Arabian Archaeology* 3 (1399/1979): 43-47.
De, Sushil Kumar. *The Early History of the Vaisnava Faith and Movement in Bengal*. Calcutta: General Printers and Publishers, 1942, 2nd ed. Calcutta: K.L. Mukhopadhyaya, 1961.
Dikshit, K. N. "Conservation: Eastern Circle, Bengal". *Annual Report of the Archaeological Survey of India 1923-24*. Calcutta: Archaeological Survey of India, 1926, pp. 32-33.
—— "Bengal and Assam". *Annual Report of the Archaeological Survey of India 1927-28*. Calcutta: Archaeological Survey of India, 1931, pp. 43-44.
—— "Bengal and Assam: Rampal, Shankarpasha". *Annual Report of the Archaeological Survey of India 1928-29*. Calcutta: Archaelogical Survey of India, 1931, pp. 40-41 and 42-44.
Dimock, Edward C. "Hinduism and Islam in Medieval Bengal". *Aspects of Bengali History and Society*, ed. Rachel Van M. Baumer. Honolulu: University Press of Hawaii, 1975, pp. 1-12.
—— and Ronald B. Inden. "The City in Pre-British Bengal". *The Sound of Silent Guns and Other Essays*, Edward C. Dimock, Jr. Delhi: Oxford University Press, 1989, pp. 113-29.
Dodd, Erica Cruikshank, and Shereen Khairallah. *The Image of the Word*, 2 vols. Beirut: American University of Beirut Press, 1981.
Duroiselle, Charles. "Excavations at Hmawza". *Annual Report of the Archaeological Survey of India, 1927-29*. Calcutta: Archaelogical Survey of India, 1931, pp. 127-35.
Dutt, Chinmoy. *Catalogue of Arabic and Persian Inscriptions in the Indian Museum, Calcutta*. Calcutta: Indian Museum, 1967.
Eaton, Richard M. "Islam in Bengal". *The Islamic Heritage of Bengal*, ed. George Michell. Paris: UNESCO, 1984, pp. 23-36.
—— *The Rise of Islam and the Bengal Frontier 1204-1760*. Berkeley: University of California Press, 1993.
Ettinghausen, Richard, and Oleg Grabar. *The Art and Architecture of Islam 650-1250*. Harmondsworth: Penguin Books, 1987.
——, —— and Marilyn Jenkins-Madina, *Islamic Art and Architecture 650-1250*. New Haven, CT, and London: Yale University Press, 2001.
Fergusson, J. *History of Indian and Eastern Architecture*, 2 vols. 1876, rpt. Delhi: Munshiram Manoharlal, 1972.
Firishta, Muhammad Qasim Hindu Shah. *Tarikh-i-Firshta*, 2 vols. Lucknow: Nawal Kishore, 1864-65, English trans. by J. Briggs under the title, *History of the Rise of the Muhammadan Power in India till the year 1612 A.D.*, 4 vols. London, 1829, rpt. New Delhi: Oriental Books Reprint Corporation, 1981.
Fischer, Klaus. "Bengal Brick Temples: Thoughts on Early Near-Eastern and Medieval Hindu Traditions during the Indo-Islamic Period". *Studies in Indian Temple Architecture: Papers presented at a Seminar Held in Varanasi in 1967*, ed. Pramod Chandra. Varanasi: American Institute of Indian Studies, 1975, pp. 179-96.

Foucher Alfred. *Etudes sur l'Iconographie boudhique de l'Inde, d'après des documents nouveaux*. Paris: Ernest Leroux, 1900, 1905.

Ghausi, Muhammad. *Gulzar-i-Abrar*, Ca. 1613. MS Pers. vol. 41, no. 259. Calcutta: Asiatic Society of Bengal.

Ghosh, J. C. *Bengali Literature*. London: Curzon Press, 1976.

Ghosh, Pika. *Temple of Love: Art and Devotion in Seventeenth-Century Bengal*. Bloomington and Indianapolis: Indiana University Press, 2005.

Gibb, H. A. R. trans. and selected. *The Travels of Ibn Battuta*. 1929, rpt. New Delhi: Goodword Books, 2001.

Godard, André. "Les anciennes mosquées de l'Iran". *Athar-e-Iran* 1 (1936): 187-210.

—— *The Art of Iran*, trans. Michael Heron, ed. Michael Rogers. London: Allen and Unwin Ltd., 1965.

Golombek, Lisa. "Abbasid Mosque at Balkh". *Oriental Art* 15, no. 3 (Autumn 1969): 173-89.

Grabar, Oleg. *The Formation of Islamic Art*. New Haven, CT: Yale University Press, 1973.

—— "The Visual Arts". *Cambridge History of Iran*, vol. 4. Cambridge: Cambridge University Press, 1975, pp. 331–63.

—— "Symbols and Signs in Islamic Architecture". *Architecture as Symbol and Self-Identity*. Proceedings of Seminar Four held in October 1979. Philadelphia: Aga Khan Award for Architecture, 1980, pp. 1-12.

Grover, Satish. *The Architecture of India, Islamic*. New Delhi: Vikas Publishing House Pvt., Ltd, 1981.

Haq, Muhammad Enamul. *Muslim Bengali Literature*. Karachi: Pakistan Publications, 1957.

—— *A History of Sufism in Bengal*. Dacca: Asiatic Society of Bangladesh, 1975.

Haque, Saif Ul, Raziul Ahsan, and Kazi Khaled Ashraf. *Pundranagar to Sherebanglanagar: Architecture in Bangladesh*. Dhaka: Chetana Sthapatya Unnoyon Society, 1997.

Hasan, Perween. "Eight Sultanate Mosques in Dhaka District". *The Islamic Heritage of Bengal*, ed. George Michell. Paris: UNESCO, 1984, pp. 179-92.

—— "Sultanate to Mughal: An Architecture of Transition in Bengal". *Journal of the Asiatic Society of Bangladesh* 23 no. 2 (December, 1988): 99-120.

—— "Sultanate Mosques and Continuity in Bengal Architecture". *Muqarnas* 6 (1989): 58-74.

—— "The Origin of Sultanate Architecture in Bengal". *Sultanate Period Architecture*, ed. Siddiq-a-Akbar et al. Lahore: Anjuman Mimaran, 1991, pp.189-98.

—— "The Footprint of the Prophet". *Muqarnas* 10 (1993): 335-43.

—— "Reflections on Early Temple Forms in Eastern India". *Journal of Bengal Art* 2 (1997): 211-24.

—— "Mosque Design and Changing Ruling Class Identities in Bengal". *Proceedings of the Symposium on Mosque Architecture*, 10 vols. Riyadh: College of Architecture and Planning, King Saud University, 1999, vol. 2, pp. 131-46.

——"Temple Niches and Mihrabs in Bengal". *Islam in Indian Regions*, 2 vols., ed. A. L. Dallapiccola and S. Z. Lallemant. Stuttgart, 1993, vol. 1, pp. 87-94, rpt. in *Architecture in Medieval India*, ed. Monica Juneja. Delhi: Permanent Black, 2001, pp. 439-55.

Hasan, Sayid Aulad. *Notes on the Antiquities of Dacca*. Dacca, 1904.

Hasan Syed Mahmudul. *Mosque Architecture of Pre-Mughal Bengal*. Dacca: University Press Ltd, 1979.

—— *Muslim Monuments of Bangladesh*. 2nd ed. Dacca: Islamic Foundation, Bangladesh, 1980.

Havell, E. B. *Indian Architecture*. London, 1913.

—— *Indian Architecture; Its Psychology Structure and History*. London, 1927.

Hill, Derek, and Oleg Grabar. *Islamic Architecture and its Decoration. A.D. 800-1500*. Chicago: University of Chicago Press, 1964.

Hillenbrand, Robert. *Islamic Architecture: Form, Function and Meaning*. Edinburgh: Edinburgh University Press, 1994.

Hoag, John D. *Islamic Architecture*. New York: Harry N. Abrams, 1977.

Hosain, Hidayet. "A Note on the Ruins of Masjidkur and Amadi". *Islamic Culture* 14, no. 4 (October 1949): 454-56.

Hunter, W. W. *A Statistical Account of Bengal*, vols. 2 and 5. Rpt. Delhi, 1973.
Husain, A. B. M. *The Manara in Indo-Muslim Architecture*. Dacca: Asiatic Society of Pakistan, 1970.
—— "The Ornamentation of the Sultanate Architecture in Bengal". *Annual Journal of the Bangladesh Shilpakala Academy* 1 (1978): 1-7.
—— "Baro Bazar: Was it the Mahmudabad of Sultani Bangla?". *Essays in Memory of Momtazur Rahman Tarafdar*, ed. Perween Hasan and Mufakharul Islam. Dhaka: University of Dhaka, 1999, pp. 228-36.
—— and M. A. Bari. "The Sultanate Mosques". *Gawr-Lakhnawti*, ed. A. B. M Husain. Dhaka: Asiatic Society of Bangladesh, Dhaka, 1997, pp. 65-98.
Hutt, Antony, and Leonard Harrow. *Islamic Architecture of Iran*, vol. 1. London: Scorpion Publications, 1977.
Ikram, S. M. "An Unnoticed Account of Sheikh Jalal of Sylhet". *Journal of the Asiatic Society of Pakistan* 2 (1957): 63-68.
Islam, Nazrul, ed. *Bangladesh Bhougalik Porichoy* (in Bengali). Dacca: Centre for Urban Studies, Department of Geography, Dacca University, 1974.
Jack, J. C. *Bengal District Gazateers (Bakerganj)*. Calcutta: Bengal Secretariat Book Depot, 1918.
Jahangir. *Tuzuk-i-Jahangiri or Memoirs of Jahangir*, 2 vols., trans. Alexander Rogers, ed. Henry Beveridge. London, 1909-14, rpt. as 1 vol. Delhi: Low Price Publications, 1989.
Jalil, A. F. M. Abdul. *Shundorboner Itihash* (in Bengali), 2 vols. Dacca: Linkman Publications, 1969.
Jones, Dalu, and George Michell. "Squinches and Pendentives". *AARP/Art and Archaeology Research Papers* 1 (1972): 9-25.
Karim, Abdul. *Corpus of the Muslim Coins of Bengal (down to 1538)*. Dacca: Asiatic Society of Pakistan, 1960.
—— "Two Hitherto Unnoticed Sultanate Mosques of Chittagong". *Journal of the Asiatic Society of Pakistan* 12, no. 3 (December 1967): 321-31.
—— "Nur Qutb Alam's Letter on the Ascendancy of Ganesa". *Abdul Karim Sahitya Visarad Commemoration Volume*, ed. Muhammad Enamul Haq. Dacca: Asiatic Society of Bengal, 1972, pp. 335-43.
—— *Banglar Itihash Sultani Amol* (in Bengali). 2nd ed. Dhaka: Bangla Academy, 1987.
—— *Corpus of the Arabic and Persian Inscriptions of Bengal*. Dhaka: Asiatic Society of Bangladesh, 1992.
—— *Social History of the Muslims of Bengal (down to A.D. 1538)*. 3rd ed. Dhaka: Jatiya Grantha Prakashan, 2001.
Kaviraj, Krishnadas. *Chaitanya Charitamrita of Krsnadasa Kaviraja*, Harvard Oriental Series, 56, trans. Edward C. Dimock. Jr., ed. Tony K. Stewart. Cambridge, MA: Harvard University Press, 1999.
Khan, Bahram. *Laili Majnu* (in medieval Bengali), ed. Ahmed Sharif. Dacca: Bengali Academy, 1966.
Khan, F. A. "Exploration in Pakistan: East Pakistan" and "Conservation of Ancient Monuments in East Pakistan". *Pakistan Archaeology* 5 (1968): 21-25 and 241-49.
Khan, M. Abid Ali. *Memoirs of Gaur and Pandua*, ed. and rev. H. E. Stapleton. Calcutta: Bengal Secretariat Book Depot, 1931.
Khan, M. Hafizullah. *Terracotta Ornamentation in Muslim Architecture of Bengal*. Dhaka: Asiatic Society of Bangladesh, 1988.
Khan, Muhammad Muhsin, trans. *Sahih Al-Bukhari*, 9 vols. Ankara: Hilal Yayinlari, 1976.
Khatun, Habiba. "Bagerhater Noy-Gumbaj Moshjid" (in Bengali). *Bangladesh Itihash Porishod Patrika*. Baisakh-Chaitra, 1382 B.S., pp. 104-13.
—— and Khoundkar Alamgir. "Satgachhia Moshjid" (in Bengali). *Itihas*, 15th year, vols. 1-3 (1398 B. S., 1992 A.D.): 128-42.
King, Geoffrey. "The Mosque Bab Mardum in Toledo and the Influences Acting upon It". *AARP/Art and Archaeology Research Papers* 2 (1970): 29-40.
Kühnel, Ernst. *Islamic Art and Architecture*, trans. Katherine Watson. London: G. Bell and Sons, 1966.

Kuraishi, M. H. *List of Ancient Monuments Protected under Act VII of 1904 in the Province of Bihar and Orissa*. Calcutta: Archaeological Survey of India, 1931.

Kuran, Aptullah. *The Mosque in Early Ottoman Architecture*. Chicago: University of Chicago Press, 1966.

List of Ancient Monuments in Bengal. Revised and Corrected up to 31st August, 1895. Calcutta: Government of West Bengal, Public Works Department, 1896.

Lohuizen de Leeuw, Joanna E. van. "The Early Muslim Monuments of Bagerhat". *The Islamic Heritage of Bengal*, ed. George Michell. Paris: UNESCO, 1984, pp. 165-78.

Louis-Frederic, pseud. *The Temples and Sculptures of Southeast Asia*. London, 1965.

Luce, Gordon, H. *Old Burma – Early Pagan*, Artibus Asiae Supplementum 25. Locust Valley, NY: J.J. Augustin, 1969.

Majumdar, R. C., ed. *The History of Bengal, vol. 1. Hindu Period*. Dacca: University of Dacca, 1943.

Majumdar, S. C. *Rivers of the Bengal Delta*. Calcutta: University of Calcutta Press, 1942.

Mannan, Qazi Abdul. *The Emergence and Development of Dobhasi Literature in Bengal up to 1855*. Dacca: University of Dacca, 1966.

Marshall, John. "The Monuments of Muslim India". *Cambridge History of India*, vol. 3. Cambridge: Cambridge University Press, 1922, rpt. Delhi: S. Chand & Co., 1958, pp. 568-640.

Martin, Montgomery. *Eastern India*. 5 vols. Rpt. Delhi: Cosmo Publications, 1976. vol. 3.

McCutchion, David. "Hindu Muslim Artistic Continuities in Bengal". *Journal of the Asiatic Society of Pakistan* 13, no. 3 (1968): 233-51.

—— *Late Medieval Temples of Bengal*. Calcutta: Asiatic Society, 1972.

—— "Origins and Developments" and "Classification of Types". *Brick Temples of Bengal*, ed. George Michell. Princeton: Princeton University Press, 1983, pp. 15-51.

Melik-Beglaroff, Joseph D. *Report of a Tour through the Bengal Provinces in 1872-73*. Calcutta, 1878.

—— *Report of the Archaelogical Survey of Bengal 1887*, parts 1 and 2. Calcutta: Catholic Orphan Press, 1888.

Michell, George, ed. *Brick Temples of Bengal: From the Archives of David McCutchion*. Princeton: Princeton University Press, 1983.

——, ed. *Islamic Heritage of Bengal*. Paris: UNESCO, 1984.

Minhaj -ud-Din Abu-Umar-i-Usman, Maulana. *Tabaqat-i-Nasiri: A General History of the Muhammadan Dynasties of Asia, including Hindustan from 810 A.D. to 1260 A.D.*, trans. H. Raverty. Calcutta: Asiatic Society of Bengal, 1881, rpt. in 2 vols. Calcutta: The Asiatic Society, 1995.

Mitra, Debala. *Buddhist Monuments*. Calcutta: Sahitya Samsad, 1980.

Mitra, Satish Chandra. *Jawshohore Khulnar Itihash* (in Bengali), 2 vols. Calcutta: Dasgupta and Company Private Limited, 1963.

Morrison, Barrie M. *Political Centers and Cultural Regions in Early Bengal*. Tucson: University of Arizona Press, 1970.

Mukerjee, R. K. *The Changing Face of Bengal: A Study of Riverine Economy*. Calcutta: University of Calcutta, 1938.

Mukhopadhyay, Sukhamay. *Banglar Itihasher Dusho Bachchar: Shaddhin Sultander Amol* (in Bengali). 3rd ed. Calcutta: Bharati Book Stall, 1980.

—— *1204-1576: Banglar Itihash* (in Bengali). Dhaka: Khan Brothers, 2000.

Nath, R. *History of Sultanate Architecture*. Delhi: Abhinav Publications, 1978.

Nathan, Mirza. *Baharistan-I ghaybi: A History of the Mughal Wars in Assam, Cooch Bihar, Bengal, Bihar, and Orissa during the reigns of Jahangir and Shahjahan*, 2 vols., trans. M. I. Borah. Gauhati, Assam: Government of Assam, 1936.

Nicholas, Ralph W. "Vaishnavism and Islam in Rural Bengal". *Bengal Regional Identity*, ed. David Kopf. East Lansing: Asian Studies Center, Michigan State University, 1969.

Niyogi, Puspa. *Brahamanic Settlements in Different Subdivisions of Ancient Bengal*. Calcutta: R.K. Maitra, 1967.

Select Bibliography

O'Kane, Bernard. "The Origin, Development and Meaning of the Nine-bayed Plan in Islamic Architecture", *A Survey of Persian Art: From Prehistoric Times to the Present*. 18 vols. Costa Mesa, California: Mazda Publishers, 2005, vol. 18, pp. 189-244.

O'Malley, L. S. S. *Bengal District Gazeteers (Khulna)*. Calcutta: Bengal Secretariat Book Depot, 1908.

Page, J. A. *An Historical Memoir on the Qutb: Delhi, Memoirs of the Archaeological Survey of India*, no. 22. Calcutta, 1926, rpt. New Delhi, 1970.

―― *A Memoir on Kotlah Firoz Shah*. Delhi, 1937.

Pope, Arthur Upham. *Persian Architecture*. New York: George Brazillier, 1965.

―― "Some Interrelations between Persian and Indian Architecture". *Indian Art and Letters* 9, no. 1 (1935).

Qadir, M. Abdul. "Eight Unpublished Sultanate Inscriptions of Bengal". *Journal of Bengal Art* 4 (1999): 235-61.

―― "Recent Excavations". *Mainamati-Devaparvata*, ed. A. B. M. Husain. Dhaka: Asiatic Society of Bangladesh, 1997.

Rashid, Haroun Er. *Geography of Bangladesh*. Dhaka: University Press Limited, 1991.

Rashid, M. H. *Paharpur*. Dacca: Department of Archaeology and Museums, 1980.

―― *Mainamati*. Dhaka: Department of Archaeology and Museums, 1997.

Ravenshaw, J. H. *Gaur: Its Ruins and Inscriptions*. London: C. Kegan Paul & Co., 1878.

Ray, Nihar Ranjan. "Medieval Bengal Culture". *Visva-Bharati Quarterly* 11, no. 2 (August-October 1945): 45-95.

―― *Bangalir Itihash* (in Bengali). 2nd ed. Calcutta: Book Emporium, 1952.

Rennell, J. "An Account of the Ganges and Burrampooter Rivers". Appendix to *Memoir of a Map of Hindoostan; or the Mogul Empire*. 3rd ed. London, 1793, pp. 335-65.

Rowland, Benjamin. *The Art and Architecture of India*. Harmondsworth: Penguin Books, 1977.

Roy, Asim. "The Social Factors in the Making of Bengali Islam". *South Asia* 3 (August 1973): 23-35.

―― *The Islamic Syncretistic Tradition in Bengal*. Princeton: Princeton University Press, 1983.

Rykwert, Joseph. *On Adam's House in Paradise: The Idea of the Primitive Hut in Architectural History*. 2nd ed. Cambridge, MA: MIT Press, 1984.

Salim, Ghulam Hussain. *Riyazu-s-Salatin: A History of Bengal*, trans. Abdus Salam. 1903. Rpt. Delhi: Idarah-e-Adabiyat-i-Delli, 1975.

Sanyal, Hitesranjan. "Religious Architecture in Bengal (15th-17th Centuries): A Study of the Major Trends". *Indian History Congress, Proceedings*, 32nd session, Jabalpur, 1970, 1: 413-22. New Delhi: Indian History Congress, 1971.

―― "Regional Religious Architecture in Bengal: A Study in the Sources of Origin and Character". *Marg* 28, no. 2 (March 1974): 31-43.

Saraswati, S. K. "Indo-Muslim Architecture in Bengal". *Journal of the Indian Society of Oriental Art* 9 (1941): 12-36.

―― *Architecture of Bengal*, bk. I. Calcutta: G. Bharadwaj & Co., 1976.

Sarkar, Sir Judunath, ed. *The History of Bengal, vol. 2. Muslim Period, 1200-1757*. Dacca: University of Dacca, 1948.

Saudi Arabia, Dept. of Antiquities. *An Introduction to Saudi Arabian Antiquities*. Riyadh: Dept. of Antiquities and Museums, Ministry of Education, Kingdom of Saudi Arabia, 1975.

Sauvaget, Jean. "Observations sur quelques mosquées seljoukides". *Annales de l'Institut d'Etudes Orientales, Université d'Alger* 4 (1938): 81-120.

Sen, Dinesh Chandra. *History of Bengali Language and Literature*. 2nd ed. Calcutta: University of Calcutta, 1954.

Sen, Sukumar. *History of Bengali Literature*. 3rd ed. New Delhi: Sahitya Akademi, 1979.

Shams-i Siraj Afif. *Tarikh-i-Firuz Shahi*, ed. Maulavi Vilayet Husain. Calcutta, Asiatic Society of Bengal, 1891. Extracts printed in Henry Elliot and John Dowson, trans. and ed., *History of*

Select Bibliography

India as Told by its Own Historians, 8 vols. Allahabad: Kitab Mahal, 1964, vol. 3, pp. 269-373.

Sharif, Ahmed. *Bangali O Bangla Sahitya* (in Bengali), 2 vols. Vol. 1, Dacca: Barnamichhil, 1978; vol. 2, Dacca: Bangla Academy, 1983.

Sharma, Y. D. *Delhi and Its Neighbourhood.* New Delhi: Archaeological Survey of India, 1974.

Siddiq, Muhammad. "Badr Maqams or the Shrines of Badr al-Din Auliya". *Journal of the Asiatic Society of Pakistan* 7, no. 1 (1962): 17-36.

Siddiq, Mohammad Yusuf. *Arabic and Persian Texts of the Islamic Inscriptions of Bengal.* Watertown: South Asia Press, 1992.

Skelton, Robert. "The Iskandar Nama of Nusrat Shah". *Indian Painting*, exhibition catalogue. London: Colnaghi, 1978, pp. 135-52.

Sourdel, Janine. "Inscriptions seljoukides et salles à coupoles de Qazvin en Iran". *Revue des Etudes Islamiques* 42 (1974): 3-43.

Spooner, D. B. *Annual Report of the Archaelogical Survey of India*, pt. I, 1917-18 (1920): 9.

Stapleton, H. E. "Contributions to the History and Ethnology of Northeastern India". *Journal of the Asiatic Society of Bengal* 18, no. 1 (1922): 25-60.

Strachan, Paul. *Imperial Pagan: Art and Architecture of Burma.* Honolulu: University of Hawaii Press, 1990.

Statistical Yearbook of Bangladesh 2000. Dhaka: Bangladesh Bureau of Statistics, Planning Division, Ministry of Planning, Government of the People's Republic of Bangladesh, 2002.

Sultan, Saiyid. *Nabi Bangsha* (in medieval Bengali), 2 vols., ed. Ahmed Sharif. Dacca: Bangla Academy, 1978.

Tarafdar, M. R. "Notes on Indo-Muslim Architecture". *Journal of the Asiatic Society of Pakistan* 11, no. 2 (August 1966): 127-41.

—— *Husain Shahi Bengal, 1494-1538 A.D. A Socio-Political Study.* Dhaka: Asiatic Society of Pakistan, 1965, 2nd rev. ed., Dhaka: University of Dhaka, 1999.

Thaw, Aung. *Historical Sites in Burma.* Ministry of Union Culture, Government of the Union of Burma, 1972, rpt. 1978.

The Forests of Bengal. Calcutta: Calcutta Revenue Department, Government of Bengal, 1935.

Tin, Pe Maung, and G. H. Luce. *The Glass Palace Chronicle of the Kings of Burma.* London, 1923.

Wali, Maulavi Abdul. "On the Antiquities and Traditions of the Jami Masjid and Rauza of Hazrat Muhammad Arab at Sailkupa, Sub-division of Jhenidah, District Jessore". *Journal of the Asiatic Society of Bengal*, 1 (1901): 15-28.

—— "On Some Archaeological Remains in the District of Rajshahi". *Journal of the Asiatic Society of Bengal* o.s., 73, pt. 1 (1904): 108-17.

—— "On the Antiquities and Traditions of Shahzadpur". *Journal of the Asiatic Society of Bengal* 1, no. 3 (1904): 262-71.

Welch, Anthony, and Howard Crane. "The Tughluqs: Master Builders of the Delhi Sultanate". *Muqarnas* 1 (1983): 123-66.

Westland, J. *A Report on the District of Jessore: Its Antiquities, its History, and its Commerce.* 2nd ed. Calcutta: Bengal Secretariat Press, 1871.

Wise, James. "Notes on Sonargaon". *Journal of the Asiatic Society of Bengal* 63 (1874): 88-92.

Zakariah, A. K. M. "Muhammad Bakhtiar's Conquest of Nudiah". *Journal of the Varendra Research Museum* 6 (1980-81): 57-72.

Zbavitel, Dusan. *Bengali Literature*, vol. 9, fasc. 3 of *A History of Indian Literature*, ed. Jan Gonda. Weisbaden: Otto Harrassowitz, 1976.

Index of Mosques

Aroshnagar Mosque, 67, 153-54, 209, 212; 121, 122

Baba Adam's Mosque, 45, 46, 54, 58, 59, 60, 65, 79, 85, 98-101, 209, 212; 29, 30, 68, 69

Baba Saleh's Mosque, 59, 67, 155-56, 209, 212; 123

Badr Awlia Dargah Jami Mosque, 48, 65, 102, 109-11, 199, 211; 77, 78

Bagha Mosque, 58, 61, 67, 92, 161-65, 170, 214, 186, 192, 193, 209, 213; 44, 127-30

Bandar Shahi Mosque, 58, 59, 60, 65, 74, 95-98, 111, 113, 153, 155, 209, 212; 65-67

Bibi Begni's Mosque, 66, 72, 120, 123-25, 212; 91-92

Bibi Chini's Mosque, 65, 87-88, 211; 58, 59

Binat Bibi's Mosque, 36, 38, 58, 59, 65, 80-82, 209, 212; 51-53

Chhota Sona Mosque, 46, 55, 59, 61, 64, 67, 73, 92, 94, 147-50, 152, 160, 162, 195, 209, 213; 112-18

Chunakhola Mosque, 66, 72, 143, 144-47, 203, 211; 111-14

Darasbari Mosque, 39, 46, 55, 58, 59, 60, 64, 65, 66, 92-95, 160, 161, 209, 213; 22, 23, 63, 64

Dhunichak Mosque, 65, 73, 105-7, 213; 73, 74

Faqir's Mosque, 58, 65, 66, 89-92, 190, 209, 211; 60-62

Fath Shah's Mosque, 48, 59, 61, 65, 101-3, 111, 199, 209, 212; 35, 36, 70

Galakata Mosque, 66, 72, 137-39, 212; 104, 105

Goaldi Mosque, 39, 58, 59, 61, 67, 74, 96, 100, 102, 157-59, 209, 213; 18, 19, 124

Gopalganj Mosque, 39, 59, 65, 82-83, 209, 212; 20, 21

Gorar Mosque, 67, 72, 169, 170-72, 183, 184, 185, 186, 224, 212; 135, 136

Hammad's Mosque, 58, 67, 188-90, 209, 211; 155, 156

Jorbangla Mosque, 58, 61, 67, 72, 178-80, 183, 209, 212; 143, 144

Kasba Mosque, 43, 66, 133-35, 211; 99, 100

Khania Dighi Mosque, 65, 73, 107-9, 213; 75, 76

Kusumba Mosque, 58, 61, 67, 162, 192, 193, 194, 195-97, 199, 209, 212; 46, 162-64

Majlis Awlia's Mosque, 54, 56, 67, 165-70, 184, 185, 188, 201, 206, 212; 131-34

Makhdum Shah's Mosque, 65, 84-87, 213; 54-57

Mankalir Bhita Mosque, 63, 75-76, 211; 47, 48

Manohar Dighi Mosque, 67, 72, 172-73, 212; 137, 138

Masjidbari Mosque, 15, 39, 58, 61, 66, 141-44, 209, 213; 108-10

Masjidkur Mosque, 43, 66, 111, 116, 127, 129, 130-33, 135, 202, 212; 96-98

Mosque adjoining Khan Jahan's Tomb, 72, 117-19, 212; 84-86

Muazzampur Shahi Jami Mosque, 54, 65, 77-79, 209, 213; 39, 49, 50

Nabagram Mosque, 61, 67, 128, 175-78, 209, 213; 141, 142

Nine-domed Mosque, 43, 66, 72, 116, 127-30, 137, 139, 177, 211; 25, 26, 95

Noongola Mosque, 67, 72, 180-81, 212; 145, 146
Osmanpur Gayebi Mosque, 67, 190-92, 213; 157, 158
Parbajpur Mosque, 67, 167, 169, 171, 183, 184-86, 188, 213; 151, 152
Pathagar Mosque, 67, 72, 181-82, 183, 212; 147, 148
Pirpukur Mosque, 67, 72, 174-75, 212; 139, 140
Qutb Shah's Mosque, 48, 68, 102, 196, 199-201, 212; 37, 38, 167
Ranbijoypur Mosque, 38, 66, 72, 120-23, 186, 202, 211; 87-90
Rezai Khan's Mosque, 67, 72, 186-88, 211; 153, 154
Sailkupa Mosque, 66, 139-41, 212; 106, 107
Shaitgumbad Mosque, 16, 46, 49, 50, 55, 64, 66, 67, 72, 94, 114-17, 120, 125, 137, 143, 144, 150, 159, 211; 33, 34, 81-83

Shankarpasha Mosque, 35, 54, 58, 67, 151-53, 206, 209, 213; 40, 119, 120
Shatgachhia Mosque, 66, 72, 128, 135-37, 139, 212; 101-2
Shatoir Mosque, 43, 65, 111-13, 212; 79, 80
Shialghuni Mosque, 68, 198-99, 201, 211; 165, 166
Shingra Mosque, 51, 66, 72, 125-27, 211; 93, 94
Shubhorara Mosque, 54, 68, 79, 99, 204-6, 212; 170-72
Shukur Mallik Mosque, 67, 72, 182-83, 186, 212; 149, 150
Sura Mosque, 67, 192-95, 196, 197, 212; 159-61
Ten-domed Mosque, 67, 72, 159-61, 211; 125, 126
Yusufganj Mosque, 65, 74, 103-4, 212; 71, 72
Zinda Pir's Mosque, 51, 68, 72, 143, 144, 186, 202-3, 204, 211; 168, 169

General Index

Reference to figures are in italics

Abbasid, 13, 43 n. 21
Abeyadana Temple, *see* Pagan
Abhaynagar, 204
ablution fountain, 46, 55
Abraham, 20
Abu Minhaj al-Din Usman ibn Siraj al-Din al-Juzjani, 9
Abul Fazl, 8, 9 n. 5
Abyssinian(s) (*habshi*), 13, 15, 16, 32, 62, 65
Adam, 20
Adina Mosque, *see* Malda
Afghan (s), 13, 15, 17, 18, 195
Afghanistan, 9
Agra, 44 n. 22, 69
Ahmad (Ahmed) Shah, 15, 61, 65, 78, 79, 207
Ahmed, A. S. M., 5, 79, 83, 87, 92, 95, 98, 107, 109, 117, 119, 123, 125, 127, 130, 133, 135, 141, 144, 147, 150, 153, 156, 159, 165, 170, 190, 195, 214
Ahmed, Shamsuddin, 76, 82, 83, 95, 98, 101, 103, 144, 150, 156, 159, 165, 178, 197, 214
Ajmer, 49, 58, 63, 175
    Arhai-din-ka-Jhompra Mosque, 49, 58
Ajyal Khan, 144
Ajyal Mina, 178
Akbar (Emperor), 3, 8, 13, 15, 18
al-Walid (caliph), 63
Ala al-Din Ali Shah (Sultan), 11, 207
Ala al-Din Husayn (Husain) Shah (Sultan), 16, 17, 139, 147, 150, 151, 153, 155, 156, 159, 165, 179, 188, 208

Alexander receiving Dara's daughter Roshanak, 26; *7*
Ali (local saint), 202
Ali, Abdullah Yusuf, 71
Ali Mardan, 10
Ali Mubarak, 11
Ali Musa Sultan, 79
Ali, son of Abi Talib, 103
al-Walid, 63
amalaka, 27, 30, 79, 170, 216
Ananda Temple, *see* Pagan
Anatolia, 102
Arab, 16, 43, 63
Arabia, 13, 43 n. 21, 63
Arakan, 9, 16
Arakanese, 15
Arhai-din-ka-Jhompra Mosque, *see* Ajmer
Arial Khan (river), 8
ariz, 11, 216
Arjuna, 20
Aroshnagar Mosque, *see* Khulna
Asher, Catherine, 5, 36 n. 13 & 14, 43 n. 19, 46 n. 24, 56 n. 35, 62 n. 43, 63 n. 45, 64 n. 46, 65 n. 49, 66 n. 50, 67 n. 54, 76, 87, 95, 101, 107, 109, 117, 144, 150, 159, 165, 195, 197, 199, 201, 203, 214
Ashraf al-Husaini, 159
Ashraf Barsbay, 15
Ashrafpur bronze stupa, 28; *9*
Ashta Sahasrika Prajnaparamita, 24, 28,
Assam, 9, 13, 67 n. 53, 153, 225
Astogram, 199
Atala Mosque, *see* Jaunpur

Atrai River, 195
avatar, 19, 20
azan, 50, 59, 81, 216

Baba Adam Shahid, 98
Baba Adam's Mosque, *see* Munshiganj
Baba Saleh, 95, 97, 98, 155, 156,
Baba Saleh's Mosque, *see* Narayanganj
Babur (Emperor), 17
Badr Alam, 18
Badr Awlia Dargah Jami Mosque, *see* Chittagong
Badrpati, 109
Bagerhat, 16, 23, 38, 42, 43, 46, 48, 49, 50, 51, 62, 64, 66, 67, 68, 72, 92, 94, 111, 113, 114-30, 137, 139, 143, 144-47, 155, 159-61, 170, 171, 177, 179, 186-88, 202-3, 204, 211, 215
    Bibi Begni's Mosque, 66, 72, 120, 123-25, 211; *91-92*
    Chunakhola Mosque, 66, 72, 143, 144-47, 203, 211; *111-14*
    Khan Jahan's Tomb, 66, 67, 72
    Mosque adjoining Khan Jahan's Tomb, 51, 66, 72, 117-19, 211; *84-86*
    Nine-domed Mosque, 43, 66, 72, 116, 127-30, 137, 139, 177, 211; *25, 26, 95*
    Ranbijoypur Mosque, 38, 66, 72, 120-23, 186, 202, 211; *87-90*
    Rezai Khan's Mosque, 67, 72, 186-88, 211; *153, 154*
    Shabekdanga, 155, 170
    Shaitgumbad Mosque, 16, 46, 48, 49, 50, 55, 64, 66, 67, 72, 94, 114-17, 120, 125, 137, 143, 144, 150, 159, 211; *33, 34, 81-83*
    Shingra Mosque, 51, 66, 72, 125-27, 211; *93, 94*
    Ten-domed Mosque, 67, 72, 159-61, 211; *125, 126*
    Zinda Pir's Mosque, 51, 68, 72, 143, 144, 186, 202-3, 204, 211; *168, 169*
Bagha Mosque, *see* Rajshahi
Baghi-Alam ka Gumbad, *see* Delhi
Bahlol, 178
Bahram Khan, 188, 190
Bakerganj, 135, 144, 198, 211
Balaganj, 190, 213
bamboo, 23, 25, 26, 29, 32, 49, 92, 116, 154, 204, 217
Bandar, 74, 95, 155
Bandar Shahi Mosque, *see* Narayanganj
Banga (Bangala, Bang), 8, 9, 10, 13,
Bangali, 9
bangla, 32, 51
Bangladesh, 2, 3, 4, 5, 7, 9, 16, 18, 28, 29, 39, 43, 46, 50, 60, 62, 63, 65, 66, 67, 71, 72, 73, 75, 87, 92, 114, 120, 147, 155, 161, 209
Bankura, 28
Bara Khan ka Gumbad, *see* Delhi
baraka, 54, 216
Barani, Zia al-Din, 8, 10
Barguna, Bibi Chini's Mosque, 65, 87-89, 211; *58, 59*
Bari, M. A., 5, 37, 107, 109, 117, 119, 123, 125, 127, 130, 133, 135, 137, 147, 155, 161, 172, 188, 203, 214
Bari Masjid, *see* Hughly
Barind, 7, 10
Barisal, 8, 43, 66, 68, 72, 111, 133, 134, 143, 98, 199, 211
    Kasba Mosque, , 43, 66, 111, 133-35, 211; *99, 100*
    Shialghuni Mosque, 68, 198-99, 201, 211; *165, 166*
Baro Bhuiyans, 18
Barobazar, 16, 58, 62, 66, 67, 71, 72, 73, 135-39, 170-75, 178-83, 188
    Galakata Mosque, 66, 72, 137, 139, 212; *104, 105*
    Gorar Mosque, 67, 72, 169, 170-72, 183, 184, 185, 186, 212; *135, 136*
    Jorbangla Mosque, 58, 61, 67, 72, 178-80, 183, 212; *143, 144*
    Manohar Dighi Mosque, 67, 72, 172-73, 212; *137, 138*
    Noongola Mosque, 67, 72, 180-81, 212; *145, 146*
    Pathagar Mosque, 67, 72, 181-82, 183, 212; *47, 148*
    Pirpukur Mosque, 67, 72, 174-75, 212; *139, 140*
    Sadiqpur Mosque, 72
    Shatgachhia Mosque, 66, 72, 128, 135-37, 139, 212; *101, 102*
    Shukur Mallik Mosque, 67, 72, 182-83, 186, 212; *149, 150*
Baror, 83,
Basu, Maladhar, 19
Bay of Bengal, 7, 15
Bayazid Bistami, 125
Bayazid Shah, 246
Bebe Paya Temple, *see* Hmawza
Bedaralgafelin, 20

INDEX

Belat Daulatpur, 174
Benaras, 13
Bengal, 3, 4, 5, 7-21, 23, 25-69, 71, 72, 75, 96,
    98, 102, 120, 130, 135, 140, 153, 190,
    198, 199, 201, 207
Bengal style, 32-69, 196
Bengal Sultanate, 11, 16, 66, 72, 75
Bengali, 4, 7, 8, 9, 12, 13, 14, 15, 19, 20, 21,
    23, 25, 31, 32, 35, 37, 41, 43, 44, 65,
    128, 188, 216
Bengali Muslim, 15, 19, 21, 41
Betagi, 87, 211
Beveridge, H., 89, 95, 135, 141, 144, 150, 199,
    215
bhadra, 27, 28, 29, 31, 216; *9*
Bhagirathi (-Hughly), 8, 18
Bhairab River, 72, 204
Bhanga, 165, 212
Bhati, 9
Bhattasali, N. K., 11, 158
Bibi Begni's Mosque, *see* Bagerhat
Bibi Chini's Mosque, *see* Barguna
Bihar, 9, 10, 13, 16, 17, 34, 57, 67, 83, 201
Bijapur, 15
bil, 8, 111, 216
Bilecik, 102; *29*
Binat Bibi's Mosque, *see* Dhaka
Bishnupur, Shyama-Raya Temple, 199
Bismillah, 59, 216
Bistam, 125
Blochmann, H., 83, 98, 101, 155, 156, 159,
    214,
Boalmari, 111, 212
Bodhgaya, 57
Bogra, 63, 75, 211
    Mankalir Bhita (Mankali-ka Kundi)
    Mosque, 63, 75-76; *47, 48*
Brahma, 40
Brahman (s), 10, 17, 18, 19, 20, 52, 216
Brahmaputra River, 7, 9, 73
Brick construction, 34-35
British, 8, 9, 69
Buddhas, 28, 31, 219; *10*
Buddhism, 30
Buddhist, 3, 14, 23, 27, 28, 30, 31, 34, 36, 57,
    65, 158, 190, 201, 216, 219
Bukhara, Samanid Tomb, 37, 120
Bulghampur, 10
Burma (Myanmar), 7, 15, 24, 29, 30, 51, 57
Burmese, 20, 31, 51, 57 n. 37, 216, 219

Calcutta, 92, 141

Cambay, Great Mosque, 59
Cambodia, 29
Cambridge University Library, 28, 29, 30
central aisle, 39, 46, 63, 64, 67, 93, 94, 114,
    115, 148, 149; *32, 63, 116*
Central Asia, 31, 37
central Islamic lands, 21, 34, 43, 63
chahar taq, 37, 216
chain and bell, 94, 133, 139, 141, 169, 182
chain and lamp, 79
Chaitanya, 19
Chakravarti, M. M., 4, 82, 83, 101, 150, 159,
    165, 197, 214
chala, 24, 25, 27, 32, 37, 69, 114, 115, 216; *14*
Chamkatti Mosque, *see* Malda
Champanir, Jami Mosque, 51
Champaran, 13
Chandi, 20
Chandidas, Baru, 14
Charyapadas, 14
chati, 12
Chatigram, 12
chau-chala, 25, 39, 46, 64, 65, 67, 75, 92, 94,
    115, 116, 142, 148, 149, 150, 167, 189,
    217; *5, 62, 82*
chhatris, 96, 217
Chhota Pandua, Bari Masjid, 50, 56, 64, 75, 87
Chhota Sona Mosque, *see* Gaur
China, 12 n. 17, 13, 19 n. 39
Chinese, 12, 15, 19, 218
Chishti, 14, 175, 217
Chittagong, 8, 9, 11, 12, 17, 19, 109, 209, 211
    Badr Awlia Dargah Jami Mosque, 48, 65,
        102, 109-11, 199, 209; *77, 78*
    Faqir's Mosque, 58, 65, 66, 89-92, 190, 209;
        60-62
    Hammad's Mosque, 58, 67, 188-90, 209;
        155, 156
Chittagong Hill Tracts, 8
Chunakhola Mosque, *see* Bagerhat
circular towers, 114, 116, 118, 120, 123, 126,
    130, 135, 157, 176, 189, 200
Comilla, 7
corbelled pendentives, 58, 63, 68, 89, 94, 98,
    108, 112, 115, 125, 126, 130, 149, 157,
    160, 162, 167, 171, 177, 187, 192, 193,
    196, 200; *44*
Creighton, H., 5, 147
Cunningham, Alexander, 56 n. 35, 75, 76, 95,
    101, 102, 103, 109, 147, 149, 150, 214
curved cornice, 23, 37, 49, 65, 68, 80, 87, 94,
    101, 102, 109, 157, 188, 196

curved eave, 27

dabir-i-khas, 17, 217
Dakhil Darwaza, *see* Malda
Damascus, Great Mosque, 50, 63
Dand-Bhukti, 29
Dani, A. H., 4, 36, 44, 46, 50, 56, 62, 63, 64, 65, 66, 67, 76, 82, 83, 87, 95, 101, 107, 109, 117, 133, 135, 141, 144, 150, 153, 159, 165, 170, 176, 177, 178, 192, 195, 197, 201, 214
Darasbari Mosque, *see* Gaur
Dargabari Shahi Jami Masjid, 101
dargah, 64, 98, 109, 217
Dargapara, 98, 139
Daud Khan Karrani (Sultan), 13, 18, 208
Delhi, 2, 3, 8, 9, 10, 11, 13, 14, 17, 18, 37, 43, 44, 46, 49, 50, 51, 58, 59, 63, 64, 66, 69, 207
  Alai Darwaza, 37, 59
  Baghi-Alam ka Gumbad, 59
  Bara Khan ka Gumbad, 59
  Jahanpanah (Begumpur) Mosque, 43
  Jamatkhana Mosque, 49, 51, 102, 200
  Kalan Mosque, 37
  Khirki Mosque, 37, 43, 50, 115, 201
  Kotla Mosque, 44
  Quwwat al-Islam Mosque, 46, 58
  tomb of Iltutmish (Sultan), 37, 51
  tomb of Sultan Ghari, 49, 59
Department of Archaeology, 5, 71, 72, 75, 92, 98, 105, 107, 114, 120, 123, 125, 127, 130, 133, 135, 138, 141, 144, 147, 153, 157, 161, 165, 170, 174, 178, 180, 181, 182, 186, 187, 192, 195, 200, 214
Devkot, 10, 207
Dhaka, 2, 4, 5, 7, 8, 19, 28, 36, 56, 65, 72 n. 2, 73, 77, 80, 81, 82, 95, 96, 147, 150, 155, 158, 165, 170, 188, 190, 192, 195, 209, 211, 212, 214, 215
  Binat Bibi's Mosque, 36, 38, 58, 59, 65, 80-82, 209, 212; *51-53*
Dhaleswari (River), 73
Dharma, 20
Dhunichak Mosque, *see* Gaur
Dighir Par, 117, 127
Dikshit, K. N., 130, 153, 197
Dinajpur, 10, 27, 44 n. 22, 82, 192, 193, 194, 199, 209, 212
  Gopalganj Mosque, 39, 59, 65, 82-83, 209; *20-21*
  Kantaji's Temple, 199

Sura Mosque, 67, 192-95, 196, 197; *159-61*
tomb of Chehel Ghazi, 82
do-chala, 25, 32, 154, 167, 188, 201, 217; *2, 6*
Dulai Khal, 80

Early Sultanate period, 63, 75-77
East Bengal, 4, 7 n. 1, 9, 18, 30
East Pakistan, 117, 123, 125, 130, 197
East India Company, 7, 9
Eaton, Richard M., 5, 12, 14 n. 24 and 26, 15 n. 28, 16 n. 32, 51 n. 29, 66 n. 51, 79, 92, 144, 190, 208, 214
Egarasindur, Sadi's Mosque, 199, 201, 202
Egypt, 15
Eklakhi Tomb, *see* Pandua
enamelled tiles, 66
engaged corner towers, 37, 49-51, 63, 65, 66, 76, 90, 98, 112, 127, 128, 133, 157, 162, 185, 191

Fakhr al-Din Mubarak Shah (Sultan, Fakhra), 11, 207
faqir, 89, 114, 217
Faqir's Mosque, *see* Chittagong
Faridpur, 15, 43, 54, 56, 65, 67, 111, 133, 165, 170, 184, 185, 188, 201, 206, 212
  Majlis Awlia's Mosque, 54, 56, 67, 165-70, 184, 185, 188, 201, 206, 212; *131-34*
  Shatoir Mosque, 43, 65, 111-13, 212; *79, 80*
Fath Shah's Mosque, *see* Sonargaon
Fathabad, 15
Fei Sin, 73
Firdawsi, 14, 217
Firishta, 15, 34
Firuz Khan, 79
Firuz Shah Tughluq (Sultan), 13, 43, 44
Firuzabad (Pandua), 11, 13
Fitch, Ralph, 73
five-lobed leaf, 125, 127, 128, 133, 185, 165, 169, 183, 185, 188
four-petalled flower, 125, 133, 156, 158, 163, 171, 172, 175, 182, 185
Friday mosque, 59, 62, 80

Galakata Mosque, *see* Barobazar
Ganges (River), 7, 8, 10, 18
Garamsir, 9
Garuda, 20
Gaur, 4, 5, 9, 10, 15, 17, 19, 39, 44 n. 22, 46, 62, 64, 65, 66, 73, 92, 105, 107, 109, 132, 133, 147, 150, 152, 160, 161, 188, 202, 203, 207, 208, 214, 215

INDEX

Chhota Sona Mosque, 46, 55, 58, 59, 61, 64, 67, 92, 94, 147-50, 152, 160, 162, 195, 209, 213; *115-18*
Darasbari Mosque, 39, 46, 55, 58, 59, 60, 64, 65, 66, 73, 92-95, 160, 161, 162, 209, 213; *22, 23, 63, 64*
Dhunichak Mosque, 65, 73, 105-7, 213; *73, 74*
Khania Dighi Mosque, 65, 73, 107-9, 213; *75, 76*
for monuments in Gaur, India, see Malda
Gaurnadi, 133, 211
Gayebi Masjid, *see* Shankarpasha Mosque
ghazis, 12, 217
Ghiyath al-Din Azam Shah (Sultan), 13, 14, 207
Ghiyath (Ghiath) al-Din Bahadur (Shah) (Sultan), 11, 195, 197, 208
Ghiyath al-Din Balban (Sultan), 10
Ghiyath al-Din Iwaz Khalji (Sultan), 10
Ghiyath al-Din Mahmud Shah (Sultan), 17, 188, 190, 208
Ghiyath al-Din Tughluq (Sultan), 11, 37
Ghiyath al-Dunya wal-Din, 61
Ghoradighi, 114, 123
Ghoraghat, 192, 212
Goaldi Mosque, *see* Narayanganj
Godard, Andre, 37
Gopalganj Mosque, *see* Dinajpur
Gorar Mosque, *see* Barobazar
Gujarat, 49, 59
Gumti Gate, *see* Malda
Gunmant Mosque, *see* Malda

Habiganj, 35, 54, 67, 151, 206, 209, 212
Shankarpasha Mosque, 35, 54, 58, 67, 151-53, 206, 209, 212; *40, 119, 120*
Hadith, 58, 59, 60, 95, 97, 101, 103, 144, 150, 155, 159, 165, 178, 179, 217
Hafiz, 14
haiyya falah, 81
Haji Baba Saleh, *see* Baba Saleh
Hammad's Mosque, *see* Chittagong
Hanafi, 15, 217
hanging motif, 79, 83, 95, 96, 98, 107, 113, 122, 125, 129, 137, 139, 141, 145, 150, 158, 162, 172, 177, 179, 183, 194, 201
haor, 199, 217
Hari, 20
Haruniyya Tomb, 128
Hasan, S. M., 5, 79, 92, 95, 98, 101, 109, 117, 119, 123, 127, 130, 133, 135, 141, 144, 147, 150, 153, 159, 165, 186, 195, 215

Hathazari, 89, 211
Haveli Khalifatabad, 66
Hazrat Haji Shah Sharif Jinnani, 175
Hindu, 3, 9, 12, 13, 14, 15, 17, 18, 20, 23, 27, 31, 34, 36, 44, 69, 73, 98, 135, 158, 201, 216, 218, 219
Hinduism, 18, 219
Hizbar Khan, 58
Hmawza, 30, 31, 51, 52, 57
Bebe Paya Temple, 31, 52; *4, 13*
Lemyethna Temple, 31, 52; *11, 12*
Hughly, 36, 44, 50, 62, 64
Molla Simla Mosque, 36, 64
Zafar Khan Ghazi's Mosque, 44-46, 56, 58, 62, 63, 64, 75; *27, 28*
Hughly (river), 8, 18, 19
Humayun (Emperor), 17, 208
Husayn Shah Sharqi (Sultan), 16
Husayn Shahi (Dynasty), 13, 16-17, 19, 32, 61, 62, 67
hut(s), 23, 25, 28, 29, 30, 32, 35, 37, 39, 49, 50, 92, 115, 116, 142, 178, 216, 217; *2, 5, 6*
hut-mosques, 35; *15*

Ibn Battuta, 9, 12, 73
Ibrahim Adil Shah (Sultan), 15
Ibrahim Sharqi (Sultan), 15
Ikhtiyar al-Din Muhammad Bakhtiyar, 9, 10
Ilyas Shahi (Dynasty), 12, 13-14, 62, 63, 64, 65, 207
imam, 13, 51, 55, 217
imam al-azam, 13
Independent Sultanate, 3, 11-18, 63, 73
India(n), 1, 4, 5, 7, 9, 10, 11, 12, 13, 14, 17, 18, 19, 27, 29, 30, 34, 36, 49, 50, 51, 57, 58, 59, 62, 63, 64, 65, 69, 73, 83, 87, 92, 107, 109, 135, 147, 185, 196, 214, 215, 217, 219
Indian Museum, 92, 141, 144
iqlim, 103
Iran, 1, 13, 31 n. 8, 37, 128, 130
Isfahan, Masjid-i Jami, 125, 128
Iskandar Nama, 26, 27 n. 1; *7*
Islam(ic), Islamization, 2, 4, 5, 9, 11, 12, 14, 15 n. 28, 16, 18, 19, 20, 21, 32, 34, 36 n. 13, 37, 41, 43, 46, 50, 52, 54 n. 33, 59, 60, 61 n. 41, 63, 66, 79, 81, 82, 85, 92, 95, 98, 101, 103, 109, 119, 120, 130, 133, 144, 150, 153, 155, 156, 159, 165, 178, 180, 190, 197, 201, 214, 215, 218, 219

Islam Shah, 17, 208 37
Islamic architecture, 1, 2, 34
Islamic art, 1

Jadu, 14, *see* Jalal al-Din Muhammad
jagir, 17, 217
Jahangir (Emperor), 13, 18
Jahanpanah (Begumpur) Mosque, *see* Delhi
Jain, 27
Jajnagar (Orissa), 13
Jalal al-Din Fath Shah (Sultan), 16, 97, 101, 103, 208
Jalal al-Din Muhammad Shah (Sultan), 15, 16, 37, 65, 207
Jalal al-Dunya wal-Din, 61
jali, 139, 175, 217
Jamatkhana Mosque, *see* Delhi
jamdar ghayr mahalli, 61, 217
jami, 48, 51, 54, 58, 65, 74, 77, 95, 101, 102, 109, 111, 125, 128, 150, 165, 199, 206, 209, 211, 213, 217, 218
Jamuna (river), 7
jangdar, 61, 83, 178, 217
Jaunpur, 13, 15, 16, 17, 49, 50, 51
    Atala Mosque, 51
    Jami Mosque, 51
Jessore, 15, 54, 66, 68, 72, 117, 133, 135, 204, 212
    Shubhorara Mosque, 54, 68, 79, 99, 169, 204-6, 212; *170-72*
Jesus, 20
Jhenaidah, 16, 66, 72, 135, 137, 139, 170, 172, 174, 178, 180, 181, 182, 209, 212
    Sailkupa Mosque, 66, 139-41, 212; *106, 107*
    see also mosques under Barobazar
Jorbangla Mosque, *see* Barobazar

Kabadak (river), 130
kabir, 58, 79
Kalan Mosque, *see* Delhi
kalasha, 79, 83, 95, 96, 107, 109, 119, 145, 150, 168, 169, 170, 193, 194, 196, 201, 205, 218
Kaliganj, 135, 170, 172, 174, 178, 180, 181, 182, 184, 212, 213
Kaliya, 20,
Kamhina, 179
Kamrup (Kamrud), 9, 10, 13
Kantaji's Temple, *see* Dinajpur
Kara, 11
Karatoya (river), 9, 84

Karim, Abdul, 5, 8 n. 4, 11 n. 12, 13 n. 19 & 22, 15 n. 27, 28 & 29, 16 n. 31 & 32, 61 n. 41 & 42, 63 n. 45, 66 n. 51 & 52, 71, 72 n. 2, 83, 87, 92, 95, 98, 101, 103, 119, 144, 150, 156, 159, 165, 178, 188, 190, 197, 215
Karrani Dynasty, 13, 17-18, 62, 67, 208
Kasba Mosque, *see* Barisal
Kathmandu, 13
Kavindra Paramesvara, 19, 20
khadem, 176, 218
khalifa(h), caliph, 13, 43 n. 21, 63, 72, 150, 218
khalifat Allah, 15, 16
khalifat Allah bil hujjat wal burhan, 16
Khalifatabad, 5, 16, 37 n. 17, 66, 72, 117, 119, 123, 125, 127, 130, 133, 135, 137, 147, 155, 161, 172, 188, 203, 214
Khalji, 9, 10, 62
khamba, 114, 218
Khan, M. A. A., 5, 73 n. 5, 95, 109, 150, 215
Khan Jahan (Ulugh Khan-i Azam Khan Jahan), 13, 15, 16, 18, 51, 62, 66, 67, 72, 123, 127, 128, 159, 172, 186, 202, 211
Khan Jahan style, 16, 37, 50, 66-67, 90, 92, 111, 113, 114-47, 159, 172, 186, 202
Khan Jahan's Tomb, *see* Bagerhat
Khan, Hamid, 188
Khan Muazzam Mubarak Khan Nazir, 178
Khania Dighi Mosque, *see* Gaur
Khan-i-Jahan Junan Shah, 43
khanqa, 62, 218
Khaqan, 83, 218
Khirki Mosque, *see* Delhi
Khondkartola, 95
Khulna, 8, 15, 43, 66, 67, 111, 116, 117, 127, 129, 130, 133, 135, 144, 153, 161, 186, 203, 204, 206, 209, 212
    Aroshnagar Mosque, 61, 67, 153-55, 209, 212; *121, 122*
    Masjidkur Mosque, 43, 66, 111, 116, 127, 129, 130-33, 135, 212; *96-98*
Khwaja Moinuddin Chis(h)ti, 175
Khwaja Nizam al-Din Ahmad, 15
kiosk mosque, 31 n. 8, 37
Kishoreganj, 48, 68, 102, 196, 199, 212
    Qutb Shah's Mosque, 48, 68, 102, 196, 199-201, 212; *37, 38, 167*
    Sadi's Mosque, *see* Egarasindur
Koch (Kuch), 9,
Kotla Mosque, *see* Delhi
Kotwali, 82
Kotwali Gate, *see* Malda

INDEX

Koyra, 130, 212
Krishna, 14, 19, 20
Krishna Mangala, 19
Krishnanagar, 159
Kusumba Mosque, *see* Naogaon

Laili Majnu, 188, 190
Lakhnawti (Lakshmanavati), 9, 10, 11, 18, 62, 73, 107, 109, 150
Lakshmansena, 9, 10, 73
Lalmai, 7
Lamapara, 190
Late Sultanate Period, 62, 67-69, 72, 147-206
Lattan Mosque, *see* Malda
Laud, 103
Lemyethna Temple, *see* Hmawza

Madhupur, 7, 8
Madina (Medina), 13, 50, 156
    Mosque of the Prophet, 50
madrasa, 13, 15, 19, 62, 92, 175, 218
Mahabharata, 19, 20
Mahananda (River), 73
Mahasthan, 63, 75, 76
Mahasthangarh, 75
Mahmudabad, 16, 73, 103
Mahuan, 73
Majampur (Muazzampur), 77
majlis al-majalis majlis mansur, 61, 218
Majlis Awlia Saheb, 165
Majlis Awlia's Mosque, *see* Faridpur
makara, 167, 201, 218
Makhdum Shah's Mosque, *see* Sirajganj
Makka (Mecca), 13, 15, 77, 98, 156, 217
Malda, 9, 36, 41, 46, 50, 65, 73, 132, 147, 188, 202
    Adina Mosque, 41, 43, 46, 49, 50, 55, 56, 63-64, 66, 67, 75, 87, 94, 95, 160, 214; *31, 32, 43*
    Chamkatti Mosque, 107, 109
    Dakhil Darwaza, 66, 132
    Eklakhi Tomb, 36, 37, 49, 65-66, 67, *16, 17*
    Gumti Gate, 67
    Gunmant Mosque, 46, 64
    Kotwali Gate, 92, 107
    Lattan Mosque, 67
    Qadam Rasul, 188, 202, 203
    Tantipara Mosque, 105, 107
    tomb of Sultan Sikandar Shah, 37
malik, 61, 98, 101, 103, 156, 179, 218, 82, 123, 125, 129, 215
malik al-muazzam, 61, 218

Malik Baba Saleh, 97, *see* Baba Saleh
Malik Kafur, 101
Malik Yuz al-Din Tughral, 9
Mamluk, 15, 62
Manasa, 19, 20
Manasa-Mangala, 19
Manasa-Vijaya, 19
Manda, 195
Mandu, Jami Mosque, 51
Mankalir Bhita (Mankali-ka Kundi) Mosque, *see* Bogra
Manohar Dighi Mosque, *see* Barobazar
maqsura, 43, 137, 172, 175, 218
Marhamat, 58, 82
Marshall, Sir John, 56
masjid, 3, 50, 56, 58, 64, 75, 87, 101, 111, 125, 128, 147, 151, 218
masjid al-jami, 58, 80
Masjida, 188
Masjidbari, 15, 39, 41, 58, 61, 66, 88, 141, 142, 143, 202, 209, 213
Masjidbari Mosque, *see* Patuakhali
Masjidkur Mosque, *see* Khulna
Masjidpara, 139Muhammad
Mawlana Muhammad Arab, 139, 141
Mawlana Muzaffar Shams Balkhi, 14
Mawlana Shah Muazzam Danishmand (Shah Dawlah), 161
Meghna (river), 7, 73
Merv, 128
mesh (pattern), 109, 125, 127, 128, 133, 139, 143, 144, 147, 179, 181, 182, 203
Middle Sultanate Period, 65, 67, 72, 77-113
Mihkhan, 179
mihrabs, 51-55; *39, 40*
minaret, 2, 46, 49, 50-51
minbar, 64, 75, 85, 87, 93, 155, 175, 218; *54, 55*
Minhaj al-Siraj (Minhaj-ud Din Abu Umar-i-Usman), 9, 10 n. 1, 62 n. 44,
Mir Bahr, 61, 178, 218
Mir Namwar Khan, 75
Mirzaganj, 141, 213
Mithapukur, 180
Modhukhali, 111
Mograpara, 101, 103
Molla Simla Mosque, *see* Hughly
Moses, 20
Mosque Adjoining Khan Jahan Jahan's Tomb, *see* Bagerhat
Mosque of the Prophet, *see* Madina
Muazzampur, 73

Muazzampur Shahi Jami Mosque, *see* Sonargaon
muezzin, 184, 218
Mughal, 3, 8, 13, 17, 18, 44, 46 n. 24, 67, 69, 73, 89, 96, 101, 102, 188, 200, 201, 216, 219
Mughal style, 69, 201
Muhammad (the Prophet), 13, 20, 50, 51, 60, 63, 81, 95, 97, 100, 103, 144, 150, 155, 156, 158, 165, 178, 179, 197, 217, 219
Muhammad Abdul Qadir, 153, 179, 180
Muhammad bin Tughluq (Sultan), 11
Muhammad Enamul Haq, 11 n. 13, 15 n. 27
Muhammad ibn Bakhtiyar Khalji, 62
Muhammad Shah Ghazi, 197
Muhammadabad, 73, 179
Muiz al-Din Muhammad Ghuri, (Sultan), 10
Mulla Hizbar Akbar Khan, 58, 159
Munawwar Ana (or Manurana), 178
Munghyr, 34, Pir Shah Nafa's tomb, 67 n. 53
Munshiganj, 34 n. 12, 44 n. 22, 45, 46, 54, 65, 85, 98, 99, 100, 206, 209, 212
    Baba Adam's Mosque, 34 n. 12, 45, 46, 54, 58, 59, 65, 79, 85, 98-101, 212; *29, 30, 68, 69*
muqarrab al-dawla(t), 61, 218
Musammat Bakht Binat, 58, 82
mutawalli, 140, 184, 218
Myanmar (Burma), 7, 15, 23, 24, 29, 30, 31 n. 6, 51, 57
Mymensingh, 7, 8, 10

Nabagram Mosque, *see* Sirajganj
Nabi Bangsha, 20
Nadiya, 9
nagara (temples) 27, 218
Nalanda, 57
Naoda, 9
Naoga, 175, 195
Naogaon, 68, 195, 209, 212
    Kusumba Mosque, 68, 69, 162, 192, 193, 194, 195-97, 198, 199, 209, 212; *46, 162-64*
Narayanganj, 65, 67, 73, 74, 77, 95, 101, 103, 113, 153, 155, 156, 157, 212
    Baba Saleh's Mosque, 59, 67, 74, 95, 155-56, 209, 212; *123*
    Bandar Shahi Mosque, 58, 59, 60, 65, 74, 95-98, 111, 113, 153, 155, 209, 212; *65-67*
    for other mosques in Narayanganj district *see* Sonargaon
Narasimha Vishnu, *41*

Narinda, 36, 80
Nasir al-Din Mahmud Shah (Sultan), 15, 65, 72, 73, 83, 95, 97, 101, 103, 144, 179, 188, 190, 208
Nasir al-Din Nusrat Shah (Sultan), 16, 17, 26, 27 n. 1, 139, 165, 178, 208
Nasir al-Dunya wal-Din, 61, 165
naskhi, 61, 218
Nawabganj, 73, 92, 105, 107, 147, 213
    see mosques listed under Gaur
Nepal, 13, 28, 29
Niamati, 87
nine-domed, 39, 41-44, 67, 111, 120
Nine-domed Mosque, *see* Bagerhat
Nishapur, 128
Noah, 20
Noongola Mosque, *see* Barobazar
North Africa, 46
north Indian temples, 185, 219
Nur Qutb Alam, 14, 15

octagonal corner towers, 68, 78, 80, 81, 89, 95, 100, 110, 111, 142, 148, 151, 152, 154, 156, 172, 175, 178, 179, 181, 193, 196, 198, 199, 200, 202
Old Dhaka, 80
Orhan Ghazi, 102
Orissa, 13, 16, 18, 67 n. 53
Osmanpur Gayebi Mosque, *see* Sylhet

Padma (River), 7, 8, 18, 111
Pagan, 29, 30, 31, 57
    Abeyadana Temple, 29
    Ananda Temple, 29, 30, 31
    Patothamya Temple, 29
pagodas, 31
Paharpur, 29, 30, 31, 33 n. 10, 34
Pakistan, 9, 117, 123, 125, 130, 170, 197, 214, 215
Pala, 28, 73
Pandua, 4, 11, 13, 14, 19, 35, 36, 37, 41, 47, 50, 56, 57, 63, 65, 66, 67, 73, 75, 87, 94, 95, 160, 207, 214, 215
    for monuments *see* Malda
Parbajpur Mosque, *see* Satkhira
pargana, 151, 218
Pathagar Mosque, *see* Barobazar
Pathrail, 165
Patna, 56 n. 35, 214
    Sher Shah's Mosque, 201
Patothamya Temple, *see* Pagan

Index

Patuakhali, 15, 39, 41, 66, 72, 87, 141, 142, 143, 202, 209, 213
    Masjidbari Mosque, 15, 39, 58, 61, 66, 88, 141-44, 202, 209, 213; *24, 108-10*
Persia, 13, 58, 63
Persian(ized), 4, 9, 14, 19, 59, 61 n. 41, 71, 72 n. 2, 73, 80, 81, 83, 125, 128, 144, 158, 197, 215, 216
Phultola, 204
pir, 12, 18, 19, 51, 72, 77, 218, 30, 38, 39, 73, 93, 99
Pir Badr, 11, 12, 109
Pir Majlis Abd Allah Khan (Majlis Awlia Saheb), 165
Pir Makhdum Shah Dawlah Shahid, 84
Pir Manna Shah Darvesh, 101
Pirpukur Mosque, *see* Barobazar
pointed arch(es), 57-58, 63, 87, 88, 108, 109, 110, 111, 112, 119, 126, 127, 128, 131, 135, 137, 141, 142, 160, 171, 191
pond, 55, 89, 92, 114, 120, 133, 135, 139, 153, 161, 165, 170, 172, 174, 178, 180, 181, 188, 217
Portugese, 17
prasada, 29, 219
pre-Islamic, 3, 9, 10, 27, 30, 31, 37, 44, 50, 51, 55, 57
pre-Mughal, 5, 9, 37 n. 16, 83, 95, 101, 123, 150, 165, 197, 214, 215
Prome, 31
puja, 52, 219
Pundranagar, 44, 75, 117, 123, 130, 147, 150, 214
Pundravardhana, 75
Puranas, 20
Puri, 18
purna kalasha, 201
Purnia, 83
pyatthat, 29, 219
Pyus, 30

Qabil, 20
Qadam Rasul, *see* Malda
Qadr Khan, 11
qibla, 3, 38, 44, 51, 52, 55, 63, 64, 218, 219
Quran, 20, 59, 71, 83, 95, 97, 100, 103, 150, 156, 158, 202, 219
Quranic, 58, 59, 60, 61, 71, 91, 190, 216
Qutb Saheb, 199
Qutb Shah's Mosque, *see* Kishoreganj
Quwwat al-Islam Mosque, *see* Delhi

Radha, 19
Raja Ganesh (dynasty), 12, 14-15, 37, 62, 65, 73, 207
rajas, 13
Rajasthan, 69
Rajbibi Mosque *see* Khania Dighi Mosque
Rajmahal, 18, 34
Rajshahi, 5, 9, 12 n. 14, 36 n. 13, 37 n. 17, 55, 60, 67, 72, 92, 153, 161, 163, 164, 165, 175, 197, 198, 209, 213, 214
    Bagha Mosque, 58, 61, 67, 92, 161-65, 170, 179, 186, 192, 193, 209, 213; *44, 127-30*
Rama, 20
Rampal, 98
Ranbijoypur Mosque, *see* Bagerhat
Rarh (Ral), 10
ratha, 55, 167, 169, 185, 219
ratna, 32, 219
rectangular mosque, 4, 44-49, 58, 62, 65
Rennell, James, 7, 8 n. 2
Restored Ilyas Shahi (dynasty), 12, 15-16, 32, 62, 65, 73, 208
Rezai Khan's Mosque, *see* Bagerhat
Ribat-i Sharaf, 128
Riyazu-s-Salatin, 9, 15
Royal Scottish Museum, 150
(Rukn al-Din) Barbak Shah, 15, 66, 83, 92, 95, 141, 144, 208
Rukn al-Dunya wal-Din, 61, 83, 144
Rup, 17

Sadi's Mosque, *see* Egarasindur
Sadiqpur Mosque, *see* Barobazar
Sailkupa Mosque, *see* Jhenaidah
Saiyid Ahmad Yasavi, 12
Saiyid Sultan, 20
Salim, Ghulam Husain, 9, 15 n. 27 & 29
Samanid Tomb, *see* Bukhara
Sanatan, 17
Sanskrit, 19, 216
Saran, 16
Saraswati, S. K., 4, 29 n. 2 & 4, 30 n. 5, 31 n. 6 & 7, 83, 95, 101, 135, 150, 159, 165, 197, 215
Sar-i-lashkar, 61, 103
Sasanian, 37,
Satgaon, 10, 11, 13, 18, 19
Satkhira, 66, 67, 72, 167, 184, 185, 188, 213
    Parbajpur Mosque, 67, 167, 169, 171, 172, 183, 184-86, 188, 213; *151, 152*
Sekh Munshi Chamiruddin, 20

Sena, 9, 73
Shabekdanga, *see* Bagerhat
Shah Badr Alam, 11, 18
Shah Jalal, 12, 18
Shah Langar, 77
shahada, 81, 219
Shah-i Bangaliyan, 13
Shahi Jami Masjid, *see* Shatoir Mosque
Shahzadpur, 65, 84, 85, 86, 213, 215
Shaitgumbad Mosque, *see* Bagerhat
Shams al-Din Ahmad Shah (Sultan), 13, 15, 61, 65, 78, 79, 207
Shams al-Din Firuz Shah (Sultan), 10, 11
Shams al-Din Ilyas Shah (Sultan), 13, 15, 73
Shams al-Din Muhammad Shah (Sultan), 17, 197, 208
Shams al-Din Muzaffar Shah (Sultan), 16, 208
Shams al-Din Yusuf Shah (Sultan), 61, 89, 92, 95, 208
Shams al-Dunya wal-Din, 61, 92, 95
Shams-i-Siraj Afif, 13
Shankarpasha Mosque, *see* Habiganj
Sharif, Ahmed, 14 n. 25, 20 n. 41
Shatgachhia Mosque, *see* Barobazar
Shatoir Mosque, *see* Faridpur
Shaykh Abdul Moudud, 184
Shaykh Ali, 12
Shaykh Muhammad Yusuf, 101
Shaykh Nur Qutb Alam, 14, 15
shaykh(s), 11, 12
Sher Shah (Khan) Sur, 17, 73, 201, 208,
Sher Shah's Mosque, *see* Patna
Shialghuni Mosque, *see* Barisal
Shibganj, 75, 92, 105, 107, 147, 211, 213
Shikarhat, 204,
shikhara, 30, 31, 219
shikhara temples, 27, 55; *8*
shikhara-shirsha bhadra, 29; *3, 10*
Shingra Mosque, *see* Bagerhat
shiqdar, 61, 83, 219
Shiraz, 14
Shiva, 20, 44 n. 22, 218
Shubhorara Mosque, *see* Jessore
Shukur Mallik Mosque, *see* Barobazar
Shundorghona, 114, 125, 186
Shyama-Raya Temple, *see* Bishnupur
Siddiq, M. Y., 61, 79, 82, 83, 92, 95, 98, 101, 103, 119, 150, 155, 156, 159, 165, 178, 190, 197, 215
Siddhartha (Prince), 29
Sikandar Khan Ghazi, 12
Sikandar Lodhi (Sultan), 17

Sikandar Shah (Sultan), 13, 43, 63, 207
silahdar, 11, 219
Sirajganj, 67, 84, 175, 176, 209, 213
    Makhdum Shah's Mosque, 65, 84-87, 213; *55, 56, 57*
    Nabagram Mosque, 61, 67, 128, 175-78, 209; *141, 142*
Sitakunda, 188, 211
Sitalakhya (river), 73, 95
Somapura, 30
Sonargaon, 10, 11, 13, 19, 26, 38, 39, 48, 50, 52, 54, 62, 65, 67, 73-74, 77, 78, 99, 100, 101, 102, 103, 104, 111, 157, 158, 159, 206, 207, 212, 213, 215
    Fath Shah's Mosque, 48, 52, 59, 61, 65, 74, 101-5, 111, 199, 209, 212; *35, 36, 70*
    Goaldi Mosque, 38, 39, 58, 59, 61, 67, 74, 96, 100, 102, 157-59, 209, 213; *18, 19, 124*
    Muazzampur Shahi Jami Mosque, 54, 58, 65, 74, 77-79, 99, 206, 209, 213; *39, 49, 50*
    Yusufganj Mosque, 65, 74, 103-4, 212; *71, 72*
south Bengal, 15, 72, 140
square domed unit, 4, 35-41, 44
Sri Krishna-Kirtan, 14
Sri Lanka, 29
Sri Krishna-Vijaya, 19
stupa, 28, 29, 219
stupa-shirsha bhadra, 29
suba, 3, 8, 96, 219
Suba Bihar, 8
Sufi, 9, 11, 14, 19, 84, 98, 217, 218, 219
Sufism, 11 n. 13, 12 n. 16
Sulayman (Sulaiman), 58, 195, 197
Sulayman Karrani (Sultan), 17, 18, 208
Sultan-i Bangala, 13
Sundarban, 7, 8, 88, 130, 141
Sur, 13, 17, 62, 67, 195, 196, 201, 208,
Sura Mosque, *see* Dinajpur
Surya, 158
Sutrapur, 80, 212
Suvarnagram, 73
Sylhet, 8, 10, 12, 67, 190, 213
    Osmanpur Gayebi Mosque, 67, 190-92, 213; *157, 158*

Tabaqat-i-Nasiri, 9
Taj Khan Karrani (Sultan), 17, 208
Tangail, 8
Tantipara Mosque, *see* Malda

Index

Tarafdar, M. R., 16 n. 31 & 33, 17, 19 n. 40, 73 n. 3, 195
Taras, 175, 213
Tarikh-i Firuz Shahi, 10
temple(s), 3, 23, 24, 32, 33, 35, 36, 37, 44, 49, 51, 52, 54 n. 33, 55, 57, 62, 64, 76, 79, 157, 169, 185, 194, 199, 216, 218, 219
temple architecture, 27-31, 69, 167, 170; *3, 4, 8-14*
Ten-domed Mosque, *see* Bagerhat
terracotta decoration, 34, 35, 37, 55-57, 66, 87, 106, 116, 137, 150, 152, 155, 162, 171, 194, 198, 199, 203
Thakurdighi, 127
thana, 92, 94
Thayethettaya (Srikshetra), 30
tilak, 17, 219
Tirhut, 10, 13, 17
tomb, 12, 35, 36, 37, 43, 44, 64, 65, 66, 71, 72, 77, 83, 84, 95, 98, 101, 109, 117, 118, 119, 139, 147, 155, 165, 175, 186, 199, 202, 211, 217
Tribeni, 44, 45, 56, 58, 62, 75
Tripura, 16
Tughluq, 11, 13, 37, 43, 44, 49, 50, 66, 201
tughra, 61, 219; *45*
Turk(s), 10, 66
Turkestan, 12
Turkic, 16
Turkish, 9, 14, 216
Turkish governors, 62-63
Turkoman, 9
Tus, Haruniyya Tomb, 128

Uchail, 151
Ulugh, 16, 66, 72, 83, 219

Ulugh Iqrar Khan, 83
Ulugh Khan Jahan, *see* Khan Jahan
Ulugh Nusrat Khan, 83
Umarpur, 92
Umayyad, 63

Vaishnava, 17, 217, 219
Vaishnavite, 19
Varendra, 10, 30
Varendra Research Museum (Journal of), 9 n. 7, 153, 175, 214
Vedas, 20
Vijaya Gupta, 19
Vipradas, 19
Vishnu, 20, 219; *41, 42*

Wali Muhammad, 147, 150
waqf, 140
wazir, 61, 83, 103, 179, 219
West Asia, 46, 63
West Bengal, 4, 5, 8, 9, 10, 18, 28, 35, 36, 41, 43, 44, 46, 47, 49, 50, 56, 58, 63, 64, 65, 66, 67, 73, 75, 87, 94, 105, 132, 147, 188

Yajnapindi Lokanatha, 29
Yasoraja Khan, 19
Yathepyi (old Prome), 31
Yemen, 12, 84
Yusufganj Mosque, *see* Sonargaon

Zafar Khan Ghazi's Mosque, *see* Hughly
zamindar(s), 8, 14, 219
Zamzam, 77
Zinda Pir's Mosque, *see* Bagerhat
zulla, 46, 219

Printed in the USA
CPSIA information can be obtained
at www.ICGtesting.com
LVHW080539120524
779928LV00007B/702